ADVANCE PRAISE
for

Ara

"Coaching is a sacred profession that gives you the opportunity to influence generations of young people. It isn't always pretty, but it's ultimately rewarding. This biography of my friend, Ara Parseghian, captures the raw essence of a legend and inspires us all to fight through any challenge to make a positive impact in this world."

— *Lou Holtz, Notre Dame Football Head Coach, 1986–96*

"*Ara* gives you the incredible opportunity to get to know the man behind the legacy. The more you read, the more you appreciate all Ara Parseghian has accomplished. I was blessed to have Ara as my coach, and I'm the man I am today because of him."

— *Joe Theismann, world champion quarterback*

"Mark O. Hubbard's book, *Ara*, about Notre Dame football coach Ara Parseghian, is an absorbing sweet read. For all his success, Parseghian has always been the most mysterious of Notre Dame's legendary coaches. Hubbard unlocks the mystery with a bright and shining light. Any fan of football will love this."

— *Buzz Bissinger, author of* Friday Night Lights *and* The Mosquito Bowl

"When I met Ara Parseghian in 1964, little did I know the impact he would have on my life. In *Ara: The Life and Legacy of a Notre Dame Legend*, Mark O. Hubbard has captured Ara perfectly on and off the field."

— *Terry Hanratty, Super Bowl IX and X champion quarterback*

"Mark O. Hubbard delivers a comprehensive account of Ara's multifaceted life. He introduces us not just to the legendary coach, but also to the son of immigrants, the mischievous prankster, the astute businessman, and the devoted husband, father, and grandfather. Amidst his family's battles with illness, Ara emerged as a beacon of hope and healing. Hubbard paints a portrait of joy, heartbreak, selfless service, and inspiration, celebrating a life truly well-lived."

— *Gregory P. Crawford, president, Miami University*

"I felt from my time as a player, and then as a combination fan, admirer, and friend, that I knew Ara quite well, and this book really captures the true Ara, as a coach and man. To read this book is to know the real Coach Parseghian, even if you never met him."

— *Peter Schivarelli, manager of the rock band Chicago*

"This book is a remarkable tribute to the history of Ara Parseghian, his background, and his soul. It is a history for all Notre Dame fans."

— *Katie Parseghian, wife of Ara Parseghian*

ARA

ARA

THE LIFE AND LEGACY OF A NOTRE DAME LEGEND

— THE AUTHORIZED BIOGRAPHY OF —

COACH ARA PARSEGHIAN

MARK O. HUBBARD

University of Notre Dame Press • Notre Dame, Indiana

University of Notre Dame Press
Notre Dame, Indiana 46556
undpress.nd.edu
All Rights Reserved

Published in the United States of America

Library of Congress Control Number: 2024937296

ISBN: 978-0-268-20851-6 (Hardback)
ISBN: 978-0-268-20853-0 (WebPDF)
ISBN: 978-0-268-20854-7 (Epub)

TO KATIE DAVIS PARSEGHIAN,

the first lady of Notre Dame Football

Ara did choose wisely.

The best quarterback that I ever had on my team was my wife.

She was a member of my team for thirty-five years and continues to serve

in that capacity. She keeps herself in excellent condition, doesn't smoke,

and occasionally has a postgame cocktail. She sets my game plan for every

contest and has executed it flawlessly. She is also very audible on occasion,

and has a conservative background but will throw a bomb occasionally.

Her overall stats are excellent and more importantly, she has let me

sleep with her for thirty-five years. To be perfectly honest,

I don't plan to recruit any other quarterback—she still has eligibility.

—ARA PARSEGHIAN, 1974
(note from his personal files, in answer to the following question:
Who was your favorite quarterback?)

CONTENTS

THIRD QUARTER (1964-1974)

FOURTH QUARTER (1975-2017)

FOREWORD

As one looks back on life, no matter how fragile or overbearing one's ego may be, I would like to believe in John Donne's meditation that "no man is an island." In that belief, we didn't get to where we are by ourselves: we got here because of a parent, a teacher, a mentor, a friend, a drill sergeant, a coach. We got here because someone cared, yelled at us, kicked us in the rear end, or demanded no breaking point. We got here because someone believed in us and gave us a sense of hope.

But hope must start somewhere, that little kernel of belief, that one can achieve something in one's life. It might start with a look, a nod of the head, a pat on the back. It may continue with a correction, an observation, or a teaching point, but it makes a difference.

And that was what Ara Parseghian was all about . . . about making a difference.

He never took an opponent nor one of his players for granted. If you were an All-American standout, or just a walk-on holding a blocking dummy, you were an essential part of his team, and he made you feel that way. Now, he was not beyond getting irritated or yelling or correcting mistakes. His voice would rise, and all heads would turn towards the tower, because he was the coach and controlled your life. You were eighteen to twenty-two years old — what did you know? Nothing. What did you have . . . nothing . . . except memories. And it was those memories that made you proud, made you special, made you part of a legacy that lives on forever . . . God, Country, Notre Dame . . . The Fighting Irish . . . Go, Ara, Go . . . Ara, stop the rain!

One man created those memories . . . but you must understand he was just a man, with fears, dreams, insecurities, like the rest of us. That is what this book is all about, a possible road map, left behind by a man that we all loved, to help us navigate our own lives.

Rocky Bleier, 2024

As a freshman arriving at the University of Notre Dame in the fall of 1967, I was greeted by a pervasive, campus-wide spirit that could not have been duplicated anywhere else in the country. The Fighting Irish football team finished the 1966 season as the national champions with a 9–0–1 record, overcoming a 10–10 tie at Michigan State in what has often been called the "game of the century" (one of a select few games with this designation before and since). Prospects for a repeat national championship ran high in the following September. The primary reasons for this were the renewed national attention Notre Dame was attracting combined with the confidence everyone had in the head football coach going into his fourth season in South Bend. Sure, many of the same quality student-athletes were returning. But Ara Parseghian had firmly established himself as a force to be dealt with in major college football. Everyone with knowledge of the game understood that.

The coaching credentials were certainly established. Success at both Miami University (Ohio) and at Northwestern University prepared Ara for the challenges in South Bend. In 1964, Ara's first year, Notre Dame almost won the undisputed national title, being only one minute, thirty-three seconds away from a final victory against the University of Southern California in a game forever marred by a series of controversial calls made by the game officials. The handsome young coach had graced the cover of *Time* magazine that year when the story line of Notre Dame's return to glory literally woke up the echoes from the successful Frank Leahy coaching era over a decade earlier. Notre Dame football teams had been seen as disappointing by an arguably spoiled national fan base in the intervening seasons prior to Ara's arrival.

As Notre Dame President Father Theodore Hesburgh so eloquently put it many years later, "Ara made the entire difference. He changed everything."

But in the fall of 1967, catching a glimpse on campus of the now-famous coach was rare — outside of watching him on the balcony of the Old Field House at raucous Friday pep rallies or in Notre Dame Stadium pacing the west sideline at the sold-out five home games. His car was usually parked in a space marked with "PARSEGHIAN" behind the Rockne Memorial Building, where the Football Office was located at that time. It was enough comfort for the students and faculty just to see his car in place and to know that he was woven into the Notre Dame fabric. To fans across America, Ara Parseghian had become the hopeful new face of Notre Dame Football.

I had no difficulty being swept up by the enthusiasm of being a freshman architecture student on the Notre Dame campus in 1967. Someone with creative photographic skills had doctored a black and white photo of Ara walking on water. This image was posted all over campus, including in my dorm room. Comparing the coach to Jesus was, perhaps, a little sacrilegious, especially at a Catholic university. And when the student body started chanting "Ara, stop the snow!" during the Navy game in early November, the spirited claim of near divinity was renewed again. Yes, Ara was our guy. And he was special.

Against this background, flash ahead forty-three years to November 3, 2010, when I found myself the unlikely choice to be riding with Joe Doyle, the retired sports editor at the *South Bend Tribune*, to visit Ara at his home. If I've learned anything, it is that life is full of surprises. If you pay close attention, many of them can be good. Joe insisted that I join him to meet his very close friend of over forty-six years with a specific purpose in mind. He was convinced that a follow-up book to author Jim Dent's *Resurrection*, about the surprising 1964 season, Ara's first, was necessary to capture the spectacular 1966 championship season. Further, he thought I was the guy who should do it. To that point in time my meager writing credentials had only included one business text and a collaboration with my brother, Donald Hubbard, *Forgotten Four*, about the 1953 Notre Dame team featuring top-ten NFL draft choices Ralph Guglielmi, Joe Heep, Neil Worden, and Heisman Award winner Johnny Lattner in Coach Frank Leahy's final season. But Joe was confident that I was up to the task. His one admonition as we pulled into the Parseghians' driveway was, "For God's sake, kid [I was sixty years old], don't tell him you're a Republican."

So it began. That day started a project that eventually came to fruition in 2011, *Undisputed: Notre Dame, National Champions 1966 (A Football Family and the Game of the Century)*.

It was obvious from the outset that Joe had also prompted his pal, Coach Parseghian, with his own admonition, something like "Give the kid a chance." When we settled into comfortable chairs in Ara's home office — awards, photos, and memorabilia adorned every wall and bookshelf — we were all a little nervous. At least, I was. I think Ara was slightly annoyed that he was going to have to placate his friend by answering questions from this novice author whom he expected to scratch at the most written about season and game in modern Notre Dame Football history. He'd had more than enough of that.

Ara led the conversation with a bombshell. "I suppose you want to hear about the tie at Michigan State." Of course, this game had been the pebble in his shoe since the final whistle when the grossly unfair "Ara played for a tie" nonsense erupted.

My answer set the table for what became a warm and close friendship with Ara for the remainder of his life. "No, Coach, I want you to take a look at this photo and tell me about it." The photo depicted Ara's starting high school football team at Akron South in 1941. There were eleven young faces, seven in front and four behind, dressed in baggy canvas pants and wearing the leather helmets of the time, devoid of face guards. Ara, in the back row as halfback, was standing next to a Black player, which for industrial Akron, Ohio, had to have been quite unusual in those days. He surveyed the photo carefully and when he looked up, he said, "That's Conwell Findley, our tailback. I wonder what became of him." I never had to ask him a question about the photo. But because I didn't, he sensed that I might write a different kind of story about the 1966 season at Notre Dame.

He wasn't disappointed with the result. After a careful reading of the final book, Ara only found one semi-factual error, which I promised to correct if ever I wrote again about his career. Many sources stipulate that Ara only lost consecutive games one time in his tenure at Notre Dame, and that is what I printed. Ara called me one morning at home and pointed out that this statistic included an Orange Bowl loss to Nebraska in 1972, after an 8–2 regular season. "Mark, I never lost two consecutive regular season games in eleven years at Notre Dame." On this page, I have now made the correction and kept my promise. Because I finally and convincingly debunked the 10–10 tie myth, with documented historical records and thorough analysis of video evidence, our relationship was cemented. As a result, I became a frequent guest at the Parseghian home and was always warmly greeted by both Ara and his wife, Katie.

Sometimes I'd call ahead and sometimes I'd just drop in. Our topics of conversation were wide-ranging. We'd talk about football — a game, a person from his past, the changes happening to the rules. Sometimes we'd drift into discussion of current events, world affairs, or family stories. He eventually accepted that I was a Reagan Republican, but in contemporary culture (when party labels were less binding) there was a lot of common ground with a Roosevelt–Kennedy Democrat. I came to appreciate that Ara was a person with an ever-curious intellect, instinctive about understanding human nature, generous and committed to causes he believed in, and resolute about character in all things.

Once, as Ara walked me to the front door of his home I commented, "Coach, you know that many of us think you were the greatest coach ever at Notre Dame." His clipped retort: "Mark, you have to stop that stuff." I'm sorry to disappoint you, Coach. A tie for first place with Knute Rockne seems a reasonable concession.

But his flippant response does set the stage for a serious examination of the entirety of his life. Ara spent over forty years as an adult not coaching football. He and his family grappled with immense challenges away from the spotlight. He was absolutely dedicated to excelling in his roles as husband, father, grandfather, family member, colleague, business associate, former coach, and friend. True, playing football and then coaching occupied Ara for a time — a long time. But it was just one of his callings. As a complete person he was so much more. His life story needed to be told.

My last visit with Ara was on May 26, 2017. I corralled one of my former students, Amber Lattner Selking, to join me for a spontaneous afternoon visit to acknowledge Ara's ninety-fourth birthday. She had just finished her PhD in sports psychology and wanted to capture some of Coach Ara's organizational and motivational philosophies — which she did. Ara was in good health and spirits that day, oblivious to the fact that he wouldn't see another football season. As Coach, Katie, Amber, and I sat around their dining room table sharing stories, I raised the subject of writing Ara's biography — a subject that I raised frequently and was just as frequently rebuffed. Then Amber innocently asked, "If there were to be a biography what should the title be?" Coach answered with a laugh, "How about Ara, A-R-A? It reads the same forward and backward."

When Katie and the Parseghian family encouraged me to write this biography I felt honored and humbled. What I lack in formal writing skills I hope is made up for by attention to details and a profound respect for the man who was my friend.

What follows is an attempt to capture the essence of Ara Parseghian, who lived a lifetime of character with no breaking point. A-R-A . . . his life reads the same both forward and backward.

ACKNOWLEDGMENTS

Writing a biography, something I've never done before, presented some challenges. It was an immeasurable benefit for me to be personally acquainted with the subject, Ara Parseghian. Over the years I was fortunate to spend many hours of quality time in his presence. There were conversations I could recall with authentic insights on how the man thought about a variety of subjects, especially those close to the heart. But there were also numerous occasions during this project when I found myself lamenting, "Ara, I wish you were still here to tell me about that."

On the other hand, having a living subject hovering in the background as one attempted to understand a lifetime could also have been a hinderance. There might have been some tendency to remember events more favorably and perhaps to feel the necessity to mention individuals out of loyalty, should they expect special treatment. Or, in Ara's case, he might have been too harsh in judgement of himself (a personality trait). Fortunately, I wasn't burdened with pitfalls of those kinds.

From the beginning it was important to set some standards relative to the information that was included — especially about a person of Ara's stature who probably is the most written about football coach in Notre Dame history, if column inches are the measure. Sportswriters and sports reporting can at times be filled with hyperbole. It is just part of the challenge of keeping the average reader engaged. Sometimes the myths grow into gross misrepresentations of the truth, be they favorable or unfavorable.

Ara would have been delighted to know that this project started with a game plan, a point of view. Of course, college football had to be part of the story. But, more importantly, I was guided by a steadfast focus on the personality and the character of the subject in historical context. The vast amount of interesting material was screened to fit and enhance this central game plan. Many stories, interactions, and published materials didn't make the cut.

The standard I set for myself in this work was to include Ara's own words where possible, contemporaneous accounts, and the firsthand recollections of those who actually knew him. This high standard ultimately made writing much easier. Some myths may have been dispelled in the process. But other character traits appear with much more clarity. What emerges is an impressionistic portrait of a very fine individual. That Ara found success in so many of the endeavors he attempted only makes the narrative more interesting, and I believe worth knowing and retelling.

Among the people who are owed a debt of gratitude for helping to make this biography both accurate and lively, one name goes to the head of the list — Kathleen "Katie" Parseghian who lived it all and whose memory was razor sharp. It would have been impossible to have done this project justice without her unlimited access to family records, constant attention to detail, and overall guidance. I would visit Katie at home and she would have coffee and a muffin ready for me. Together we assembled over thirty hours of audio worthy of archives. The COVID-19 pandemic interrupted those sessions, but not the constant communication that cemented a deep friendship.

Immediate family members still living added substantially to the story. They are: Kriss (Parseghian) Humbert (daughter), Jim Humbert (son-in-law), Jim Burke (son-in-law and widower of daughter Karan Parseghian), and Linda (Parseghian) Runyon (Ara's niece).

Brian and Micki Boulac were deeply involved with the project from the start. As the only remaining member of Parseghian's initial coaching staff, Brian added insights into many of the day-to-day aspects of Ara's character. Unfortunately, he wasn't able to enjoy the final telling of this story to which he contributed so much. But Micki stepped in after Brian's death and provided me with the encouragement I needed to continue when my unexpected confrontation with kidney cancer interrupted the process. Their daughter, Denise Boulac, added valuable research.

It is dangerous to write in a vacuum. I was fortunate to have a loyal set of experienced eyes review my work through the entire writing process, Walter Nicgorski, PhD. Now retired, Walt was a young faculty member in the Parseghian years at Notre Dame and became an invaluable sounding board for adding content and texture — in addition to keeping my writing style fresh and grammatically on track.

Another contributor, Joe Bride, helped start me down the path of writing about Notre Dame Football (with his friend the late Joe Doyle). He was a steady influence for me since our days sharing an office in Cincinnati years ago. Joe worked in Notre Dame sports information as a student and had a distinguished career doing public relations starting with *Life* magazine, the Baltimore Orioles, and then spanning over four decades of corporate clients. Unfortunately, Joe also passed away before completion of this project.

Recognition is also deserved for the people who assisted the project at the archives of Miami University, Northwestern University, and of course, the University of Notre Dame.

There was a cadre of interested readers of the text as it was parsed out incrementally. I had these folks in mind as I attempted to keep the work readable and interesting. They include: Bert Bondi, Dave Brenner, Father John Connoly, Tony Jeselnik, Bob Kloska, Father Doug Smith, and Mike Vogel — all contemporaries of the Parseghian years at Notre Dame.

A project of this scope and duration would have been tedious without the constant support and encouragement of immediate family, my spouse, Bridget O'Rourke Hubbard, and my son, Dr. Matthew Hubbard.

Of course, books don't assemble and publish themselves. The University of Notre Dame Press was a supportive partner, especially the care and attention paid by Rachel Kindler. Copyeditor Rachel Martens carefully added clarity and luster to the finished manuscript.

When I started this project, I was warned by Rocky Bleier, "Mark, you are taking on a monumental task." His warning was prescient. But with his help and that of a number of former players I was able to press on. My thanks to all of them, especially Terry Hanratty, who was able to check the accuracy of the "inside football" aspects of the book.

It would have been impossible to have mentioned in the text all of the people who entered Ara's life in some meaningful way, especially all the players he coached over twenty-four years. Those who either knew or only casually met Coach Parseghian told me countless stories. Many of his players may be disappointed that their football heroics or individual anecdotes weren't included in this volume. I apologize for that and I hope they forgive me. My hope is that by including a few blank pages at the end, readers may add their own memories for posterity and personalize this volume in a special way that I never could have.

And finally, I need to thank Ara Parseghian himself. Over time I was fortunate to have a number of friendly conversations that eventually found a place in my personal memory notes. More importantly, Ara left a very rich set of personal files, all of which were provided to me by Katie. He was a prolific writer and saver of the written word. In so many instances I didn't have to imagine what he thought at a specific moment in time because it was all there in his own words.

Toward the end of the project, after exchanging the chapters for review, I received the following short email: "Sounds like you know the guy. Love, Katie."

My hope is that readers will come to the same conclusion.

INTRODUCTION

In October 2019, the home office of Ara Parseghian (also used as a TV room) was essentially unchanged from the final day he occupied it in the summer of 2017. It was a veritable museum of personal effects and artifacts assembled and curated under Katie Parseghian's care to remind the occupants of cherished memories and the people most important to them.

Immediately upon entering, a visitor was drawn to a wall on the right side, full of awards received by Ara over a lifetime of coaching college football. There was one predominant exception. This was a large (two feet by three feet), carefully framed color photo of the entire Parseghian family taken for Ara's seventy-fifth birthday in 1998. The family portrait is the centerpiece of this space. In a tree-lined setting, Katie and Ara are surrounded by their children, their children's spouses, and all of their grandchildren. One can only imagine how many times Ara gazed up from his desk to be reminded of the thing that truly mattered most in his life, his family. But the photo also served as a bittersweet reminder of happier times for Katie and Ara. Some of the smiling faces had been called from this life so early and tragically. Their oldest daughter, Karan Burke, had succumbed to multiple sclerosis after a valiant battle to raise a family and live as normally as possible. Son Mike and daughter-in-law Cindy Parseghian had only three of their four young children still with them when the photo was taken.

Only one child survives now: Ara, named after his grandfather. The other three grandchildren, Michael, Marcia, and Krista, all died in childhood from the ravages of Neimann-Pick type C (NPC), a very rare genetic disease currently without a cure. Close examination of the prized family photo revealed a photo of the missing grandson, Michael (named after his father and Ara's father), had been lovingly attached and seamlessly integrated by Katie. He was the first of the Parseghian grandchildren to be stricken by NPC. A reminder of these unfortunate events might be enough to break a lesser family and its patriarch. But gazing back at Ara were all the faces that demanded courage and reinforced his guiding attitude, first used in the context of his football teams, that "We have no breaking point."

A closer survey of this same wall revealed the dimensions of Ara's college coaching success. The induction plaque from the College Football Hall of Fame (1980). Three silver plaques presented by the National Football Foundation in honor of national championships in 1964, 1966, and 1973. Yes, three, though the University of Notre Dame has never claimed a national championship in 1964 because the title wasn't undisputed. Many would argue it is a slight that deserves correction while many members of the 1964 team are still living. There was a citation from the American Football Coaches Association naming Ara as "Coach of the Year" in 1964. Propped up against this wall, and unframed, was a black and white photo of the entire Navy recruit training unit (over one hundred strong) that Ara commanded at the Great Lakes Navel Training Station during World War II.

Adjacent, on the far wall with a window, were other awards and photos. A bachelor's degree (1949) and a master's degree (1954), both from Miami University. The President's Medal awarded by Miami University in 2016 rested framed but unhung against the wall. The Honorary Doctor of Letters degree Ara received from Miami (1978) and the companion honorary doctorate from the University of Notre Dame (1997) were hung one above the other. A shelf overhead displayed a large collection of footballs with dates and scores proudly painted on them to designate key victories.

Directly opposite, next to the doorway, there was a wall of religious memorabilia, all related to the Catholic Church. Included were designations from Pope Paul VI and Pope John Paul. There were personal photos with Father Theodore Hesburgh, Notre Dame's president, and Father Edmund Joyce, executive vice president and Ara's de facto boss for his eleven years of coaching. There was also a handsome color photo of the Golden Dome.

File drawers flanked Ara's large, double-pedestal wooden desk on both sides, and the wall behind boasted custom, built-in bookcases. The shelves were chock full of memories from a long and storied career in college football as a player and a coach. More footballs. More photos. Books and miscellaneous memorabilia joined the display because each recalled a person or an event important to Katie and Ara. Furthermore, there were closets and a basement full of other interesting objects that didn't quite make the cut. Many of these items are destined to be added to the archives at Notre Dame, Miami University, and Northwestern University.

Ara's oversized desk was centered off this wall. A blotter had some more recent family photos tucked in at the edges. The file drawers were just as he left them. Even the pencil drawer had the slightly disorganized appearance of imminent use — paper clips, a magnifying glass, a letter opener. There was a large, white desk lamp of a bear climbing a tree, the significance of which no one can quite explain, except that it migrated north when the family's Marco Island condo was sold. There was a Cross pen and pencil desk set — a gift from the 1966 National Championship Team — which appeared to be more ceremonial than used. A coffee cup holding pencils, pens, and Sharpies used to sign autographs was within easy reach.

On the top, left-hand side was a short stack of papers, obviously important because of their easy accessibility for the left-handed coach. Perhaps prompted by my scheduled visits to collect information for Ara's biography, Katie Parseghian had finally begun sorting through these papers after over two years of neglect. Upon my second visit, she handed me what looked like a typed essay with an anxious invitation to read it immediately, "I think this might have been left for you." It is a deeply personal and insightful document that speaks loudly in Ara's own words. It is included herein transcribed exactly as it was written and discovered by Katie Parseghian.

When I finally came to Notre Dame in December 1964, Moose Krause our Athletic Director quipped as he introduced me at the second press conference, "We expect Ara to be with us a long time, after all he signed twice." He was referring to my departure from Notre Dame when the first press conference had been cancelled. I had left the Morris Inn without addressing the press. The only comment I made was the premature announcement of my hiring had not allowed us to agree on a number of issues. There was much speculation on the hows and whys of my departure. Salary, staff size, scholarships, and several other conjectures, none of which came close to the real reason.

Joe Doyle, Sports Editor of the *South Bend Tribune* and longtime historian of Notre Dame's athletics, particularly football, had been following events very closely. He did some excellent detective work and guessed I'd be named the new coach. He elected to print the story before the University had made an announcement. This did not make the Notre Dame Administration very happy. Father Hesburgh and Father Joyce had not consulted with the Board for their approval and a hasty conference call was made approving my hiring.

Hugh Devore, the Notre Dame Head Coach in 1963 was named interim coach. I had been at Northwestern eight years and felt Notre Dame would be a great opportunity. I called Father Joyce and indicated my interest and said if he was contemplating a change, I would like to throw my hat into the ring and if he had already made a decision to disregard my phone call. He said no decision had been made but appreciated my call and said he may be in touch. My call had been an exploratory one with a reasonable response. I had made a decision to leave Northwestern and contrary to some rumors, I had been offered a five-year contract but chose not to sign. A short time after my phone call to Father Joyce, I had made arrangements to an interview at [the University of] Miami Florida. Andy Gustafson, their coach, was stepping aside and they expressed an interest. I made reservations for a trip to Miami. I told my wife that I would be checking in to see if Father Joyce had called. The flight schedule to Miami from Chicago made a stop in St. Louis. I called back home and sure enough, Father Joyce had called. I cancelled my flight to Miami and returned home to Wilmette. I returned Father Joyce's phone call and we set up our first meeting in Chicago after the annual Knute Rockne dinner. This was scheduled for Dec. _____. Subsequently, we had several phone calls and met in New York when we were both to be there for different functions. After we had returned home, we visited by phone. Then came a call from Father Joyce indicating he wanted to set up a meeting with Father Hesburgh, the President of the University. It was then that I felt I had a good chance. The meeting took place in a hotel on the south side of Chicago. Apparently it went well, and Father Joyce was to let me know in a day or two what my status would be. Then came the Saturday and Joe Doyle's story. Father Joyce called, upset and wanted to meet Sunday and then have a press conference on Monday. I drove to South Bend Sunday and checked in at the Morris Inn on campus. Father Joyce and I had dinner at the Inn and discussed a number of issues and the press conference was set for Monday morning. The early press release had triggered some congratulatory phone calls and telegrams from my friends. Overnight, my mind was whirling. The campus was very quiet. The students were home for Christmas break. So what was my problem? To be brutally honest, I panicked even though I had told Father Joyce in our first meeting that I was a fallen-away Catholic. My mother was born in France and when her mother died, she was nine. She and her siblings were placed in a Catholic orphanage in Nantes, France. Upon coming to this country to marry my Armenian father, she found that he was not a religious person and yet the Armenian country was the first to adopt Christianity as a nation. However, my siblings and I became closet Catholics and my mother raised us in her faith.

Interestingly enough, her church in Nantes, France, was St. Pierre or "Saint Peter." The church I attended in Akron was St. Peter's. That is where I was baptized, did my catechism, made my first communion, was confirmed, and attended regularly.

I made all of this clear to Father Joyce in our first meeting. If he had any objection, I knew my chance for the job would end there. He told me it would be nice if I could return to the Church and wouldn't disqualify me as a coaching candidate. I was pleased to hear his response. At least I still had a chance. Yet overnight, doubt set in. The congratulatory communications along with my respect for the Catholic Faith confused me. It made me realize that many in my hometown knew of my Catholic background. I was fearful it would not be well received by the faculty, students, alumni and Notre Dame fans. The next morning, I met with Father Joyce and Moose Krause. They tried to convince me that all would be OK.

I told them I needed to clear my head and we agreed to cancel the press conference. The reason given was that all the details had not been worked out. Little did I realize the furor that would accompany the cancelling of the press conference. It was not Father Hesburgh, Father Joyce, or Moose who were at fault. It was my fear of not being what the Notre Dame Family would expect in a coach. The Catholic Faith is very strong and would they embrace a fallen-away coach? That morning, Father Joyce and Moose did everything they possibly could to convince me. I am sorry they had to take some heat and I want to make it clear it was me, not them.

I returned home and mentally wrestled with my concerns and finally came to the conclusion if Father Hesburgh, Father Joyce, and Moose Krause all felt it would not be an issue, then I should respect their judgement. Yet we never made the real reason known. Still, I wonder if we had made my Catholic background known, would I have been accepted by the Notre Dame faithful? At age 19, I went into the Navy and Church became an option rather than what it actually was, an obligation. In retrospect, given the eleven great years I had at Notre Dame (and I almost missed the opportunity) would the Notre Dame faithful have embraced me as their coach?

First impressions have significance. After my stunned surprise, I became oddly comforted by the revelation in the document I was holding. Ara Parseghian was raised as a Catholic. It would be irresponsible, in the journalistic sense, to bury the lede. This piece of new information would have been breaking news at any point in Ara's lifetime. My suspicion is that many readers of this authorized biography, especially those intimately aware of Notre Dame's prominence in American Catholic history, will share in this sense of comfort.

At a place like Notre Dame, where faith is a central identity, the conventional wisdom was that Ara was the first nongraduate (since Jesse Harper in 1919) and the first non-Catholic (Knute Rockne converted during his coaching tenure) to be the head football coach. Ara was formally introduced as a Presbyterian, likely harkening back to Katie's home church in Greenfield, Ohio, where they were married.

Notre Dame sports historian Cappy Gagnon was working as a student in Sports Information Director Charlie Callahan's confined office in December 1963 when the press releases were being composed.

Someone asked, "How do you spell that?" The answer came back, "P-A-R-S-E-G-H-I-A-N." The retort was, "No, I got that. How do you spell Presbyterian?"

Ara himself would have been quite conscious of the relationship that coaching at Notre Dame had to the Catholic Church. A prevailing colloquial sentiment, starting with Knute Rockne, was that the two most visible positions in the American Catholic Church were the pope, followed by the head football coach at Notre Dame. The American Catholic Church had been coming of age since the 1920s and success at Notre Dame was a rallying point and source of pride, giving rise to the now accepted designation of "subway alumni" for countless followers.

In providing a personal account of his hiring, Ara was likely seeking comfort for himself. Certainly, it was not an attempt to rewrite history to create a good impression (as many prominent persons are tempted to do as they survey their life). The temptation to further psychoanalyze the mindset of Ara must be cautiously avoided. However, unpacking the significance of this original manuscript does reveal a great deal about its author. In truth, Ara Parseghian conveniently wrote an introduction to his own biography without even knowing it.

Ara communicated in a straightforward manner without guile or nuance, especially in the written word. I believe this document was a sincere attempt to set the record straight by a thoughtful man who undoubtedly understood that the sands of time were passing through his hourglass. Nothing more and nothing less.

The authenticity of this being authored by Ara Parseghian is not in doubt even though Katie Parseghian had no clue that this document existed prior to its posthumous discovery. Ara did not use a computer, so this wasn't word processed by him at the keys. Ara's granddaughter Taran Humbert Conyers confirmed that he dictated this to her about eight years before his passing. It is obviously not a first or rough draft. To, or for whom was it written? This is equally unclear since the document does not include a salutation. Katie and the immediate Parseghian family would have known the content of Ara's revelations from oral tradition. He wasn't divulging any family secrets to them, so they would not have been his intended audience. What is definite is that Ara assumed his exact words would eventually be found and shared in some fashion. It was written to be read by others.

Why would Ara generate such a detailed statement? Coach Parseghian, as anyone who ever knew him would attest, would not have engaged in making this statement without a purpose. Perhaps he simply wanted to provide precise clarity to the events surrounding his hiring at Notre Dame — a subject about which many hot takes have been offered by various sportswriters and others since 1963. Many of these were speculative, and we now know that they had minimal foundation in the truth.

In part, Ara may have been providing his explanation to absolve people he cared a great deal about in his lifetime and who carried the burden of protecting him from adverse criticism when he became the head coach and during his tenure in the job. He writes with great respect about Father Hesburgh and Father Joyce. One is struck that he doesn't use the abbreviation "Fr." when referring to them. His fondness for Athletic Director Edward "Moose" Krause also shines through. It is unlikely that Ara's friend Joe Doyle had any inkling of the truth. The temptation to go public with the information would have been too overwhelming to an experienced sportswriter in South Bend. It could have been a signature story late in his career.

The profound character and priestly instincts demonstrated by both Fathers Hesburgh and Joyce are on clear display. They weren't judgmental about a person who admitted to being fallen away. It was a fundamental element of their calling to provide comfort and perspective to the fallen away. More to the point, they were charged with identifying the best possible candidate for a key position at the University of Notre Dame. Ara's football coaching credentials were rock solid, with the bonus of his thoughtfulness and character. The hiccup and delay over Ara's uncertainty and the two press conferences probably only added to their resolve that they had found a quality guy — the right guy.

As progressive young priests for their times, Fathers Hesburgh and Joyce also would have had empathy for a thoughtful young family trying to make sense of their Catholic Church in transition. This was a time of renewal under Pope John XXIII and Vatican II. There was a move away from hardline dogmatic adherence to rules and regulations and toward a fundamental understanding of the broader Christian message. Every person is a child of God, encouraged to live a good life, and eligible for salvation through the sacrifice of Jesus on the Cross. At Notre

Dame, requirements such as regular Mass attendance were being re-laxed toward a policy of volunteer participation in the faith life on cam-pus. This "kinder and gentler" Catholic Church post–Vatican II was a big tent. There was a place for the Parseghian family. That place was the University of Notre Dame.

This document reveals that in the end, Ara wondered if the Notre Dame family would have accepted him if they knew the full truth in 1963. Embedded in this rhetorical query is his clear understanding that he was indeed embraced, respected, and loved at Notre Dame.

FIRST QUARTER

(1923–1943)

CHAPTER 1

ROOTS

Ara Raoul Parseghian was born on May 21, 1923, in the family residence, an apartment on Pine Street in Akron, Ohio.

Ara's father, Mechitar (pronounced mick-eh-tar), son of Parsegh Ganjoyan (which means "son of Ganjo"), was born in 1892 in Teal in the Moush Province of Armenia. Following the convention for adult males in Armenian culture, he assumed the last name Parseghian ("son of Parsegh") when he immigrated to America, circa 1916. The addition of "ian" to a name was a common suffix for immigrants at the time and generations later still continues to identify a person as Armenian by family origin. "Michael" was officially substituted as his first name at the time of debarkation from the ship, although inside the Akron Armenian community he continued to be known by his birth name. It is interesting to note that because of the naming convention used and the records kept at ports of entry, there are other Parseghian families in America and virtually none are related by blood; this is because Parsegh was a common male name.

Ara's mother, Aimee Louise Bonneau, was born on November 26, 1897, in Reze, France. Her mother was Marie Clergeau. Her father, Jean Baptiste Bonneau, only twenty-eight at the time of her birth, was a carpenter and rural farmer in the village. The family lived in a small stone structure with a dirt floor that included two stories of dwelling and an attached barn — a building type common to the region. Aimee was the third of six children. Two died as infants. Her mother and the youngest sister, Cecile, died in 1906, when Aimee was nine (it is thought because of typhoid). Aimee and her sisters Felicite and Marte Marie were sent to the convent orphanage of Saint Vincent de Paul, in Nantes, France. Her father and brother continued to operate the homestead and farm. Her brother, also named Jean Baptiste, was later killed in World War I as a French Navy sailor when his ship was sunk (1917). Upon reaching an appropriate age, Aimee was sent from the convent school to become a domestic housekeeper for a wealthy family in Paris, probably just after the war.

Ara's first name in Arabic means "king," after the king of the mythical Kingdom of Ararat. It was a common Armenian name. His middle name, Raoul, is French (translated as "strong") and therefore believed to have had some significance to his mother.

Ara was the second-born child of the marriage with an older brother, Gerard "Jerry" Alban (1921–2010), and a younger sister, Isabelle "Zabell" Therese (Atwood) (1925–2008). As with any family, simply stated facts fail to fully capture the depth of the embedded histories that inexorably factor into the personality and character development of an impressionable young person.

FATHER: MICHAEL PARSEGHIAN
(1892-1968; Born Mechitar Ganjoyan)

To fully appreciate the events leading up to Michael Parseghian's arrival in America, a condensed background in Middle Eastern history is essential, focusing on what has now been designated as the Armenian Genocide or Armenian Holocaust.

Armenians are an ethnic group native to the Armenian Highlands of Western Asia. Today, the Republic of Armenia, founded in 1991 after the collapse of the Soviet Bloc, is located in the South Caucasus region of Eurasia, and is bounded by Türkiye, Iran, Azerbaijan, and Georgia. It is a country of thirty thousand square kilometers with a population of about three million. For a rough comparison, it is perhaps most similar to the state of West Virginia with respect to size, population, geography, and climate — but without mineral resources.

In the late 1800s, prior to the tensions in many parts of Europe and Asia that eventually precipitated World War I, Armenians were a loose ethnic confederation with historically tribal origins that occupied a larger footprint which included parts of present-day Türkiye, Syria, Lebanon, Iraq, Iran, Russia, Georgia, and Azerbaijan. Armenians were officially part of the Ottoman Empire, but until late in the nineteenth century they were mostly ignored and allowed a modicum of provincial self-governance. These almost exclusively poor rural farmers were dispersed and somewhat isolated, and they were the first ethnic group in the region to designate Christianity as their national religion. There were three denominations, Armenian Catholic, Armenian Protestant, and Armenian Apostolic (the church of the vast majority of Armenians).

A peaceful status quo was disrupted around 1890. Ottoman officials intentionally provoked rebellions (often as a result of overtaxation) in Armenian populated towns and villages. Paramilitary regiments were increasingly allowed to deal with the Armenians by way of oppression and massacre. It was the beginning of four decades of ruthless and systematic atrocities aimed at the extinction of the Armenian people. Without an organized military or modern weapons, Armenians were largely defenseless. These events accelerated and culminated in the Armenian Genocide, a term coined by historians after the fact in 1943. Most Armenian diaspora communities around the world formed as a direct result of people attempting to escape the genocide. Akron, Ohio, was one such community.

As of 2019, governments and parliaments of thirty-two countries, including the United States, Russia, and Germany, formally recognized the events as the Armenian Genocide. Today, there is a wide-ranging diaspora of around five million people of full or partial Armenian ancestry living outside of modern Armenia.

With this broad historical background, it would have been impossible to construct a history for Ara's father, the young Michael Parseghian, without significant speculation. Fortunately, a handwritten, first-person account of events was provided to Ara after his father's death. It dramatically chronicles a family in turmoil. The letter is presented here in transcription almost exactly as written by Mike Miktarian, whose father was from the same village as Ara's father (lightly edited for clarity).

Your Father Leaving Village of Teal, Moush:

Moush was destroyed in 1915, by the Turks. Ten thousand persons were massacred or fled into exile. There were schools & 7 Armenian churches. The Moushetsis raised tobacco & were farmers & traders. South of Moush were the mountains of Sasoun, where the Armenians would fight the Turks. To the north is St. John the Baptist, the monastery of the patron saint. The yearly pilgrimage to the church was as much a festival, as a religious move. Dad says St. John's head was buried in this church. During the Turk uprising, one hundred Armenian women carried the Church Door to Yeravan, where it is in the museum today, along with the Armenian Flag.

Your father was born in Teal, which is a village in Moush. Your father had four brothers: Katchig, Gaspar, Avedis, Melkon & two sisters: Noemzar & Yeghsa.

Your family name in Moush was "Ganjoyan." Remember "Ganjoyan Aram" from a long time ago in Akron, when we were little children & he sang songs? He was your father's first cousin. Araknas from California was his cousin, also she was a "Ganjoyan."

Your father's father was an important official in the Teal Village (like a Town Manager). He took care of various problems for the village people. He was paid in return with food & goods.

Katchig, your father's older brother, was an AYF member (fought Turks) & Melkon, Gaspar, and Avedis were farmers in the fields.

Their home was in a compound of Ganjoyan homes near my father's family, which was the "Artenian Family." They lived in the same area — like next door — they were like one family, doing many things together, on their farms. Homes were on one floor built of stone & mud walls, dirt floors with an oven built on the floor where they cooked their food. The fuel was dried cow dung. The floor oven was called a tundir.

An incident happened where three Turks were killed & Kachig, your uncle, had to leave Moush quickly to avoid arrest. He went to Ismir, Smyrna, & stayed until 1913. (My mother saw Kachig there.) He worked for a rich rug dealer there. Your father went to Ismir, Smyrna, in 1908 to be with his brother Kachig. Kachig helped to place him in school. The name of your father's college was "St. Mesrobian Boy's College." He stayed there & attended school until 1914. He became very well educated with many languages. Went to Greece in 1914.

Then he went to France for a year & came to America in 1919. In 1913 Kachig, your uncle returned to Moush. His mother & father & sisters & brothers were all there. Two years later, in 1915, the whole family, except for Noemzar, were killed by the Turks. First the men were taken out to the fields & shot in front of the women, and then the women were drowned. (Kachig's grandson Antronig Dicran is in Eyravan, Armenia & you have many relatives there.) Travel was by means of caravan from Moush.

Your father never returned to Moush. He was in Greece when Moush was destroyed in 1915.

In those times, when the Armenians came to America (all of them), they took their father's first name for their last name. Therefore, your father took Parsegh, his father's first name, to be his last name, Parseghian.

Noemzar, your aunt, married Solomon, who was my father's first cousin. (Solomon's father & my grandfather were brothers.) They had two children: Marmar & Asnou. In 1914 Solomon came to America, leaving Noemzar & the children behind with my father's family as she had married into his family, the Artenian Family.

In 1915, when Moush was massacred, Noemzar & her two daughters and my father's sister, Shooshanne, escaped from a barn that the Turks were burning. They ran, hiding along the way when the Russians came along & tried to help them to Yeravan. The Turks followed to kill them. General Antranig came to fight the Turks in 1919 & took Zoemzar, Shooshanig, & Marmar to Eyravan. Along the way to Eyravan, Noemzar's daughter Asno died. (She just had to leave her & flee with group.) Your aunt & my aunt stayed with wealthy Armenians in Eyravan for two years. Then family sent money to Noemzar so that she & her daughter could go to Ismir.

In 1922, my father sent money to Noemzar & her daughter, Marmar, so that they could come to Akron, to be with her husband, Solomon.

My father did see your father in Ismir in 1913 when he was on his way to America. Your father was in college at that time.

Moushetsis settled in Akron. Solomon was in Akron — this influenced your father & my father to come to Akron. Your father went to work for the bank, translating foreign languages.

My father (Hachig Miktarian) left Moush in September 1913 at the age of 15. The Turks were beginning to cause more trouble & taking Armenian youth into their army. Dad's family wanted him to leave for his safety.

Dad went to Ismir by caravan. While there he met with your father & your uncle Kachig. Your uncle Kachig helped my father. (Then Kachig decided to return home, to Moush & he was killed there in 1915.)

My father stayed forty days at the waterfront port for his ticket to America, but ticket did not come. Dad went back to the city of Ismir for another one to two months. Then your father helped my father by giving him 6.00 [denomination unclear] which helped him to continue his journey via Naples, Italy. He, Joe, spent two months in Naples. Finally passage came from cousins in America & he continued his voyage. It took six months for my dad to reach America.

Your father & mine landed in New York, & went from there to Akron.

Note: Marmar, your cousin & mine, has photos of your father's family from Moush. Contact her.

Re: Your father's visit to Russia:

Mom & Dad invited your father over for dinner when he returned from his trip to see his relatives. He was very sad & depressed! He told my parents how sad it was to know that his relatives had been living in the same eight-story apartment building in Yerevan and did not know that each lived there. They were afraid to try to contact anyone.

Your father found each family and brought them together. The living conditions were very poor. It made him cry.

Hope this information is of some help.

If you need more, please come to see Mom & Dad when you have time. They have so much to say & they know all the little background stories. It is hard to write it all down.

Regards to all — Mike Miktarian

P.S. Took this down fast. Excuse any errors in spelling.[1]

This account is spellbinding in its detail. The Armenian Genocide is an event that very few Americans, then or now, have had any profound awareness of — unless, of course, you are Armenian. This region of the world has been engaged in near continuous conflict for centuries and remains volatile and dangerous. It is a historic tragedy that almost all of the death and displacement for thousands of years has been done in the name of organized religion (or using religion as a premise to cover other motives). Unfortunately, such persecution also continues.

It is a little unclear as to the exact route Michael Parseghian took to arrive in America. Michael was the youngest son and the one chosen to go to school in Izmir, Smyrna (Türkiye). He went there by a donkey trading caravan run by an older brother. He was a student at school in Izmir when the troubles broke out at home. Many of his family were killed in his village. Family oral history has him escaping Izmir in 1914 by "borrowing" a rowboat to reach a Greek freighter in the harbor. It is known that for a time he was in Athens working for a prominent businessman, perhaps staying a year or more. From there he made his way to Marseilles where there were other friends and relatives who had escaped the carnage. The assumption is that Michael departed for America from Marseilles; he arrived in New York around 1916. From there he went on to Ohio, where others had gathered in the Akron area. There is a photo of Michael in a US Army uniform from when he served as a translator during World War I. He never returned to the village where many of his family had been killed. Years later he went back to Armenia with the president of his bank to look for family survivors, but not to that village. There he found some distant relatives living in squalid conditions under Communist rule.

Michael shared very little of the story above with his immediate family during his lifetime. During one of our many conversations about this project, Katie Parseghian lamented, "Now I wish I'd asked him more about his family history when we had private time together."

MOTHER: AIMEE "AMELIA" BONNEAU
(1897-1992)

The arrival of Aimee "Amelia" Bonneau in America is easier to trace. According to immigration records, the S.S. France departed Le Havre on May 22, 1920, and arrived in New York on May 29. (She was assigned the name Amelia at the US Immigration checkpoint.) There Aimee was met by Michael Parseghian. It was the first time either had laid eyes on the other, although they had been in contact previously.

The story goes that Michael had an Armenian friend in Akron with a French wife who he thought was very nice. He inquired if that young woman knew someone she thought was just as nice and might want to marry him. As it happened, she did. The friend's wife was happy to make an introduction to her friend Aimee back in Paris. A pen pal relationship ensued between Michael and Aimee, and photos were exchanged. All written correspondence was in French, their common language. Michael eventually suggested in a letter that Aimee join him in America. According to family lore, her response was straightforward, "Send money for a ticket." When she arrived, they went straightaway to the Municipal Building in Manhattan to get married (certificate #21571) in a civil ceremony.

Upon their return together by train to Akron, they were married in a Catholic ceremony at the Church of the Annunciation on May 31, 1920. Their first recorded residence was an apartment on Pine Street in Akron.

ARA: EARLY YEARS
(1923-1943)

Michael was employed as a travel consultant at the First Central Trust Company, later the First National Bank of Akron, because of his written and spoken facility in multiple languages. (Michael was fluent in Armenian, French, English, and Greek and had passible communication skills in Arabic, Turkish, Italian, and Hungarian.) In the Parseghian home, French was the language initially spoken. This persisted until Ara's older brother, Jerry, went to school, where fluent English was suddenly required. As a result, Michael, a learned man who valued education, insisted that the family begin speaking English at home since he wanted his children to have every advantage in his new homeland. Into his nineties, though, Ara was still able to string together phrases in French, his first language.

The family moved to a home on Longview Avenue in Akron, sometime after 1923 (listed as the date of construction). This is the only home that Ara remembered growing up in as a boy. It was still the address he used on his Selective Service Registration (US Army draft card).

Ara's niece, Linda Parseghian Runyon, is interested in family ancestry and found the record of the Parseghian family in the 1930 census. In an email to the author, she wrote, "If the census taker was getting the information from Nanny [as she was known to her grandchildren], she still had [even into her nineties] a very thick French accent. You'll see that the family is listed as: Mike, Amelia, Gerald A., Henry R., and Isabell. I feel like the poor census taker had to ask her several times to list her family members. After hearing her say 'A-R-A' he just wrote down 'Henry.' We teased Uncle Ara about being Henry."

The Parseghian children all attended Margaret Park Grade School (later demolished for an expressway), which was within walking distance of their home. As the oldest, Jerry was expected to be the studious child. He was required to take violin lessons for a time — not something he relished. In their later years the Parseghian brothers would joke about sliding down the hill in front of their house using the violin case as a sled.

Michael was an active member and a leader in the large Armenian community in Akron. The men religiously met every Sunday morning as a social event. Michael never embraced a formal religion after reaching America. In contrast, Amelia retained affiliation with her Catholic upbringing and sought to raise her children in her faith. The local parish was Saint Peter's (long since demolished). Church records from the diocese show that Jerry was baptized in 1930. Ara and Isabelle were both baptized in 1932 when Ara was nine years old. The presumption is that after parish catechism classes the children were brought up to date with their sacraments in rapid succession. In parish records, both parents are listed as Catholic. It is highly unlikely that Michael was supportive of Amelia's desire to raise her children in her faith. It was allowed, more likely conveniently ignored, under the premise that having a happy wife leads to a happy life.

While education was highly valued in the Parseghian household, participation in athletics was not. However, Ara demonstrated exceptional athletic ability at an early age. He spent his free time as a "gym rat" at the local YMCA. He played basketball and baseball at Akron South High School, but not football — at first. His mother was against him playing that sport because of possible serious injury. As he entered college, Jerry forged his parents' football consent form on Ara's behalf in

Ara's junior year. The first their mother knew about this was after seeing Ara in the team photo in the local newspaper. Whatever disharmony at home transpired must have been resolved because Ara continued to play as a junior and then as a senior for Coach Frank "Doc" Wargo. Ara recalled that his games were on Saturday afternoons. This afforded his teammates and him time on Friday nights to visit Massillon, Ohio, to watch high school games where the new stadium had lights. This was his first recollection of Coach Paul Brown, the coach of the Massillon High School Tigers, who became a key influence later in his life.

When he was of working age, Ara worked as a caddy at Loyal Oak Golf Club, eventually rising to become head caddy. This work is where he learned to play the game of golf. Even using right-handed clubs, the left-handed Ara was a natural. Later in his teens he worked for a time at Firestone Country Club, a championship course owned by the tire company for use by their executives and guests. Ara's high school employment set into motion a lifetime passion for golf.

Ara's son-in-law, James Burke, recalled in a phone conversation: "Ara told me he caddied at Loyal Oak. He said he used to hitchhike there and would pack his lunch and put it in a tree while he caddied. One day another caddy took his lunch from the tree and ate it. Ara was furious and thrashed the other caddy. Ara said that taking another guy's lunch was really crossing a line during the Great Depression."

While it would be easy to sketch the image of a carefree life for a young person during these years, the world around Ara was anything but carefree. It was the depth of the Great Depression. As the head of the household and primary breadwinner, Michael Parseghian absorbed enormous responsibility to keep his family afloat. Ara had two distinct memories of his father in those years. One day Michael came home in the middle of the day and spoke in quiet tones to Amelia, revealing that he had been laid off at the bank. Witnessing that hushed disclosure made a lasting impression on their young son. The other memory shared was attending a parade in Akron and hearing the song "Happy Days Are Here Again." This was the theme song of Franklin D. Roosevelt, and the event was most likely a local victory parade after the 1932 presidential election. Eventually economic conditions improved and Michael was able to return to the bank, where he was employed for the remainder of his working life. The family loyalty to the Democratic Party was established and embraced by Ara throughout his lifetime.

In the 1942 Akron South High School Yearbook, *The Sohian*, there are the customary photos of the graduating class of seniors along with written notes about activities and comments. For Ara Parseghian the final prophecy was, "Destined to become the head football coach at Notre Dame." This job was considered to be a pinnacle position in sports. College football was considerably more important than the professional game in the mid-twentieth century, and Notre Dame had distinguished itself as the most prominent media brand, embraced by millions, following the success of Coach Knute Rockne.

Ara Parseghian graduated from high school in 1942. In the fall of that year, he enrolled at the University of Akron, joining his brother, Jerry; they both lived at home. Ara played on the football and basketball teams, a fact rarely mentioned in any biographical profile. The military demands of World War II cut short his time in college. He enlisted in the Navy in the spring of 1943 and was assigned to Great Lakes Naval Training Station north of Chicago.

The Parseghian parents moved to a home on South Hawkins Avenue, Akron, in 1949. This remained their home for the remainder of their lives.

In the early 1960s, the Parseghians were on the daily newspaper (*Cleveland Plain Dealer*) route of Jimmy Burke. As such, he was required to collect the weekly paper money from his customers and turn the cash in to the Circulation Department. Knocking on the door of the Parseghian home asking for money proved to be an adventure. If the stoic Mr. Parseghian answered the door, he seemed to Jimmy to be semiannoyed by the intrusion. However, if Mrs. Parseghian answered he would be greeted warmly and provided with an additional ten-cent tip. Little did anyone know at the time that an adult James F. Burke Jr., would marry Ara's first daughter, Karan, the granddaughter of his paper route customers. Unfortunately, Michael Parseghian didn't live long enough to appreciate this irony. But Amelia Parseghian did. Karan and Jim Burke returned to Akron to raise their own family.

The only extended family member with Armenian blood Ara knew was his father's sister Noemzar, her daughter, and her son. Ara never made a trip to Armenia to seek out his family roots, even after it became an independent country.

Amelia did travel by ship with the three Parseghian children to visit her family in France for a couple of months one summer prior to the outbreak of World War II. The manifest for the S.S. Paris shows the family of four returning to America in September 1926. Ara was eventually able to reconnect with some of his mother's French relatives when he and Katie made two trips to France many decades later.

As with so many families, the Parseghians endured ups and downs as they navigated the challenges of surviving an ethnic cleansing, others' premature deaths, two world wars, and the Great Depression.

Michael and Amelia's first son, Jerry, graduated from the University of Akron as an engineer. He married Margaret "Maggie" Saus in 1943. Because of Jerry's poor vision he wasn't able to join the armed services. He was initially employed by the National Advisory Committee for Aeronautics, the precursor to NASA. Maggie and Jerry had two children, Thomas and Linda (Runyon). Eventually Jerry found his way into private industry as a cofounder of a specialty brush manufacturing company in Toledo. Today this company is still operated as a family business. Ara's younger sister, Isabelle "Zabell" (Atwood), married Howard and had three daughters — Loraine (Ingrassi), Michelle (McGuire), and Diane (Smith). That family stayed closer to home near Akron. Tragically, Zabell developed multiple sclerosis. Fighting the disease through research funding efforts became her lifelong cause. Ara was very supportive of his sister and the Multiple Sclerosis Foundation, giving speeches at fundraisers in the off-season, many years before his own daughter, Karan Burke, was diagnosed with the cruel disease.

How much Ara's parents fully processed and appreciated his eventual success at the time is impossible to gauge. Their son's image appeared on the cover of *Time* magazine in 1964 and thereafter in countless other publications. It would be hard to argue that Ara didn't become one of the most recognized Armenian descendants in America. Even now, when a web search is done for "Parseghian," the very first entry of over one million results is "Ara Parseghian," followed by many pages of citations about his life and legacy. Michael and Amelia had every reason to be proud.

The threads of Ara's dominant character traits that were engendered during his youth are easier to spot through the lens of his family history once he left home in 1943 and entered adulthood. They include determination, focus, self-reliance, perseverance, competitiveness, teamwork, patriotism, loyalty, fairness, gratitude, and generosity. College football would become the cloth where these threads would be woven tightly together.

CHAPTER 2

KATHLEEN

Greenfield, Ohio, is located approximately equidistant between Cincinnati and Columbus and about 180 miles southwest of Akron (Ara's birthplace) as the crow flies. The two locations have little in common. How two young people with divergent Ohio backgrounds were able to find each other is a story in itself.

Kathleen "Katie" (no middle name) Davis was born in Greenfield on February 27, 1928, at her family home on South Street. She was the daughter of Eunice (Jury) Davis (1895–1989) and John Edgar Davis (1894–1943) and the youngest of four siblings (in birth order): Richard, Mariellen, and Janice. In contrast to Ara's family, Katie could trace her roots back three generations in Ohio. Her parents were both born and raised in Greenfield. At the time of Katie's birth, the family of six, plus her two maternal grandparents, all lived under one roof in a two-story wood frame house on the edge of the town, with just a single bathroom. In 1928, the population of Greenfield and the surrounding community was about 3,800 souls. It was many miles to the next village.

Most of Kathleen Davis's forebearers descended from English or Dutch stock before arriving in America. There was one notable exception. Her father's grandmother, Mary Ann McSweeney, was the daughter of an Irish immigrant, Patrick McSweeney. Therefore, Katie's great-great grandfather was one hundred percent Irish. This fact was brought to light at Ara's ninetieth birthday celebration in 2013, when the Consul General of Ireland traveled from Chicago to present him with honorary citizen status — on the premise that he was worthy of the honor because "he had the good sense to marry an Irish girl." The crowd of over five hundred former players, family, and friends reveled at this presentation.

Driving into and through Greenfield today (population about 4,500) it isn't hard to imagine what it was like one hundred years ago. It is ripe for historical preservation. The downtown area, with a radius of a couple of blocks in all directions from the center of town, is richly endowed with turn-of-the-century brick facades on buildings that house commercial offerings on the first floor with office or residential space above on a floor or two. The public buildings and churches are still stunning in their external details. Most of them were built using limestone cut from local Rucker's Quarry, a source of architectural stone throughout southwest Ohio, including many buildings in Cincinnati. The few prominent residences are stone as well. The town must have been something to behold in its heyday. Today it is hanging on instead of thriving, looking for benefactors to return it to its former glory. Driving out of town in any direction you find simple one- and two-story frame homes on streets lined with mature trees, many of them built in between 1880 and 1930. These cozy neighborhoods then yield to miles of vast, rich farmland (the green fields).

The prosperity of Greenfield at its peak isn't hard to trace. The American Pad and Textile Company, founded by Edward Lee McClain, drove the economic prosperity. McLain's notable career evolved from working at his family saddle shop in town as a boy to inventing and manufacturing a national product that made him exceedingly wealthy: a more convenient and comfortable detachable collar for horses working the fields or pulling wagons. The factory (now demolished) was located at the edge of town, only a couple blocks from the Davis home. A single rail line, including a small passenger station, connected the factory and the town to outside markets. With the advent of the automobile, demand for the collars eventually weakened. So, the factory added life jackets (almost four million), sleeping bags, and hammocks to the product mix under contracts with the US armed services using the TAPATCO brand name. Greenfield was a company town surrounded in all directions by family farms. By all accounts the company, and therefore the town, enjoyed a measure of stability relative to the rest of the nation during the Great Depression.

The McClain family distinguished itself in another significant way. They donated a new high school to Greenfield (opened in 1915) at an estimated cost of over $1 million, a fortune at the time. It became the centerpiece of the town, and it still is. Admission was based on an annual tuition of sixteen cents per student. Six years later the McClains added athletic fields and a natatorium, making it the first high school in Ohio with an indoor pool. The pool is still in use and holds the honor of being the oldest in America. The McClains also endowed the high school with over two hundred works of art — paintings, murals and statues — many of which are still on display.

Considering its small size and being remote from population centers, Greenfield's history is quite rich. Established in 1799, it attracted abolitionist farmers to settle there by design prior to the Civil War. It was one of the stops on the Underground Railroad, as formerly enslaved persons escaped across the Ohio River on their way to Canada. In the early 1900s, Frederick Douglas Patterson established a factory in town and became the first Black man in America to manufacture automobiles. After making a total of 150 cars (none survive), the company switched to making trucks and buses. Patterson had previously attended Ohio State University and was the first African American to play football for the Buckeyes (1891). Another local made a name for himself in the country music industry, Johnny Paycheck (born as Donald Eugene Lytle, 1938–2003), famous for his rendition of "Take This Job and Shove It." More recently, when the B&O Railroad sought to abandon the twenty-five miles of track that connected Greenfield to trunk lines, the town bought the section of tracks for over $2 million, thus becoming owners of the shortest railroad company in America, including valuable fiber-optic connectivity in the rail bed.

The Davis family soon outgrew their wooden frame house on South Street. Around the time Katie was in second grade (1934), Mr. Davis drove Katie and her sister Janice to attend an auction in the county seat of Hillsboro. Returning home, he announced that the family would be moving to South 2nd Street to the home he had purchased for $5,050 cash. This was a much larger, stately stone house with a big front porch and on one of the best streets in town. The family was able to spread out in the large common rooms, along with five bedrooms and four bathrooms.

When she was about ten years old (circa 1938), Katie remembers her dad taking her to her first football game at the high school, which was a comfortable stroll from their home. The game was at night. Thanks to the generosity of the McClains, the local football field had lights, an extremely unusual feature at the time, especially for such a small town. Mr. Davis had played football for the local high school and maintained an interest in the fortunes of the hometown team. Katie's father preferred to view the game from the end zone with his friends and away from the crowd, so he deposited Katie in the stands near midfield. Once the game ended, Katie waited for her dad while the stands and the field completely emptied. Abandoned and alone, she walked down the street to the auto repair garage owned by her dad, and the people there walked her home to an embarrassed father. This formative moment was Katie's introduction to the game of football.

Katie's father, John Davis, was a local success story. He married Eunice on August 7, 1917, in Hillsboro, Ohio. Eunice was a local farm girl and someone he probably had known for most of his life since they attended the same local schools (although they were one grade apart). After high school she trained as a schoolteacher at Ohio University and returned to teach all eight grades in a one-room schoolhouse outside of Greenfield. John and Eunice married and immediately started a family; they welcomed four children in eleven years. John's success came as a result of his business acumen. He advanced at the McClain factory to become the superintendent, one of the most prominent positions in town. But his sense for business and his investment skills extended to include ownership of local farmland, residential rental properties, an automobile dealership, and a local food market. The family lifestyle was well supported, and this included the expectation of eventually sending all the Davis children to college.

Tragedy befell the family when John Davis died suddenly on December 26, 1943. Katie remembers it this way:

It was the day after Christmas. I was with my friends, and somebody said, "Let's go to Hillsboro to a movie." We said, "Great." In we drove. My father went down to stoke the coal in the coal furnace. He came up and had some chest pains. Dr. Jones's light was on. Mother called him. He came down, chatted a while, and said Dad was fine. After they went to bed my mother heard the gurgle and he was gone. They couldn't find me to tell me. I'd gone to Hillsboro with the other girls. By the time I got home there were all these cars out in front of the house. My aunt was waiting for me at the door. She told me, "Go up and see your mother." I was a sophomore in high school. It made a big change. It was hard.

The Davis family certainly was not destitute, but changes were required without a steady source of household income. By this time, Katie and her sister Janice were the only children still living at home. Mrs. Davis, now widowed at age forty-six, downsized to a home they owned in the same neighborhood and still on South Street. She returned to teaching school (with one of her students being Donald Lytle, the above-mentioned future singer known as Johnny Paycheck). All the other properties were sold except for the food market, which became the surviving family business through the remaining war years. Janice and Katie both worked in the store. Katie became quite adept at driving the only family vehicle, a stick-shift, paneled truck with "Davis Grocery" painted on both sides, around town to make deliveries until she finished high school.

Katie enrolled in 1946 at Western College for Women, a small, private college located in Oxford, Ohio. The annual tuition was $1,000. After one year, it was determined that this private school would unnecessarily strain the family budget. Katie transferred to Miami University (also in Oxford) in the fall of 1947, which was substantially more affordable — about $250 per year. This move changed the direction of her life forever. Katie was destined to see many more football games.

CHAPTER 3

CONWELL FINDLEY

The first time I met Ara in 2010, I handed him a photograph and asked him to tell me about it. Ara gazed intently at a photograph of his 1941 high school football team at Akron South. It was obvious that it was a picture he had never seen before, or one he just could not recall. When he finally looked up, he simply said, "That's Conwell Findley, our tail-back. I wonder what became of him." He was referring to the person standing right beside him in the second row — seven linemen were in front and four backs stood behind. Conwell Findley was the only person of color on the team.

What can't adequately be captured is the sense of melancholy in Ara's voice when, almost without thinking, he verbally expressed his innermost thoughts as if he were the only person in the room. Embedded in his reaction was the realization that his life, even with its ups and downs, had been filled with more opportunities than he could have imagined at age eighteen. But his teammate's life may not have gone nearly as well. It was a realistic concern given the slow, but improving, trajectory of race relations in America over the intervening seventy-five years since he had played high school football with his friend. There, for a brief time, the only thing that mattered to both was success on the field. More importantly, this response reveals Ara's sensitivity to the subject.

Ara's understanding makes sense in light of his own experiences. As a youngster growing up in a first-generation immigrant family, cross-cultural experiences abounded in the Parseghian household. Ara spoke only French at an early age. This was the language spoken at home since it was common to his French mother and his Armenian father who spoke many languages. But it would have been perceived as "different" to the outside world. Eventually the entire family, all five members, embraced English as the language of their new homeland. His mother and father, while remembering their pasts, were dedicated to building the life of safety and opportunity afforded to them and their children in the United States of America. Hardship propelled them toward a better future. And hardship was not to be used as an excuse for laziness or complacency — or prejudice toward others. These immigrant parents understood bigotry all too well in their daily lives as they attempted to overcome it and assimilate into their Akron community.

Athletics can be a useful catalyst toward acceptance. Children are born innocent of prejudice, and soon enough become aware of their surroundings. Ara Parseghian was a gifted athlete growing up, although it is hard to pinpoint exactly when this became readily apparent to his parents and siblings. Other family members were neither athletically inclined nor particularly interested in sports as a cultural component of American life. Memories of Ara as a child, an adolescent, and as a young man by family and among friends in Akron center around his athletic abilities. But opportunities to participate in organized sports before high school didn't really exist as we know them today. For example, Little League baseball wasn't established until 1939, the first of the organized youth sports. Sandlots, school playgrounds, recreation centers, and gyms at places like the YMCA were the venues for aspiring athletes, and participation was local, almost exclusively by young males. Ara Parseghian would have played with boys of all ages and from a variety of backgrounds. His noteworthy athletic skills prevented him from struggling with jealousy. As a result, he learned to respect the talents of others regardless of their race or religion. He saw and judged "players," and that is how he wanted to be judged. Ara's acceptance by and of other people matured naturally and comfortably.

Professional sports in Ara's youth were limited mainly to baseball, and there were sixteen teams in two leagues. Many, if not most, of the professional players needed off-season jobs to survive. Professional football hadn't developed in the 1920s and '30s. Parents believed the secret to their children's success was a college education. Michael Parseghian understood that very well and steadfastly guided his sons, Jerry and Ara, toward that goal. The fact that colleges had athletic teams, some with notoriety, eventually tapped into Ara's strengths. At the time, college athletes in all sports were almost exclusively white. The Navy was segregated, so when Ara joined the Navy and played on the Great Lakes team, he would have had only white teammates. When Ara was assigned to deliver boots (military recruits) from Great Lakes Naval Training to Miami, Florida, for deployment, the trains went through the heart of the segregated South. The sight of separate bathrooms and water fountains offended Ara's sensibilities. The unfairness of how multiple hurdles existed for some of the young players he remembered from his neighborhood would have been impossible to ignore. Ara knew it and felt it and was determined to personally overcome it.

After Ara's discharge from the Navy, the choice of Miami University as a place to study using the GI Bill proved to be a life-changing event in dramatic ways — as historical perspectives now confirm. The change of environment from Akron, an industrial city close to home, to Oxford, Ohio, a bucolic, small college town away from home, was liberating. Ara's natural athletic abilities were appreciated as he participated in football, basketball, and baseball. There was only one Black player on the Redskin (now Red Hawk) football team, Bill Harris from Cleveland. He and Ara decided to become travel roommates for away games. They remained lifelong friends. The rub came after the 1947 season when the team was invited to the Sun Bowl in El Paso, Texas. Ara's roommate was allowed to travel with the team, but not allowed to play because of his race. This was a slight that Ara knew was patently unfair, and he never forgot it.

The integration of professional football was slightly further along by the time Ara joined the Cleveland Browns in 1948. As head coach, Paul Brown was keenly focused on winning in the new American Football Conference, something he did four consecutive times until the conference folded into the NFL. Brown's success was enhanced by giving talented Black players an opportunity to play when some of the established NFL teams were reticent. The two most prominent Black players were fullback Marion Motley and end Horace Gillom. Traveling to the away games in the new, and therefore underfunded, league presented challenges. In 1949, when the Browns played an exhibition game against college all-stars in Houston, hotel accommodations at the new Shamrock Hotel were not extended to the two Black starters on the team. Both Motley and Gillom were housed by families away from the team hotel. The other team members, including Ara Parseghian, never forgot this injustice — or the name of the hotel (since demolished).

Ara's playing career ended abruptly after the 1949 season due to injury. A football coaching opening materialized at Miami, first as freshman coach and then as head coach. In Oxford a relaxed atmosphere welcomed students of color onto campus, but not many were financially able to take advantage of the opportunity. The sports teams, including football, naturally reflected the general campus population. The resulting teams included very few Black players. There was a smattering of Black players over Ara's five years. With increased success ethical challenges reemerged for the team.[1] The 1955 team, in Ara's last season, was his best with a 9–0 record, named Mid-America Conference Champions, and ranked top 20 in the polls. They were invited to the Tangerine Bowl played in Orlando, Florida. Ara asked for a team vote on whether or not to accept the invitation. When the team was informed that teammates of color would not be able to play in the segregated state, the team voted no. With support from the Miami University Administration, Ara turned down the prestigious bowl invitation.

Meanwhile, at Notre Dame some progress toward integration was being made, but at a snail's pace. Coach Frank Leahy's early teams were largely composed of returning veterans (all white). When that pool of talent evaporated, competition for high school recruits heated up in the early 1950s, and the net to attract players naturally expanded with the assistance of the national network of Notre Dame alumni. Having a national reputation in football helped, but it hardly offset the perception of other potential negatives where Black players were concerned — substandard high school preparation for a rigorous institution, an unfamiliar religious orientation, and a northern location not geographically known for open-mindedness. The Ku Klux Klan (KKK), which disdained non-white Protestants along with Catholics and Jews, re-emerged in a second wave in 1920 in Evansville, Indiana.

The first Black athlete to earn an ND monogram (varsity letter) was Wayne Edmonds from Canonsburg, Pennsylvania. The assistant coach who recruited Wayne promised his parents that he would personally provide transportation every Sunday for Wayne to attend the church of his choice in South Bend, a promise he dutifully honored. Getting a haircut proved more troublesome as Wayne was initially denied access to the (privately run) Notre Dame campus barber shop located on the ground floor of Badin Hall. An official intervention was required to correct that slight. With the naming of the socially progressive Father Theodore Hesburgh as president of Notre Dame in 1952, increasingly more corrective attention was paid to issues of racial equality on campus.

Moving to Northwestern and the Big Ten Conference in 1956 changed the equation for Ara. Attracting Black players yielded more attention across this collection of large, mostly state-sponsored schools in what was perceived as the dominant college conference. Now Ara could compete for football talent in a prominent conference, at a college located on the outskirts of metropolitan Chicago. But the issue of higher academic standards at the only private university in the conference remained a definite recruiting impediment.

When Ara arrived at Notre Dame in 1964, he was faced with evaluating the talent on the team he inherited from a zero-based perspective. Everyone had a chance to showcase their skills. But the coach knew that many of the players from the previous season were misplaced in positions. Because of a return to more liberal game substitution and two-platoon football (having different players on offense and defense), there were double the number of slots to fill. Players' skills could be managed precisely for offensive or defensive teams with special teams woven in. A couple of Black players found their stride under this system, Dick Arrington and Alan Page.

But recruiting Black student-athletes in the spring of 1964 for their eligibility as sophomores in the fall of 1966, a national championship season, proved to be challenging. No Black athletes were recruited. In fact, matters didn't improve substantially for many years.

Katie Parseghian recalled having a 1969 summer cookout at the Parseghians' home on Washington Street with Fathers Hesburgh and

Joyce among the guests. Father Ted pulled aside Ara and quizzed him about why so few Black players were on the football team. Ara provided a straightforward answer. "We are recruiting qualified 'kids' and the Admissions Office is turning them down." A message was delivered to the highest university authority, and a notation made. After that, recruiting cycles were a little more accommodating. Call it what you will, but think of it as "Hesburghian" affirmative action for the football team. Father Ted knew that Notre Dame would benefit from a more diverse student body. But in particular he may have been sensitive to the images, now clearly seen nationwide on television, of his team without diversity. He was, after all, on the United States Civil Rights Commission and his personal credibility was also being judged by what was displayed in full view of the nation on televised Notre Dame football games.

It would be entirely incorrect to believe that Ara engaged in any form of affirmative action once practices began. All of his former players point to his intrinsic fairness as one of the hallmarks of his successful coaching style. His favorite players were the young men who worked hard and earned their way onto the team and into the lineup. In that sense alone, he played favorites.

Prospects for the team improved as better players joined. More of them were Black. It all came together with a national championship in 1973. Then the tide turned without warning. Over the summer school period in 1974, six Black football players, all rising sophomores, were suspended for what was publicly termed a "dormitory violation" — in reality, women were present in an all-male dorm and engaging in consensual sex. Ara fought hard to keep his guys in school. But in the end the high standards of behavior expected at Notre Dame resulted in a meaningful punishment. Ara took it hard. He viewed it as a personal failure that he hadn't prepared the players to make better choices or that he hadn't expected enough of these young men whom he, Father Hesburgh, and the larger Notre Dame community desperately wanted to succeed. Without the additional talents that these young players might have provided to the team in the 1974 season, Ara's last, the Irish were shorthanded to defend their national title. The incident was one of the contributing factors that led Ara to resign after that season. Five of the six suspended students returned one year later to play at Notre

Dame and ultimately became part of the nucleus that won the National Championship in 1977 under Head Coach Dan Devine.

Unknowingly, Ara made history late in his Notre Dame career (1972) when he hired a former Irish player, Greg Blache, as an assistant coach. Blache is believed to be the first coach of color for any of the Notre Dame varsity sports teams. He went on to have a successful career in coaching, primarily in the NFL.

The lingering question of what ever happened to Conwell Findley remained unanswered for many years. Credit goes to Kriss Parseghian Humbert (Ara's daughter) for some diligent detective work. She eventually discovered a Conwell Findley living in Akron who qualified age-wise as possibly being the son of her father's teammate. So, she boldly reached out. Success! The younger Conwell, now in his seventies, was able to provide a heartfelt summary of his father's life to Ara and the rest of the Parseghian family.

The Findleys were still an Akron family, having lived there for three generations. Ara's friend Conwell went from graduation at Akron South High School to employment as a welder at Goodyear, where he worked for forty-four years until his retirement. He was a family man: married to Ann Louise Findley, the father of two children (a daughter, DeHavilland, and the son who bore his name), and ultimately the grandfather of five grandchildren. Conwell the elder was known as a quiet man who lived a very productive life. He died in 1994 and is interred at Mt. Peace Cemetery. When Kriss asked Conwell if his father followed sports at all, the answer came back, "Not much, but he did follow the career of his friend 'Arie' Parseghian." Today, the younger Conwell and his wife, Frances, still live in Akron, very close to the home where Ara's parents resided in their later years.

CHAPTER 4

THE PLAYER

Ara Parseghian enlisted in the Navy in the spring of 1943. He reported for duty at Great Lakes Naval Training Station on April 1. New recruits were assigned for rotation around the first of every month.[1] As Ara stepped off the train in Chicago for the Navy bus north to the Lake County military campus, playing football might have been the furthest thing from his mind, and with good reasons.

America had been at war for 490 days since the Japanese attack at Pearl Harbor on December 7, 1941. The Parseghian family first heard the news on their home radio on that Sunday. Troubles that had also been brewing in Europe for almost a decade had erupted in 1939 with the Nazi invasion of Poland. Ara finished his senior year of high school, graduating in 1942, and then entered the University of Akron that fall for two full semesters where he played football and basketball. With the war ramping up, every able-bodied young man was being pressed into military service. Thoughts of pursuing a normal life were definitely put on hold as the entire nation focused on the war effort that was taking place now on two fronts thousands of miles apart.

Great Lakes Training Station was created to serve the needs of the Navy right after World War I. Under the false belief that the "war to end

28

all wars" had already happened, the facility closed in 1933. With the advent of Nazi aggression, the training station was reopened in December 1940 and has remained open ever since. The base campus in 1943 included over thirty buildings and operated as a small city. When war was declared in 1941, there were about six thousand sailors in training. That amount grew overnight to about sixty-eight thousand. At the height of the war there were over one hundred thousand trainees and seven hundred trainers on the base. As the Navy's only training center for enlisted personnel, it became the largest military training facility in the world; over one million persons were trained there by the war's end.

The year 1943 was one of transition for a world at war. On April 1, Ara did not know that it would be 769 days until Victory in Europe Day and 867 days until Victory over Japan Day. The Nazi Army had stalled in its advance into Russia and started retreating from the Battle of Stalingrad. The Eastern Front gave the Allies enough breathing room to regather resources, but at a cost of millions of Russian lives. In the Pacific, the Doolittle Raid had surprised the Empire of Japan and the naval Battle of Midway in June 1942 had altered the balance of power on the Pacific Ocean. In the spring of 1943, the entire nation was on full anxious alert and the historical outcomes were far from certain. Moreover, families and communities were becoming increasingly aware of mounting casualties, with no end in sight. In complete secrecy from all but a select few, physicist Robert Oppenheimer sold his tract of remote ranch land in New Mexico to the US government in 1943 for the purpose of creating Los Alamos Laboratories. The decisive weapon of the war, the atomic bomb, would be developed there.

As part of the Great Lakes Station there were teams of enlisted men created to improve physical training and base morale. They would compete with college teams primarily in football and baseball. The 1943 Great Lakes Bluejacket football team coached by Tony Hinkle (Butler University) made a name for itself with a 10–2 record, including a final win against defending national champion Notre Dame (19–14). The touchdowns for the Irish were scored by Johnny Lujack and Creighton Miller, both future College Football Hall of Famers. As a result, the Bluejackets were ranked sixth by the Associated Press. This was serious, college-level competition, and trainee Ara Parseghian would have been keenly aware of the Notre Dame team and its success.

Many years later Ara described his experience at Great Lakes in this way:

> I went through recruit training at Great Lakes in March of 1943. Then I went to Bainbridge, Maryland for training as a company commander and then they shipped me back to Great Lakes. Depending on how badly they needed the group, we would take about 120 to 140 recruits — starting from the time they came in — and we would get them out of there in six weeks, or sometimes twelve weeks. We took them through the whole routine. We would take them to classes — various nautical things that they'd be working on — and made sure that all of the protocols of Navy discipline were adhered to in the barracks. That's what we did; it was a lot like being a head coach. And as it turned out, in 1944, I had enough time off I could go out for the team — which they allowed at the time.

Of course, players on the successful 1943 squad were cycled out to active duty, as was the head coach. In April 1944, Ohio State Head Football Coach Paul Brown was commissioned a lieutenant and assigned to coach the Bluejackets in 1944. However, Paul Brown did not return to Ohio State after the war but became the first head coach and namesake of the professional Cleveland Browns in the new All-America Football Conference. Playing for Paul Brown would have profound professional consequences for the young sailor from Akron. Sidelined for most of the 1944 season with an ankle injury, Ara absorbed the coaching discipline and techniques of Paul Brown. The 1944 Great Lakes team finished with a 9–2–1 record and nationally ranked 17th. They lost the final game in South Bend to Notre Dame (28–7) on December 2, 1944. For the record, that date would have been the first time that Ara Parseghian set foot in the legendary Notre Dame Stadium.

In the spring of 1945, returning by train from one of the assigned trips delivering newly minted sailors to Florida, Ara was able to stop in Cincinnati and visit his first cousin Haig Avedinian (son of his father's only surviving sibling, sister Noemzar), who was in military training at Miami University. Oxford, Ohio, located about twenty miles north of Cincinnati, was the quintessential small college community. Miami had an athletic heritage of competing regionally and on occasion with larger midwestern colleges, including those in the Big Ten. Ara was immediately attracted to the bucolic, red-brick campus and decided that he would like to attend Miami if and when his Navy days were over. The war finally ended on August 15, 1945 — only days after the second atomic bomb was dropped on Nagasaki. Ara was discharged on December 1, 1945, and immediately enrolled at Miami in the spring semester of 1946, taking full advantage of the GI Bill.

Of course, Ara went out for the Redskin (the mascot at the time, later changed to Red Hawk) football team in the spring of 1946, with three years of eligibility. Ara's year playing at Great Lakes did not count against Ara. The fog of history obscures that Ara actually played on two other Miami sports teams: baseball and basketball. He received varsity letters in all three sports — highly unusual at the time and virtually unheard of by today's standards.

In 1946, the team went 7–3 under Head Coach Sid Gillman, playing against Purdue University, the University of Memphis Naval Air Technical Training Center (NATTC), the University of Dayton, Bowling Green State University, Xavier University, Ohio University, Bradley University, the University of Miami (Florida), Western Michigan University, and the University of Cincinnati.

The following year was even better, with an 8–0–1 record and an invitation to play in the Sun Bowl in El Paso against Texas Tech. Miami won 13–12. The schedule included Murray State University, State University, Kent State University, Bowling Green, Xavier (this was the tie game), Ohio, Bradley, Dayton, Wichita State University, and Cincinnati.

Katie Davis attended college across town at Western College for Women as a freshman in 1946, and she went to Miami home football games with her girlfriends. She was familiar with the name "Ara Parseghian" from the public address announcements during games. She transferred to Miami in the autumn of 1947. Walking across campus that fall on what is known as the Slant Walk, she caught the attention of a passing Ara, who mentioned boldly, "It is snowing down south" — a reference to the fact that her slip was showing. Slightly embarrassed, Katie had no idea who had made the comment. But Ara remembered the incident and decided he wanted to get to know this young lady. So, he called her on the phone for a date.

Katie told me her side of the story:

> He swears it's not true, but I had known who he was because my first year
> at Western, in the same town as Miami, I'd gone over to see some football
> games. When I moved over to Miami, he had spotted me and tracked me
> down and called me on the phone out of the blue. I swear he said, "This is
> "Art" Parseghian." I figured later that he thought I would be scared off by
> his first name. Anyway, he said he didn't do that, but I think he did.

When asked seventy years later if it was love at first sight, Katie responded, "No, I had about four boyfriends at the time." Yet the other
guys never had a chance. Things moved along swiftly for Katie and Ara.
Returning from his final college game as a player, the January 1948 Sun
Bowl in El Paso, Texas, Ara stopped in Greenfield, Ohio, to formally
meet Katie's mother, Eunice. He brought a gift of souvenir linens from
the Texas border town for the occasion; Ara made a good first impression, which lasted.

Ara was an outstanding player at Miami. In 1947, as only a junior,
he achieved national recognition as a First Team "Little" All-American
at fullback — a designation for players from smaller schools and conferences. At the end of the 1947 season, Ara was elected captain for
what he expected to be his final year of football at Miami. But Ara's college football career took an unexpected turn in the spring of 1948. In
the 1948 National Football League Draft, Ara was selected in the 13th
round as the 109th overall pick by the Pittsburgh Steelers. Simultaneously, during his spring baseball season, as a left-handed pitcher, he was
being scouted by the Pittsburgh Pirates of the National League. He was
also recruited by the upstart Cleveland Browns in the newly-created
All-America Football League. Some off-season negotiations transpired,
the details of which are unrecorded. Ultimately, Ara reported to the
Cleveland Browns for the 1948 season, thus terminating his college eligibility. Katie estimates that his salary and bonus amounted to about
$10,000. The financial incentives must have been too substantial to ignore
because Ara went out and purchased a brand new 1948 Pontiac sedan.

The 1948 Cleveland Browns were a legendary team and part of a
legendary dynasty. The Browns crafty head coach, Paul Brown, remembered Ara from his playing days at Great Lakes and lobbied for him to

join the team. Ara was one of four rookies that made the Browns roster. The team was loaded with talent, including All-Pro selections Otto Graham (a quarterback and future Hall of Famer), Marion Motley (fullback), Mac Speedie (left end), and Lou Groza (lineman and Hall of Fame kicker). The Browns finished undefeated at 14–0–0 and won the league championship 49–7 against the Buffalo Bills. The Browns were the champions in all four years of the new league (1946–1949). In 1950, they were added to the National Football League along with the San Francisco 49ers and the Baltimore Colts — and won league championship honors again.

Given the expectations of a demanding coach and staff and the quality of the starters on the team in 1948, Ara's personal statistics were beyond respectable. Recall that this was still the era of single-platoon football (the same players played on offense and defense) with limited substitutions. Here is how he fared:

Games played (12) and started (1)
Rushing attempts (32) and yards gained (135)
Pass receptions (2) for yards gained (31)
Punt returns (2) for yards gained (41)
Interceptions (1) for 56 yards gained
One rushing touchdown and one passing touchdown for a total of
   12 points

Thus Ara's first season in the pros was considered very successful. He was named his team's Rookie of the Year. It was convenient to live at home with his parents and commute to Cleveland for practice and games. Cavernous Cleveland Memorial Stadium, home of the Browns, was the third largest sports venue in America, behind the Los Angeles Coliseum and Chicago's Soldier Field. Katie was able to attend a couple games driving up from Greenfield, where she and her mother were planning a wedding for after the season ended. Ara's parents also attended home games. His mother, still concerned about her son's well-being, frequently uttered, "It makes me so nervous!" with her French accent.

On December 30, 1948, Katie and Ara were married at the First Presbyterian Church on 457 Jefferson Street in Greenfield, Ohio. Both families were well represented and plenty of photos were taken to remember the event. The wedding reception, featuring tea and cookies as refreshments, was held in the church basement. This was a common practice at the time in the Midwest.

As for "Art" Parseghian, he was never heard from again.

The newly married Parseghian couple left Greenfield in the gleaming Pontiac, initially driving to Cincinnati for the night and then on to New York City for their honeymoon. They arrived in the city without reservations and stayed one night at the Claridge Hotel. This hotel (now razed), located at Broadway and 44th Street, was famous for the Camel Cigarette smoking billboard. But because it felt like a stuffy retirement home they relocated to the Hotel Edison, which is still operating at 228 West 47th Street. Katie remembers seeing *Kiss Me Kate* on Broadway and dining at the Blue Ribbon Restaurant and Schrafft's.

Ara and Katie returned to Miami University after their honeymoon as married students, and they were assigned to the Vetville compound for a semester. This was temporary housing created for returning veterans. Their home was one half of the typical duplex with two rooms and a bath for each side and the heating and cooking by kerosene. Ara completed his remaining six credit hours and graduated from Miami University in the spring of 1949.

With their belongings packed into their Pontiac in late May of 1949, the young couple's future looked very promising. Driving toward Akron, Katie and Ara may have logically thought that their time in Oxford was now in their rearview mirror. Soon enough fate would enter the picture.

SECOND QUARTER

(1944–1963)

CHAPTER 5

OXFORD

While Ara was finishing up his degree at Miami University in the spring of 1949, the football team welcomed a new head coach. Taking over for George Blackburn was the former head coach of Dennison University (Granville, Ohio), one Wayne Woodrow "Woody" Hayes. He was assisted by Warren Schmakel, Woodrow Willis, William Hoover, and Ben Ankney.

Of course, since Ara had been named captain for the 1948 team before leaving for Cleveland, he knew many of the returning Miami football players. He became a noncontact fixture, getting in shape at spring practices in 1949. His presence and his natural leadership abilities were not lost on the new head coach. Perhaps more significantly, Miami had named a new athletic director, John Brickels, in 1949. He had been an assistant coach for Paul Brown in Cleveland during the 1948 season. He knew Ara well.

Katie and Ara initially lived with Ara's parents during the summer of 1949, occupying the basement with a shared first floor bathroom. Getting in shape for the Browns' summer camp was job one. There was no rush to move to Cleveland and have their own place until Ara's pro football career was more established. Cleveland was a reasonable commute from Akron. With rare exceptions, professional athletes in all sports could not live off of their playing salaries, so offseason jobs were required. Ara elected to try his hand at selling automobiles. Whether or not he sold many cars isn't known today and is immaterial. What he did learn were the valuable skills of salesmanship. Being familiar with the culture of car sales would also pay future dividends when Ara needed to supplement his coaching income with work on auto advertisement campaigns. Ara went to the 1949 preseason camp for Paul Brown and the Cleveland professional team with confidence and optimism. Katie was busy looking at apartments closer to the Browns' practice facilities.

The Browns had three preseason games, and Ara was settling into his positions as fullback (offense) and defensive back (defense). Things were going well, as hoped, until the second game of the regular season against Baltimore, September 11, 1949, in Cleveland Stadium. The exact moment that caused Ara's injury in the game isn't recorded. He finished his "day at the office" and treated Katie to a movie that evening. Katie recalled that as they left the theater, Ara started to register significant pain in his hip. It was so painful that he had to lean on her for help getting to their car. Ara was intent on returning to game action during the 1949 season and sought medical treatment from several doctors. Paul Brown was at first skeptical about the extent of the injury. This only made Ara more anxious since he didn't want to be branded a slacker. Unfortunately, his hip never improved significantly. Ara kept going to practices and even traveled with the team to away games although he didn't play. Finally, after the season's end, an experienced orthopedic doctor diagnosed the problem. Ara had lost all cartilage in his hip. The prospects of him ever returning to play professional football were dim and medically ill-advised.

The depth of winter, from January through March 1950, in gloomy northern Ohio, was one of uncertainty with moments of despair for the young Parseghian couple. They had finally found an apartment of their own close to Cleveland and were in the process of moving. A happy complication occurred: Katie was pregnant. Then a lifeline arrived. Woody Hayes was looking for a freshman football coach. John Brickels, now the athletic director and head basketball coach at Miami, stepped in and recommended Ara. Hayes, taking cues from his immediate boss and remembering Ara favorably from the previous spring, acquiesced to the suggestion. Woody Hayes called Ara personally and offered him a position on his staff. Paul Brown also weighed in to advise Ara that it would be a good move for him, all things considered. Without other viable options, Ara and Katie grabbed the lifeline. After only two weeks in their new apartment, they repacked the Pontiac and retraced their route back to Oxford in the spring of 1950.

Woody Hayes was a guy quite comfortable with his militaristic image. He was also a guy intensely focused on achieving success, which translated into advancing up the ranks of college coaching rapidly. In his mind, Miami would not be his last stop. His entire focus was winning the varsity games, which he did during a successful second season in 1950. In two years at Miami, he amassed an overall record of 14–5. He wasn't overly concerned about the record of his freshman team. They were more useful as a practice squad for his Saturday players. Along the way a surprising thing happened. Under Ara's leadership the freshmen went 4–0, with victories over the University of Cincinnati, Xavier University, Ohio University, and the University of Dayton.

Ara's relationship as an underling on the Hayes coaching staff wasn't ideal. Woody preferred to snap orders at people, and the young assistant was a prime target: "Ara, go get coffee for us." Hayes had an explosive temper and was known to take out frustrations at staff meetings by banging, throwing, and kicking things. Those encounters didn't endear Ara to his new boss. But Ara had a job, and he was still working in the football realm at a place where Katie and he were both familiar and comfortable. He was grateful for the opportunity.

The following is a letter dated March 4, 1983, from Ara to Woody Hayes, Athletic Office, Ohio State University.

Dear Woody:

   Just a note of congratulations on being elected to the College Football Hall of Fame. Your record speaks for itself, and I personally know of the concern and attention that you gave your players. The mark of a great coach is the respect he commands from his players and that respect has been earned. Your players respect for you is to be envied.

You and I may not have agreed on every issue, but my memory is not so hazy that I don't remember who gave me my first coaching job, and also was instrumental in influencing the powers-to-be at Miami to hire me as your replacement. You've earned your place in the Sun and as the old Yiddish saying goes, "Enjoy."

Give my best to Anne and Steve.

Sincerely,

Ara

Minimal pay went to a freshman football coach. To supplement this income Ara signed on as the freshman basketball coach under John Brickels. Katie recalled Ara voicing a preference for coaching basketball over football in those months—perhaps due to the divergent personalities of his bosses.

Katie also remembered their first real home, which was an apartment in a two-family home on Locust Street and close to campus. She described it as "one of those Sears-Roebuck catalog homes that was delivered as a kit and built before the Depression." They were on the first floor and had one bedroom. Ara and Katie welcomed their first child, daughter Karan, into this home on June 6, 1950.

After the 1950 season, Woody Hayes bolted to take the head coaching job at Ohio State University on February 18, 1951—a school known at the time as the graveyard for college coaches. Hayes took all of his loyal assistants with him and assumed incorrectly that Parseghian would follow him to Columbus. At first, the mercurial Hayes was miffed at Ara for not being loyal to him. Woody Hayes turned things around at Ohio State and became a coaching legend in the process with five national championships and thirteen Big Ten Championships. Later, when Ara had obvious coaching success, Woody pridefully took some of the credit. The two remained cordial and respectful friends but intense competitors when their teams played against each other.

A mellow Ara Parseghian told his story almost fifty years after the fact as follows:

I was with the Cleveland Browns in 1948 and '49 and I got hurt in '49. I was working on my master's at Miami of Ohio. Woody Hayes was the coach there then and I had helped out the spring before in '49. He called me because he knew of my injury and said he had an opening as Freshman Coach. Of course, back in those days you're going to coach the basketball team, the golf team, everything but drive the bus. So, in any event, I decided I'd go and I'd be able to work on my master's at the same time I was coaching. Well, the bug jumped right up and grabbed me.

I had good fortune. A lot of coaches have to wait years before they can become a head coach. Some people never get it. I accepted the freshman job in February of 1950. Then Woody Hayes went to Ohio State and in less than a year I went from not even being in coaching to coaching the freshman football and basketball teams to Head Coach. One of the things that probably influenced it was that we were at the banquet and when they introduced me as the Freshman Coach, my entire freshman team stood up and gave me a standing ovation. I have a feeling that ovation had a big influence on the alumni that were there, the sports fans that were there, the people in administration. The next thing you know, in less than a year I'm the Head Coach at Miami at the age of twenty-seven.[1]

The President at Miami University of Ohio had some ideas about who should be named head coach. But Athletic Director John Brickels listened to voices of influential alums in Cincinnati who were advancing Ara's name. A limited search was conducted. For example, Ara's former Miami teammate Paul Dietzel was interviewed for the job and made awkward overtures to Ara that he would like to have him on his staff. Yet Ara already knew he was the lead candidate and Brickels had all but offered him the job. In early March, the offer became official and twenty-seven-year-old Ara Parseghian was named the head football coach at Miami University.

Paul Dietzel, a native of Fremont, Ohio, played center for Miami, graduating in 1948. He had assistant coaching jobs at Army under Earl "Red" Blaik, the University of Cincinnati under Sid Gillman, and the University of Kentucky under Bear Bryant. His head coaching credentials are impressive: Louisiana State University (LSU), 1955–1961; US Military Academy (West Point), 1962–1965; and the University of South Carolina, 1966–1974. In 1958, his LSU team went 11–0 and was named consensus national champion. He was 9–1 in 1959 (ranked 3rd) and 9–1 in 1961 (ranked 4th). He later became a successful athletic director at South Carolina, LSU, and Samford University.

Ara and Paul intersected again, but in a different capacity from coaching. During the 1963 season Dietzel (at Army) and Parseghian (at Northwestern) were paired for a Saturday evening syndicated TV show reviewing the games of that weekend. Ara did his portion from studios in downtown Chicago and Dietzel made his way to studios in New York City. It was one of the very first interactive TV sports shows. The final show featured the coaches meeting together at studios in New York (and happened to be on the Saturday after the assassination of President John F. Kennedy). The show lasted only this one season.

With only one year of college coaching experience as an assistant, now Ara was a head coach. Quite a change from the previous year to the day from when he was essentially floundering without a job! Ara's rapid advancement even surprised Paul Brown. At the time Ara remembered him saying, "Ara doesn't know what he doesn't know." That can be true of almost anyone starting a new job. But Ara wasn't just anyone. He was a good student. He'd been respectfully making mental notes of the good and the bad qualities that made Paul Brown and Woody Hayes tick. More to the point, Ara was a quick learner. With his reputation now on the line, Miami Athletic Director John Brickels was counting on Ara to deliver.

CHAPTER 6

FOOTBALL IS A COACHES' GAME

It is difficult to place enough emphasis on the importance of coaching in college football success. John Underwood, a gifted writer for *Sports Illustrated*, summarized it well in a coaching film script he composed in 1978 for the first College Football Hall of Fame located near Cincinnati:

> More than any other, football is a coaches' game. It is a product of the ability of the men who teach it, a tribute to their genius and their dedication. It is a sport shaped in the image of these men — unique, vigorous, oft-times noble individuals who found in coaching not only a meaningful life's work but a means of expression. A purpose and a fulfillment. The best of coaches did not inherit winning teams, they made them. Winning coaches come in all sizes, shapes and personalities. They have only one common trait: the ability to hold a team in the palm of their hands.[1]

Ara was a head football coach for twenty-four years. His first assignment at Miami was the result of exceedingly good luck, and undeserved based on any track record. He had never been the head coach of anything — not even a high school team. Contemporary, conventional wisdom is that it takes about ten thousand hours to become proficient at any complicated job. At most, Ara had about one thousand hours under his belt when he took over for Woody Hayes.

There must be something in the water in Oxford, Ohio, because Miami University has earned a reputation for being the "cradle of coaches." Ara was one of the early infants in that cradle. Efforts to explain the special environment at Miami may miss an important truth. Coaching isn't taught there, but it can be learned there. This applies to all sports, not just football. While some of the coaches who eventually became successful elsewhere matriculated at Miami as students, the baton of success hasn't passed seamlessly from one to another. The magic is in the quiet lack of national attention that has been afforded to Miami, a fairly good-sized college (with about eight thousand coeducational students in 1951, five thousand of which were males) with modest aspirations to beat traditional rivals and finish respectably in conference play in the second-tier Mid-America Conference (established in 1946). In other words, Miami is an ideal setting for newer coaches to develop and grow. Failure isn't fatal as long as there is a pattern of improvement and room for hope. It became an incubator for many talented but inexperienced young coaches trying to learn their craft, and it became a natural feeder for openings in college coaching ranks at higher levels. Ara was at the right place. Had he not been a Miami man himself, his career may have never taken this fortuitous course.

There is an official Cradle of Coaches Association at Miami and new members are elected periodically, across all sports. For example, the Los Angeles Dodgers' Hall of Fame Manager Walter Alston, a Miami graduate, is included as a baseball coach. Those with football credentials are (in order of induction): Weeb Ewbank, Bill Narduzzi, John Pont, Paul Brown, Ara Parseghian, Paul Dietzel, Bill Mallory, Carmen Cozza, Earl "Red" Blaik, Woody Hayes, Bo Schembechler, John Harbaugh, and Jim Tressel.

Ara didn't enter the first meeting with his team as an unknown quantity. The seniors on the team knew him from watching him practice with them in 1949 when they were rising sophomores. No doubt they admired him as an accomplished professional player from their own ranks. The sophomores knew him as their freshman coach. So, he started in 1951 with a platform of shared experience and goodwill. This may have been the most important factor during that first year as head coach. Ara might make mistakes with the Xs and Os, but the team and coaching staff were on the same page regarding discipline, confidence, and respect from the first day. Cincinnati business leader Roger Howe was an undergrad at Miami during Ara's first year as head coach. He clearly recalls sitting on the fire escape of his fraternity house watching the football team practice within his gaze. What surprised him the most was that Ara actively engaged himself with coaching the physical aspects of the game, participating in blocking and tackling drills. It made a lasting impression.

Ara's first season finished with a respectable 7–3–0 record (3–1 in Mid-America Conference play). His first game was on September 22, an away contest against Wichita State University. Upon arrival in Kansas on the Friday before the game there was a confrontation at the registration desk. Tom Pagna, a player on that team and later a Notre Dame assistant coach for Ara, recalled the scene:

> I noticed a delay as we walked through the lobby to get our room keys. A crowd had gathered around Ara and the hotel manager. Bailey, one of our top players had his picture in the paper the day before, and some of the hotel residents told the manager they didn't want him on the same floor with them. We had other Blacks on the team, but the hotel guests only knew about Bailey from his publicity. Ara was incensed. "If we can't stay together as a team he shouted, then none of us will stay here." The manager finally gave in.[2]

The Black players were assigned to the hotel ballroom and slept on rollaway beds. The Miami team won 21–3.

Coach Parseghian's second game was the home opener against Bowling Green State University on September 29, which yielded another strong win (46–7). The winning momentum stopped abruptly in week three with a home loss to Xavier University (Cincinnati) of 14–32. The remaining wins were against Western Michigan University (34–27),

Ohio University (7–0), the University of Buffalo (27–7), the University of Dayton (21–20), and Case Western Reserve University (34–7). The remaining losses were to Marquette University (7–27) and traditional rival University of Cincinnati on Thanksgiving Day (14–19). Only the game against Marquette wasn't a close loss. A couple of the wins might even be considered lopsided.

An interesting thing happened after the home loss to Xavier. Athletic Director John Brickels (also listed in the Media Guide as an assistant football coach) took the stage to criticize certain aspects of play and some coaching decisions made during the game in front of the players and the press. (Readers might recall that Brickels had been an assistant coach under Paul Brown at Cleveland, and therefore had serious football credentials of his own.) Ara walked out and led John into the coaches' office. According to Katie, in private, Ara said, "Don't ever do that again." Mark the date, October 6, 1951, when Ara demanded complete responsibility for his team and established himself forever, for better or worse, as a head football coach.

This event demonstrates a defining aspect of Parseghian's coaching style and character. Over the course of his entire twenty-four-year career, there isn't a recorded instance of Ara criticizing a player or one of his assistant coaches in public, especially after a tough game. He could be very critical with his teams in practices and behind closed gates, often using colorful language to make a point. But Ara's players and coaches always knew his style came from a positive desire aimed at improvement. On Saturday afternoons they were in a battle as one team with a leader who cared deeply. He would personally take any heat after a game, whether or not the team had been successful. That was part of his job.

For the next four years at Miami, his teams had consistent success with wins, losses, and a lone tie: 1952 (8–1); 1953 (7–1–1); 1954 (8–1); and 1955 (9–0). Ara eventually beat Cincinnati, the team's most heated rival, in his final two seasons. In 1954, Miami played Indiana in Bloomington and won 6–0. This was Ara's first game against a Big Ten opponent and was considered to be a significant step up in level of difficulty. Katie recalls that the result prompted an Indiana official to comment that "Ara could have a bright coaching future somewhere, if it weren't for his last name." Prejudice has many faces, in many places.

But Ara learned a serious coaching lesson after this game. The following week Miami experienced its only loss at home against Dayton (12–20), a mediocre 3–6–1 opponent coached by second-year Head Coach Hugh Devore (who reappears later in the narrative of Ara's time at Notre Dame). Determining how to manage the team's emotional letdown from a loss on the heels of a big win made a lasting impression on the young coach. In 1955, Miami opened against Big Ten opponent Northwestern in Evanston and won 25–14. Lesson learned, with no letdown in the second game of the season, Miami finished with a perfect 9–0 record, and ranked twentieth nationally.

On the family front, things were also going well. While still at the Locust Street apartment, daughter Kristan (nicknamed Kriss) was born on February 27, 1952. With the addition of a second child, Katie and Ara built a new home just out of town on Contreras Pike, across from the Oxford Country Club golf course. A son, Michael Ara, was born on February 27, 1955. The astute reader may have noticed that mother Katie Parseghian, daughter Kriss Parseghian, and son Michael Parseghian all share the very same birthday, February 27. While this might be a matter of unusual convenience for family birthday celebrations, it is also a statistical anomaly. The chances of this happening are about one in 4.5 million.

All three Parseghian children were born during the Miami years at Hamilton Hospital. They lived in a congenial neighborhood of young families. Among their good friends and neighbors were the Rohrs. Bill Rohr became the head basketball coach at Miami (replacing Brickels) in 1951. Parseghian and Rohr had parallel coaching careers that eventually took both families to Northwestern University in Evanston, Illinois. Bill Rohr is a basketball inductee in the Miami University Cradle of Coaches Association.

The five-year summary sheet of the Miami team under Ara is impressive. There were only six losses in five seasons. Ara never lost back-to-back games. In an era of single-platoon football (meaning the same players played offense and defense), Ara's teams were especially stingy on defense. The same players on offense made defense much easier by playing keep-away, resulting in some high-scoring games. Coach Ara Parseghian was making a name for himself, in spite of his last name.

A move away from the friendly confines of Oxford to the Big Ten Conference was earned and imminent.

Meanwhile, 225 miles northwest of Oxford, Ohio, in South Bend, Indiana, events were transpiring that would eventually cascade into an opportunity for Ara.

In 1951, Father Theodore M. Hesburgh was the executive vice president at Notre Dame, and one of the departments under his direct purview was athletics. In 1952, he became the university president and he named Father Edmund P. Joyce to fill his former position. They were a solid team for thirty-five years and both remained intimately involved with athletics. That meant Notre Dame football first and foremost. In 1953, the Irish were 9–0–1 in what was to be Head Coach Frank Leahy's final season. A convincing argument could be made that this team should have earned at least a share of the National Championship title that year, but didn't. Leahy appeared on the cover of *Newsweek* magazine early in December. By February 1954, two months later, Frank Leahy was no longer the head coach. Leahy's declining health was cited as the reason; he had collapsed during the 1953 Georgia Tech game and was even given last rites in the Notre Dame locker room by Father Joyce. But make no mistake, retiring wasn't Frank Leahy's idea. Instead, twenty-five-year-old Terry Brennan was named as Leahy's replacement. Brennan, a former Notre Dame player and an assistant coach to Leahy, had turned twenty-six when football resumed.

Notre Dame Football has not been a forgiving environment since the era of Coach Knute Rockne. From day one, everything about the job was too intense for Brennan to achieve success as head coach. Given his youth and inexperience, Brennan got off to a surprisingly good start. In 1954, the team went 9–1 and finished ranked 4th. Terry Brennan amassed what today would be considered a reasonably decent 32–18 record: 1955 (8–2, ranked 9th); 1956 (2–8, unranked); 1957 (7–3, ranked 10th); and 1958 (6–4, ranked 17th). Along the way he coached a Heisman Trophy winner, Paul Hornung (1956), and broke the historic NCAA forty-seven-game winning streak of Bud Wilkinson's Oklahoma Sooners in 1957. But the Notre Dame faithful had been spoiled by four national championships under Leahy, and Brennan's record proved not quite good enough. The Notre Dame Administration did not renew Brennan's five-year contract.

Coach Joe Kuharich left his job as head coach of the Washington NFL team to replace Brennan, and led the Irish to a disappointing 5–5 record in 1958.

The careers of two talented, energetic, and young head coaches, Brennan and Parseghian, began on parallel tracks but headed in opposite directions during the mid-1950s. Looking back, one can see the irony, unfairness, and aspects of luck that also lurk in the shadows behind the notion of football being a coaches' game.

CHAPTER 7

NORTHWESTERN

A good case could be made that Ara Parseghian saved the Northwestern University football program. The proof is one simple fact. They are still playing football in Evanston, Illinois, and the Wildcats are still members of the Big Ten Conference almost seventy years later.

Consider this passage from a 1992 article by Lou Somogyi in *Blue & Gold Illustrated* (taken from a copy in Ara's personal files):

> Parseghian accepted Holcomb's offer (to coach at Northwestern) without checking out the campus. The opportunity to ascend to the Big Ten after coaching in the Mid-America Conference was all that mattered. "You have to take risks in life," Parseghian reflected. "No risk, no reward. But when I accepted the offer over the phone, I didn't see it as a risk. I was confident, full of energy and young. You have to assume the facilities will be at the level of the other schools in the Big Ten. Well, when I got there, I was appalled. I entered through a screen door that must have been put up in 1919, and the training room had one light bulb hanging from the middle of the ceiling. As I looked around, I thought, my God what have I done?

The following text comes from "Wildcats — A History of Football at Northwestern" — posted online by the university's public relations department.

1955, the year before Ara Parseghian came to Northwestern, was a major low in the history of the University's football program. The team, coached by Lou Saban, finished with a record of 0–8–1 — the worst (at that time) in the history of Northwestern Football. To make things even more bleak, their dismal record came at the end of the three-year slump which forced Bob Voigt's retirement after the 1954 season. The 1955 schedule promised nerve tingling action, versatility, power, and spirit — but all the small crowds who went to the games saw were losses.

Near the end of the season, talk began about Northwestern's place in the Big Ten — more specifically, leaving the Big Ten for a different conference. On November 1, 1955, *The Daily Northwestern* ran a front-page editorial which endorsed the move:

"The time has come for all those concerned with football at Northwestern — students, faculty, alumni, and administration — to do a little sober thinking.

The university's gridiron fortunes, steadily on the downgrade for the last four years, reached a low ebb with last Saturday's 49 to 0 trouncing by Ohio State. That game was the twentieth Big Ten defeat the Wildcats have suffered since the start of the 1952 season.

During that period, they have won a grand total of three games . . .

Should we go winless, we will be the first Big Ten team since 1918 to do so, and the first Northwestern team since 1887, when only one game was played.

What does all of this mean?

To us it proves one thing — that for some few years now Northwestern has not been fielding a team capable of meeting Big Ten opposition week after week.

We think that, under the present conditions, there are three courses open:

Northwestern can let things ride as they are and continue to lose six or seven conference games each year.

Northwestern can make some drastic changes in its athletic policies and start fielding Big Ten caliber teams once more.

Northwestern can get out of the Big Ten.

We doubt anyone concerned with the Wildcats' plight would be in favor of the first alternative.

We think the third solution is the much more logical.

Northwestern did not, of course, leave the Big Ten. In 1956, Ara Parseghian took over as Head Coach, and while he may not have transformed the Wildcats into conference champions or bowl participants, he certainly brought them to respectability. From a 0–8–1 1955 season, Parseghian and captain Ted Ringer led the team to a 4–4–1 finish in '56, including wins over Wisconsin, Purdue, and Illinois.

Northwestern fans, ready for a turnaround of football fortunes, must have been quite shocked when Parseghian's 1957 team lost every single game by devastating margins — Minnesota scored 41 to the Wildcats' 6, the Ohio State game finished 47–6, and both Purdue and Illinois beat Northwestern in 27-point shutouts.

The 1957 season, however, was a temporary jolt in Northwestern's recovery. In 1958, the team went 5–4, with tackle Andy Cverko gaining All-American honors — in 1959, 6–3. For the latter season, the team chose four captains: James Andreotti (All-American center), Ron Burton (All-American halfback), Gene Gossage, and Mike Stock. The season began with six straight wins, over Oklahoma, Iowa, Minnesota, Michigan, Notre Dame, and Indiana — but after a 24–19 loss to Wisconsin, the Wildcats could not pull off another game. Michigan State slipped by with a 5-point lead, and Illinois won their annual game against Northwestern 28–0.

The real highlights of the next few years were wins over Notre Dame — Northwestern "rivals" who were usually good enough that a Wildcat win was cause for celebration. Northwestern topped them by one point (7–6) in 1960, ending the season 5–4 — the 1961 squad beat the Irish 12–10, and ended their season 4–5.

1962 was another stunning season for Parseghian — the team, led by captain Jay Robertson, went 7–2 (this time trouncing Notre Dame 35–6), with big wins over Illinois (45–0), Miami (29–7), and Minnesota (34–22). The following year's squad ended 5–4, and in 1964, Parseghian moved on to a coaching position at Notre Dame.

When Ara Parseghian arrived at Northwestern, the school was on the brink of dropping out of its conference — by 1963, the Wildcats had been transformed into true competitors. Parseghian has since been enshrined in the College Football Hall of Fame — as has Ron Burton, his star halfback.[1]

The on-the-field record of Ara at Northwestern is adequately summarized above, and there is no need to say more. However, the personal circumstances and consequences of the eight years the Parseghians spent at Northwestern are meaningful.

The fact that Northwestern football was on the edge of extinction in 1955 wasn't a secret. The administration took immediate corrective action, as evidenced by the hiring of Stuart "Stu" Holcomb as athletic director. Holcomb had previously been head football coach at Miami (1942–1943) and at Purdue (1947–1955) in the Big Ten Conference. He was immediately tasked with finding a new head football coach for the Wildcats, one who would stem the tide. Undoubtedly, he consulted with Otto Graham (Hall of Fame quarterback) then with the Browns, who is still considered the all-time greatest player at Northwestern. The convergence of Otto's respect and friendship for Ara along with Stu's previous affiliation at Miami led toward one logical candidate for the position. Added to the resume was that Ara's 1955 Miami squad finished ranked 20th in national polls, including a home victory over the Wildcats. Northwestern yearned for that kind of success. So, Ara was offered the position early in 1956 and accepted.

The decision for Ara was just as pragmatic. If he had learned college coaching at the "undergraduate level" at Miami, it was time to get a "master's degree" at a big-name school in an important conference. With reluctance, Katie and the family prepared for a move to the Chicago area. They immediately started construction on a new home in Wilmette on Locherbie Lane — a ranch with three bedrooms and a large family room. Thankfully, Ara's coaching at Northwestern didn't add significant new stresses at home for the Parseghians. Katie and the family made the transition with relative ease; as they grew, the children eventually went to public schools in the highly thought of New Trier School District.

The immediate, official expectations for the Northwestern football program under Ara were low, given the starting point. Chicago was the second largest US metro area at the time and boasted a long history of successful professional sports. When college football had to compete for media share of mind, Northwestern wasn't much of a local fan favorite. It was generally viewed as a small (about 6,500 students), elite university located north of town in the suburb of Evanston. At the time, although in the largest media market of the conference, Northwestern was considered the perennial weakest team of the Big Ten. The predominant loyalties of the Chicago college sports audience were firmly (and appeared permanently) entrenched ninety miles away at the University of Notre Dame.

The introduction of Coach Ara Parseghian to Chicago came in a dramatic but unexpected way prior to his first game coaching at Northwestern. The *Chicago Sunday Tribune Magazine* published a multipage feature article with color photographs on September 23, 1956, titled "Can Northwestern Ever Win Again?," by Robert Cromie.

> Ara Parseghian, a dauntless and capable young man who hopes to lead Northwestern out of the football badlands before he himself falls prey to the wolves, is no believer in gridiron miracles. At least not over a full season and against seven Big Ten opponents, plus a couple of non-conference ones who many times have played "David" to the Wildcats' "Goliath."
>
> "You need a certain type of boy to put together a good team," he says, "there is truth to the adage about a rotten apple making a darn poor bushel. You need loyalty in a boy, and desire. I mean the burning desire to do a good job. The physical characteristics are obvious: you want them big and fast. But desire is most important if you expect success."
>
> "I've always felt," he says, "that if a boy has athletic ability, he should utilize it to get what should be his primary objective — an education. When you lose sight of that, you're steering down the wrong channel. If a boy wants engineering and is qualified to take it, that's what he gets. His wishes are what count."
>
> Ara's coaching philosophy can be summed up quickly: "The harder you work the fewer mistakes you make, and the fewer mistakes you make the better your chances of winning."
>
> His handpicked assistants: Paul Shoults, former Miami and professional halfback, as backfield coach; Doc Urich and Bruce Beatty, also from Miami, as end and tackle coach, respectively; Alex Agase, former Illinois and Purdue All-American guard, who played with the Browns and was

coaching most recently at Iowa State, as defensive line coach, and Ed Schembechler, former assistant at Bowling Green University, as freshman coach. Schembechler is also a Miami man.

Ara later recalled, "The first game of the 1952 season I wore an old brown suit which my lost weight let me get into again, and we won. I kept wearing it at each game, and we won all but the last. In fact, after I began wearing that suit once more, we won thirty-two games and lost only three." When he mentions the suit, he laughs and adds: "It doesn't really mean a thing, yet when you win you don't want to do anything different. I wear the same tie and socks too. I'm not superstitious outside of football. I'll walk under ladders, and Friday the 13th is nothing to me."

Parseghian, an earnest type, 5 feet 10 inches tall, 210 pounds (when free from worry), and darkly handsome, not only enjoys football but has a genuine belief in its value to those who play it as it should be played — honestly and wholeheartedly. "It teaches loyalty and hard work," he says slowly when asked to describe those rewards. "It teaches sportsmanship; gives each man a chance to make his own decisions; and develops confidence and poise."

Whether he can return Northwestern to the golden seat remains to be determined, but if he fails it won't be for lack of trying. What Parseghian starts, Parseghian pursues like a hungry hawk. That goes for coaching, piano playing, golf (he shoots in the 70s or below), and working his way through college, a journey he helped finance by becoming a freelance barber.

You have to string along with a guy like this.[2]

Also featured in the article are multiple black and white photographs — some at practice but many of Ara's family at home. At the time, the children — Karan (6), Kristan (4), and Mike (1) — seemed cooperative with the photo shoot. Katie Parseghian glowed and was described as pretty. In fact, Katie bore an unmistakable resemblance to the idealized housewife Betty Crocker who was artistically created by General Mills and used liberally on products and in advertisements. The entire attractive family appeared to be recruited straight out of a modeling agency.

This particular article set the stage for events to come. A very large midwestern audience was now acquainted with the name Ara Parseghian and the supporting visuals were warm and friendly. References to his philosophy and education-first approach would ring authentic years later when a bigger opportunity would come his way. Additionally, this article is the first real exposure Ara had to major media. It was a step into what would become a constant distraction until he embraced broadcasting as a career path after coaching.

Through eight years of coaching at Northwestern, Ara learned a great deal. Recruiting for the smallest school with the highest academic standards in a conference and then competing against some of the largest schools required innovation and creativity. Matching wits, week in and week out, against some of the most successful coaches in the business was challenging. In addition to Ara, four of the other nine coaches in the conference eventually would be inducted into the College Football Hall of Fame: Duffy Daugherty (Michigan State University), Forest Evashevski (University of Iowa), Woody Hayes (Ohio State University), and Jack Mollenkopf (Purdue University). Additional travel and playing in front of large hostile crowds was something new. Being part of the coaching fraternity in one of the dominant college conferences created occasions for Ara to informally learn all about big-time football. Increased respect followed. Woody Hayes was no longer directing Ara to go fetch coffee.

It went along well, for a time. Even a 0–9 season in 1957, Ara's worst by far, didn't create clamors for a change. Ara freely admitted later that he learned a great deal from the experience of a losing season. There were signature wins that demonstrated coaching savvy in the face of inferior personnel. Ara especially relished beating the Ohio State University team coached by Woody Hayes, which he did three times out of six attempts.

But the most significant games for his eventual career advancement came against a non-conference yet geographic rival, the University of Notre Dame. Parseghian's Wildcats, thinner on depth and talent, beat the Fighting Irish four consecutive times from 1959 to 1962 (they did not play in 1963), much to the displeasure of the many carnivorous Notre Dame alumni living in Chicago. This victorious stretch occurred during some down years for Notre Dame, often referred to as the "Period of Penance." And in many ways, these losses proved to be the most fortunate losses in Notre Dame football history.

Exactly how Ara's time ended at Northwestern is largely forgotten, because it deserves to be. Tensions started to emerge between Athletic Director Stu Holcomb and the now popular head football coach. Holcomb's son was a quarterback on the Wildcat team, which became a flashpoint. He wasn't the best quarterback, at least not in the opinion of the head coach and staff. Holcomb was purported to say that he respected Ara as a coach, but that as a father he was disappointed. Before the start of the 1963 season Ara notified the administration at Northwestern that he would not renew his contract. The rest of the football world didn't know this. Only a few people did, including Katie. Things were set in motion for the next move.

In summary, a good case could be made that Ara Parseghian saved Northwestern football. He was about to get an opportunity on an even bigger stage — perhaps the biggest — to repeat this performance.

CHAPTER 8

TED, NED, AND MOOSE

In 1952, the Congregation of Holy Cross (C.S.C.) entrusted its jewel, the University of Notre Dame, to Reverend Theodore M. Hesburgh, known with affection as "Father Ted." Father Hesburgh, who had been the executive vice president under Reverend John Cavanaugh, remembered receiving the envelope containing his new assignment at the Congregation's annual gathering where all member priests were informed of their duties under their vow of obedience. Inside that envelope was a small card with a single word, "president." The case could be made that this modest piece of paper is one of the most important documents in Notre Dame history. The initial term was limited to six years under Congregation rules. Father Ted's term was renewed five consecutive times.

Father Hesburgh immediately turned to his close friend Reverend Edmund P. Joyce, "Father Ned," to fill the vacant position of executive vice president, essentially the person second in charge of managing the university. In addition to his constant counsel as a collaborator, Father Ned was assigned three areas of responsibility: business affairs, athletics, and fundraising, especially as it related to aggressive plans to expand the physical plant and build the endowment.

Of course, that job would be too large for one person to handle without help. Fortunately, when it came to athletics there already was a trusted person on board, Athletic Director Edward W. Krause, who also went by "Moose."

Those three men, Ted, Ned, and Moose, would transform Notre Dame and preserve the integrity of the football program leading up to the arrival of Ara Parseghian. It was not a smooth ride. Almost immediately, the Frank Leahy Era was forced into a sudden conclusion following the disappointing 1953 football season. Father Joyce proposed making the twenty-five-year-old Notre Dame grad and freshman coach, Terry Brennan, the head coach. Father Hesburgh approved. What were they thinking? When asked if he thought he was too young to be named head coach at the age of twenty-five, Brennan is reported to have replied casually, "Oh, I don't know. I'll be twenty-six in a few months." Looking back, the talented but young Brennan never really had a chance to mature under the immediate pressures at Notre Dame. He would have been the perfect candidate had he already been a successful head coach at another college and possessed the skills to understand and navigate the politics of major college football. But on-the-job training proved costly for him personally.

In fact, Leahy, smarting from his sudden noncelebrity status, fueled some of the internal discontent, something not fully understood until decades later. Brennan's five-year term as head coach ended without fanfare after the 1958 season. Without having to overcome the historical baggage, he may have become a successful long-term head coach at Notre Dame. Dick Hackenberg of the *Chicago Sun-Times* said it well in 1966, "The tactical terminus of Terry's tenure will forever remain a barnacle on the Notre Dame ship of state."

Many have suggested that the new Notre Dame administration was actively trying to de-emphasize the football program. The facts suggest that if there was a strategy at all, it was more subtle. It was time for the new administration to pay increased attention to academics, to the role of the university in the global Catholic Church, and to vocal alumni who would be called upon to restock the university's postwar coffers. It was a time to grow Notre Dame beyond a singular football image. Looking back, it is impossible not to be impressed by the wisdom of a strategy that encompassed a wider vision or the dimensions of its successful execution.

For example, football scholarships were rationed with more accountability. Under Father Hesburgh, Notre Dame elected to follow the Big Ten guidelines of offering thirty maximum grants per year and an overall maximum of 120. The Big Ten was the dominant conference at the time. There were no NCAA regulations and other, lesser conferences had much higher limits, with some as high as forty-five new scholarships per year. Under Coach Leahy, scholarships had been a bit ad hoc and fluid; they were awarded and taken away annually to suit his private needs for the program without informing the administration.

Under the new regulations, once a young man had grant-in-aid it was to remain in effect even if the player was injured and could no longer perform on the field or if a player was demoted to the prep team. This approach was revolutionary at the time, and at many major college football programs scholarships still remain a year-to-year award. That measure handcuffed Brennan, who inherited legacy commitments to honor. The effect was that in his first season only seventeen scholarships were awarded, and Brennan rarely had more than twenty to give to incoming freshmen. But stricter rules were necessary improvements after Leahy's largesse and those rules put Notre Dame on the vanguard of national policy reforms. Without recent national championships to prove the university's commitment to football excellence, the perception of de-emphasis gained some acolytes, especially among ill-informed members of the press with Notre Dame bias — either good or ill.

After Brennan's uneven tenure as an unseasoned coach, the knee-jerk response was to hire a replacement coach from the professional ranks, Joe Kuharich from the Washington Redskins (now the Commanders). The thinking was that the experienced Kuharich, also a Notre Dame grad, would blunt the criticism that the new coach didn't have prior coaching credentials. But for a number of reasons, far too many to recount, Kuharich never really was able to take advantage of the great opportunity he had at Notre Dame. He left after the 1962 season and returned to professional football, first as an assistant to NFL Commissioner Pete Rozelle and later as head coach of the Philadelphia Eagles. Hugh Devore was named interim coach for the Irish's 1963 season, and he was as loyal a Notre Dame man as ever was. It was obvious from the beginning of his tenure that "interim" was the operative word. With an entire year to find a permanent head coach at Notre Dame, interesting possibilities opened up.

At Northwestern University, a hot young coach was making a name for himself, including his team's four consecutive wins against the Irish. But the career-minded Ara Parseghian knew he had gone about as far as he could at Northwestern, something acknowledged by the administration there as well. So, in a 1963 telephone call to Father Joyce, Ara indicated his interest in the Notre Dame coaching job. Other candidates emerged as well. Today it is unclear who else may have been on the short list, but the often-mentioned name is Dan Devine, who later coached the Irish to their national championship in 1977. After learning about Ara's call to Father Joyce, Father Ted personally recounted to the author calling the president at Northwestern, Dr. J. Roscoe Miller, and asking for permission to talk to Coach Parseghian. President Miller was impressed by the civility of the call, acknowledged that Parseghian had outgrown Northwestern's program, and provided Father Hesburgh with a strong recommendation. Things moved ahead rapidly after that.

Working in secrecy, Fathers Ned and Ted met with Parseghian in a private hotel room in Chicago on a snowy evening in early December 1963. The drive from South Bend over the Indiana Toll Road and the Chicago Skyway was harrowing due to the weather conditions. Father Ted remembers listening intently as Father Ned led the discussion, but asking only one direct question himself, "Will you follow the strict guidelines we've established at Notre Dame?" When Ara answered in the affirmative, Father Ted was satisfied.

Those close to the situation insist that the final decision to offer Ara the job, by the only person holding the power of final veto, was made that night after that answer was provided. But in matters like this, especially at Notre Dame, contractual negotiations don't follow a straight line. As we now know from Ara's own account (see the introduction of this book), it took a number of phone calls and at least one false start before Parseghian agreed to be named the new head football coach at the University of Notre Dame on December 17, 1963.

Ara's initial annual salary was $20,000 (not including outside endorsements, speaking fees, and appearances on radio or TV shows), or roughly eight times what a Notre Dame student was paying for room, board, and tuition at the time ($2,500). Although penurious by today's standards, this made Parseghian one of the highest paid employees at Notre Dame, considering that Fathers Hesburgh and Joyce and most of the top administrators at the time were Holy Cross priests who officially drew no salaries. Through all the negotiations, Athletic Director Moose Krause hovered in the background, and he had to make it all work.

REVEREND THEODORE M. HESBURGH, C.S.C.
(1917-2015)

The student staff of the 1967 *Dome*, the Notre Dame yearbook, provided the following quote from Robert Hutchins (the chancellor of the University of Chicago) to launch the introductory first section: "Notre Dame's efflorescence has been one of the most spectacular developments in higher education in the last twenty-five years. I suspect that Notre Dame has done more than any other institution in this period, possibly because there was more to do."[1] It was an accurate summary and assessment of the changes both past and in motion under Father Hesburgh's leadership by the start of 1964.

The student yearbook authors expounded further:

> One hundred and twenty-five years after its founding in 1842, the University of Notre Dame is the outstanding Catholic institution of higher learning in the United States. Although this is by no means obvious to all, Notre Dame is unquestionably at the forefront of Catholic education, and its president, Father Hesburgh, has been instrumental in gaining for Notre Dame this position.
>
> Prior to the appointment of Father Cavanaugh to the presidency in 1948, there was little to indicate the academic prominence that Notre Dame now enjoys.
>
> Notre Dame was, quite simply, a financially poor university, and merely keeping the doors open was an all-embracing task.
>
> Although far from a scholarly activity, football provided the only reliable source of income in the university's history, thereby indirectly aiding its academic pursuits.

Notre Dame, today, despite a slow beginning and continued conservatism, is vastly different from the institution it was ten years ago. It is physically larger, ten times as wealthy, academically respected, and with the new lay board of trustees, structurally reformed.[2]

The prevailing joke on campus in the 1960s was: "How are God and Father Hesburgh alike?" Answer: "God is everywhere, and Father Hesburgh is everywhere but at Notre Dame." That joke still garnered an eye roll from Father Ted late in his life, because it highlighted an acknowledged truth. According to records, Hesburgh logged 120,000 miles of travel and visited fifty nations in the calendar year 1964 alone, a pattern he repeated year after year. Sports writer Joe Doyle recalled Father Ted's response at the time, which was: "The president of a large university today has to make his university present to the world in all major questions of the times."

Arguably no educator or priest before or since has had more simultaneous influence on a university, a nation, or the world outside. Father Ted was the subject of a *Time* magazine cover story on February 9, 1962. He holds the Guinness World Record for honorary degrees received at an astonishing 150, and no one is a close second.

Theodore "Ted" Hesburgh was raised in Syracuse, New York, and left his close family to attend the seminary at Notre Dame. He was furthering his collegiate studies at a seminary in Rome when he was called home upon the outbreak of World War II. He graduated from the Catholic University of America in 1945 with a doctorate in sacred theology, his only earned academic degree. It may surprise readers to learn that Father Ted wasn't himself a Notre Dame graduate (although one of his honorary degrees is from the university).

Father Hesburgh served with distinction on many US presidential commissions, notable among them the Civil Rights Commission (where he was chairman), the Atomic Energy Commission, and the Commission on Immigration Reform. He similarly was called upon by his personal friend Pope Paul VI to represent the Vatican internationally in areas of science, especially nuclear energy. Representing the interests of higher education, he was a member of the International Federation of Catholic Universities and the Rockefeller Foundation. Even after retirement he was a member of the Knight Commission, assisted by Notre

Dame Sports Information Director Roger Valdiserri, which provided guidance to college presidents on ways to overhaul college athletics. Father Hesburgh was honored with both of the two highest civilian awards from a grateful nation, the Congressional Gold Medal and the Presidential Medal of Freedom. After his death in 2015, the United States Postal Service honored him with a commemorative postage stamp in 2017.

Generations of students at Notre Dame knew when Father Ted was on campus. They saw his lights on, burning throughout the night from his second-floor corner office in the Administration Building. When those lights weren't on, the university was being carefully monitored by Father Ned Joyce, a role he performed capably and without complaint for thirty-five years.

REVEREND EDMUND P. JOYCE, C.S.C.
(1917-2004)

If Father Hesburgh was Notre Dame's "Mr. Outside," then Father Joyce was its "Mr. Inside." Both were as important to Notre Dame football as Doc Blanchard and Glenn Davis (the original Mr. Outside and Mr. Inside, respectively, and both Heisman Award winners) were to the Army football teams in the 1940s. Father Ned held the dual positions of executive vice president and treasurer of the university.

Edmund "Ned" Joyce was from Spartanburg, South Carolina. He graduated from Notre Dame in 1937 and became a certified public accountant in 1939 before deciding he had a vocation to the priesthood in 1945. He then studied at Congregation of Holy Cross seminaries and completed a year of graduate studies at Oxford University. Father Joyce was ordained in 1949.

The financial books at Notre Dame were nothing to cheer about in 1950, when Father Joyce was named the assistant vice president for business affairs. So, he knew what he was getting into when he accepted Father Hesburgh's invitation to join his management team and forge a new era of changes at Notre Dame. He would have been intimately knowledgeable about the cash contribution football was making to the operational budget every year, which was significant at the time. The rumor on campus was that football profits paid for athletics and the annual heating and electric bills for the entire university, no small matter in cold and snowy South Bend. In reality, the contribution of cash from football may have been even greater than surmised by outsiders. The university's operating budget in 1964 was approximately $30 million. Football contributed between $3 and $4 million in unrestricted cash after paying for the athletic department. Thus assigning athletics (including football) to the purview of Father Joyce made perfect sense.

People remember Father Ned as a tall, impeccably dressed man, an impression difficult to achieve when your entire wardrobe is monochromatic by design. He was soft-spoken, conservative, and had an appetite for detail. Those qualities made him the perfect complement to Father Ted as the bookends that held Notre Dame upright until they retired together in 1987.

A fresh administrative attitude and emerging wealth from postwar alumni translated into increased prosperity at Notre Dame. You can see it physically in the building program, starting with O'Shaughnessy Hall in 1951. The march continued with the construction of Fisher, Pangborn, North Dining Hall, Keenan-Stanford, Stepan Center, Hammes Bookstore, Center for Continuing Education, Lobund Center, the Computing Center, the Notre Dame Post Office, and numerous other renovations scattered around campus. The most ambitious building projects were Memorial Library (the largest collegiate library structure in the world at the time) in 1964 and the Athletic and Convocation Center, on which construction started in the fall of 1966. This building eventually was renamed the Joyce Center in honor of Father Ned.

Generations of freshmen and parents in the 1960s will remember Father Joyce as the celebrant of the Mass that welcomed new students during Freshman Orientation. Father Hesburgh had a perennial conflict in mid-September. Enter Father Joyce, who, as Mr. Inside, was frequently seen around campus — and therefore not compared to God, even in jest.

In one of our many conversations, sports writer Joe Doyle recalled asking Father Joyce at the end of his career if he ever lamented not being a priest (in the traditional sense, caring for a flock). He paused for a moment, and then answered, "Yes, I suppose so. When I got here, they turned me into a bean counter." There were lots of beans to count. He may have entered Notre Dame as an accountant, but he became so much more. His flock was Notre Dame Athletics.

EDWARD W. "MOOSE" KRAUSE
(1913-1992)

Moose Krause made fast friends with virtually everyone he met. The process was further accelerated if you provided him with a fresh cigar. He liked good ones. This is how everyone pictures Moose, with his friendly arm draped over somebody's shoulder and puffing on a cigar. He was the ideal person to execute the athletic plan for the strategists Fathers Hesburgh and Joyce. Essentially, he was the brand manager for football.

As anyone who works in the business of athletics will attest, it is a small community based on relationships and trust. Moose Krause understood that and was the designated ambassador of good will. He knew athletics because he was an athlete himself.

Moose Krause arrived at Notre Dame from Chicago in 1930 as a freshman to play football for Coach Knute Rockne. Physically, he was the largest person ever to suit up in a Rockne locker room. After Rockne's accidental death Moose stayed and went on to letter in three varsity sports: football, basketball, and track. His most notable accomplishments actually transpired on the basketball court. He is often identified by name as one of the players who forced college basketball to adopt a radical rule change in 1938. Before this change, there was a jump ball at center court following each basket or foul shot. This slowed the game down and gave an unfair advantage to a team with at least one very tall player — Moose was the poster boy for changing the rule.

His successor as athletic director, Dick Rosenthal, told me this story: "Moose once won a key basketball game against Butler in the last second of play after being knocked to the floor. The ball bounced into his hands and, while lying flat on his back, he lobbed up the winning basket. As legend has it, the next morning the team left the hotel and boarded a bus for South Bend. While standing near the door of the bus selling his newspapers, a young paperboy shouted, 'Morning *Star!*' Moose replied, 'Morning, son.'" Moose Krause was inducted into the Basketball Hall of Fame in 1976.

In the football game programs from the 1960s, Moose is improperly credited with being an All-American in both football and basketball. When the College Football Hall of Fame was eager to induct Krause, his friend Joe Doyle was put on the case to establish the bona fides; an inductee must have been an All-American to be made a Hall of Famer. Try as he could, Doyle couldn't find official evidence, however remote, that Moose had been so honored. (This same rule applies to Joe Montana, who sailed into the Professional Football Hall of Fame, but can never enter the College Football Hall of Fame under their current rules.)

After short coaching stints at St. Mary's College in Minnesota and Holy Cross in Massachusetts, Moose Krause returned home to Notre Dame in 1942. He became head basketball coach for a time, was the assistant athletic director to Frank Leahy in 1948, and became the athletic director in 1949. He was made for the job and the job was made for him.

Of the many roles an athletic director assumes at Notre Dame, two don't usually get written on the job description. The head of athletics has to be the "shock absorber" for many of the public shots taken at how the university is doing both on and off the field. Some of these are friendly fire. Moose had the personality and the knack to diffuse criticism. Even the most hostile faultfinder had to like the guy. The second unwritten role is that of "confessor" and motivator to the key coaches. At Notre Dame, that meant football coaches — first, second, and third. Ara Parseghian had a particularly close working relationship with Krause, something he readily acknowledged.

In 1969, after Notre Dame started going to bowl games again (hiatus after 1924 season), the Cotton Bowl became a frequent stop for Irish teams. It was during this period in the 1970s that Moose started wearing the cowboy hat that many associate with his persona. It fit him perfectly. Everything about the guy was Texas-sized.

Moose was well-known and respected throughout the nation and in all quarters of the university community, which Rosenthal reflected in his letter to alumni at the time of his friend's passing, "His unfailing goodness was, indeed, the principal reason for his greatness. He was incapable of malice and never turned away from someone in need. His love affair with his wife and family was the manifestation of a man whose capacity to love was boundless." People who knew him well are quick to mention the dedication he displayed for his wife Elizabeth when she was confined to a nursing home for many years. He and Elizabeth were the parents of three children: Edward (now a Holy Cross priest), Mary, and Phillip.

In December 1992, the open casket containing the body of Edward "Moose" Krause was laid in state inside the Basilica of the Sacred Heart, the main church on the campus of Notre Dame. In it were placed two Krause trademarks, his cowboy hat and a cigar. According to Dick Rosenthal, Notre Dame football legend George Connor (who played tackle from 1946–1947 and is in the College Football Hall of Fame) noticed the brand of the cigar wasn't up to Moose's usual high standards. So, he walked over to the nearby Morris Inn in the cold darkness, purchased the best cigar available, and returned to make the substitution without fanfare. It was a tender gesture from one big Notre Dame man to another.

THIRD QUARTER

(1964–1974)

CHAPTER 9

FIRST THINGS

Different versions of the story of how Ara Parseghian came to be named head football coach at Notre Dame have seeped into unofficial accounts, many based on nothing more than conjecture. The events surrounding Ara being hired at Notre Dame in 1963 follow this approximate timeline as taken from several reliable sources, including weather records. Reliance on the memories of living sources, especially those of Katie Parseghian, add special credibility.

> November 28, Thanksgiving Day, Ara and his family are with his brother, Jerry, and Jerry's family in Toledo. Jerry suggests that Ara call Father Joyce and indicate interest in the head coaching position, which is widely known to be open.
> Also on Thanksgiving Day, Notre Dame plays its final game of the season against Syracuse at Yankee Stadium, losing 7–14. This ends the head coaching term of Hugh Devore. (He later becomes associate athletic director working for Moose Krause.)
> Monday, December 2, Ara calls Father Joyce's office and leaves a message with his assistant that he is interested in the coaching job and would like to discuss it, if it is still open.

71

Tuesday, December 3, Ara takes a morning flight to Miami, Florida, to interview with the University of Miami. The intermediate stop is in St. Louis, Missouri. Ara calls home and finds out from Katie that Father Joyce has received his message, returned Ara's call, and is interested in meeting with him about the head coaching position. Ara immediately returns to Chicago instead of going to Miami.

Wednesday, December 4, Ara and Father Joyce meet in person for the first time that morning to become acquainted. (Father Joyce had stayed in Chicago overnight after the annual Knute Rockne Dinner the night before.)

Thursday, December 5, as a courtesy, Father Hesburgh calls the president of Northwestern asking about Coach Parseghian's availability. The president grants permission to officially communicate with Ara about the open position at Notre Dame.

Saturday, December 7, at the Army–Navy game Father Joyce encounters Northwestern Athletic Director Stu Holcomb, who acknowledges that he was informed about the permission granted to negotiate with Ara.

Telephone discussions lead to scheduling an evening meeting with Fathers Hesburgh and Joyce at a hotel south of Chicago on Monday, December 9. All parties remember traveling in a snowstorm, thus confirming the date of this meeting since the 9th is the first and only night of recorded snow in Chicago in early December 1963.

Father Joyce attends the annual National Football Foundation Awards Dinner in New York on the evening of Tuesday, December 10.

Presumably, the final decision to offer the position to Ara is made in the December 11–13 timeframe. Sometime in this window, the Board of Trustees is informed and in agreement.

Ara checks in to the Morris Inn on Notre Dame's campus on Sunday, December 15. He meets with Father Joyce over dinner that evening.

A press conference scheduled for Monday, December 16, is canceled at the last minute, with the university citing ongoing negotiations for the delay. (As explained in the introduction, it is now known that Ara was having doubts about being worthy of the position because he viewed himself as a fallen-away Catholic and didn't want to embarrass the university.)

Ara returns home to Wilmette, Illinois. Many telephone conversations ensue with family members and Notre Dame administrators.

Ara decides to accept the position in a telephone conversation with Father Joyce on the afternoon of December 17, from his home. He immediately leaves Chicago on a late flight to San Francisco to fulfill his coaching duties at the annual East–West Shrine Game. He appears at the Shrine Game luncheon the following day with the all-star players and other coaches.

The morning of December 18, Notre Dame Athletic Director Moose Krause makes the formal announcement of Ara's hiring, quipping, "Ara should be with us a long time since we hired him twice."

After returning from California on December 29, Ara makes arrangements to return to Notre Dame on December 30 to handle details for the transition into his new job scheduled for Thursday, January 2. On that day, he announces hiring three assistant coaches, Paul Shoults, Richard "Doc" Urich, and Tom Pagna, all from Northwestern.

Ara Parseghian officially joins the Notre Dame payroll backdated to December 15, 1963. A three-page employment contract is exchanged mid-January. Father Joyce makes a special note in the cover letter to start the contract early as a gesture of appreciation and goodwill.

Returning to Notre Dame on December 30, Ara was now a coaching staff of one. His computer-like mind would have been sorting through a long list of priorities — probably written in his tiny print on pocket-sized note cards, as was his habit. The items of highest importance, those at the top of his list, can only be speculated about after so many years. Fortunately, what Ara actually did first is well-documented and quite consequential, but not something he would have written on any list.

The Notre Dame Football Office was located on the ground floor, northern side, of the Rockne Memorial athletic building — bookending the extreme western boundary of what is known on campus as the South Quad. It was inconveniently located on the other side of the sprawling campus about as far away as possible from Notre Dame Stadium and the football practice fields.

Ara was curious about his new headquarters. First things first. Someone provided him with a set of keys. He made his way across the frozen campus into what he logically believed would be an empty building with a locked office door. The students were all away on Christmas break, so the campus was eerily quiet.

When he opened the door to his new, not-so-spacious office area, he was surprised to see a fellow, a hulking shadow, seated in the back spinning films on the flickering film editor with a stack of metal film cannisters on the table. He asked the surprise occupant, "Who the hell are you? And what are you doing here?"

Looking up, the stranger replied, "Hi Coach, I'm Brian Boulac. I'm one of the grad assistants for the football team, or at least I was. I'm here grading all these films we've received from high school recruits. Nobody else is around, Coach, and I didn't have anything better to do." The conversation quickly expanded. Ara wanted to know all about this person in his office, and he wanted to know why grad student Brian Boulac believed he was qualified to grade films of potential recruits. Satisfied with the answers, Ara told Brian to continue and informed him that he now had a spot on the new football staff, should he want it. The deal was sealed for the lifetimes of both. History records this as Ara's first decision as head coach at Notre Dame.

Bear in mind that the 1963 season was a study in "lack of attention" from the time when Hugh Devore had been named the interim head coach. The season effectively ended on a sour note when the scheduled game at Iowa was suddenly and appropriately cancelled after the assassination of President John F. Kennedy on Friday, November 22, 1963. The team had already checked into a hotel in Iowa City when the news broke. The country was suddenly thrust into an extended period of mourning and uncertainty, understandably so. The Irish were spared what would likely have been a loss at Kinnick Stadium. A week later, the last game of the season was the forgettable loss to Syracuse University at Yankee Stadium on Thanksgiving Day. The final 1963 season record was a disappointing 2–7. Without having a true head football coach in place, the month of December in 1963 would have added to the deep uncertainty surrounding the future of Notre Dame Football. Why anyone associated with the football program would be in the office in late December would have been a mystery.

Call it serendipity. Call it providential. Either way, that afternoon meeting between Ara and Brian changed lives. Consider the circumstances. There was no reason for anyone on the paid Devore coaching staff to be energetically working on recruitment. They were presumed to be terminated, although a couple staff members were ultimately retained. They couldn't make firm offers to potential players. The convention at the time was that binding offers could only be made after a high school student finished playing in his senior year. How were any players being groomed to arrive in the fall of 1964 to play on the freshman team and then become eligible for the 1965 season? Who was making visits? Who was contacting high school coaches? Theoretically no one, yet there was loyal Brian Boulac sitting in the dark believing he might continue to be helpful, with nothing better to do. Right time, right place.

Perhaps without this well-timed initiative, talented players would have found other collegiate homes. Recruiting for this class was a chore. Yet a list of names now familiar to Irish fans were recruited in 1964: Tom Schoen, John Pergine, Mike McGill, Kevin Rassas, Jerry Wisne, Rocky Bleier, Dan Harshman, Tom O'Leary, Jim Smithberger, and Dave Martin. Recruiting became much easier after the unexpected explosive success of the team in 1964. With an organized recruiting effort put into place by Ara and administered by Brian, one year later the incoming 1965 class was transformational. This set the table for even greater success in 1966, the year the drought ended at Notre Dame after seventeen years without a national championship. Consider this: of the thirty-two players who saw game action at Michigan State in the famous 10–10 tie of that 1966 season, ten were sophomores who had been recruited in 1965.

Brian Boulac ultimately spent his entire professional career at Notre Dame as an assistant football coach, physical education instructor, head softball coach, and associate athletic director. He often wondered what would have happened had he not been quietly working in the office when Ara walked in. He and his wife, Mary Ann (Micki), thrived along with their four daughters in South Bend; every family member earned degrees at Notre Dame. Brian is the answer to an interesting trivia question: Which coach at Notre Dame has the most National Championship rings? Leahy's teams won four National Championships, but in those days, championship rings weren't awarded. So, the correct answer is Brian Boulac, with four (1966, 1973, 1977, 1988)!

Recruiting players for Big Ten teams had been competitive for some time, but generally confined geographically to regions surrounding the individual universities. This had more to do with state pride and the cost of transportation for the travel by teams and the parents of players wanting to see their sons in action. Ara was at a disadvantage at Northwestern because of its status as the smallest school in the Big Ten and the one with the highest academic standards. But he managed to recruit in the talent-rich Chicago area and often found himself competing with Notre Dame, only ninety miles away, for young men with the same student-athlete profile.

College recruiting became much more competitive nationally just about the time Ara arrived at ND in 1964. A number of factors contributed to this. The reemergence of two-platoon college football (using separate players for offense and defense) encouraged the cultivation of more position specialists, and the best players were scattered across the nation. The "need for speed" became an important criterion and difficult to find in potential recruits. Television emerged as another recruiting factor in 1966. National broadcasts of college games leveled the playing field for recruits nationwide; they could be seduced by national exposure at particular institutions as a prelude to now-lucrative professional football careers. Talented Black players were finally able to participate widely and with a wider range of geographic options. Finally, air travel was just starting to become affordable for average parents wanting to be part of the college experience of their sons. Putting all of these factors together, some traditional advantages of Notre Dame disappeared at that time while competitors became more effective at the recruiting game.

Successful recruiting now depended on having a strong plan, organizational clarity, and solid strategies of communication. Ara Parseghian brought high competency in all of these categories to South Bend. Some colleges saw how recruiting was changing and figured it out. Some didn't because they were tied to out-of-date thinking. Inconsistency in these respects at some big-name schools led to resentment and jealousy, and regrettably, an outbreak of questionable ethical behavior.

One of the most illuminating incidents of these times occurred in 1969. It provides a clear window onto the character of Ara Parseghian. For this reason alone, it merits full exposure, even after over sixty years. A summary of the situation is required to appreciate the entire picture. The names of the individuals involved in questionable behavior will be withheld out of courtesy. No practical purpose would be served by mentioning them today.

The president of Michigan State University registered an official written complaint with the president of Notre Dame, Father Hesburgh (and by extension, Father Joyce), relative to the recruitment of two players highly sought after by both schools. The charge was that Notre Dame acted inappropriately. Of course, the intent was to raise the issue to the highest court at Notre Dame — the one occupied by guys with clerical collars who would be sensitive to institutional integrity. The plot, hatched by the coaches at Michigan State, was far less altruistic, hoping that fallout would at the very least slow down the aggressive recruiting behavior of Ara and his staff. A copy of the complaint landed without comment or prejudice on Ara's desk for a response.

Two highly recruited young men were coveted by both Notre Dame and Michigan State. After completing a standard recruiting process at both schools, including visits and interaction with coaches, both made verbal commitments to Notre Dame in the December–January timeframe after their senior seasons. Weeks later, around the official signing date, both suddenly reneged on their promises, and almost in unison. This prompted the Notre Dame coaching staff to determine the reason behind the reversals. What was uncovered by indirect communication with one of the parents (who later clammed-up for fear of reprisals) was that significant incentives were added to the recruitment package from MSU. The incentives went beyond the prevailing NCAA guidelines. Upon verification of this information, the Notre Dame staff wrote both boys about the situation and the possible jeopardy for each. When Michigan State got wind of this, the official complaint emerged. Their opening position: it was inappropriate under NCAA rules for Notre Dame to be tampering with their now-committed recruits.

Defending his integrity was something foreign to Ara. Basically, he was such a straight arrow that he may never have needed to before. But because he valued his integrity above all things, Ara spent considerable time defending himself in writing to his bosses, Fathers Hesburgh and Joyce. The complete document survives as a carbon copy and is taken from his files. It is about ten pages in length, and there are additional supporting exhibits (A through G). It is written completely in Ara's voice. Turning the other cheek was not an option when his reputation, and by extension that of Notre Dame, was concerned. The organization and detail of his response befits any legal brief. An excerpt is included below, to prove the point.

First of all, before I get into the discussion of the events of this issue, I would like to outline the intense competition that is taking place in the recruiting of blue-chip athletes by all universities around the country. The pressures have increased and particularly by teams that have had a disappointing fall. Michigan State had a down year and felt it mandatory to have a successful recruiting year. To accurately describe the circumstances as they took place one must be aware of the fact that there are two boys involved in this, rather than just one. I will try in this letter to outline the details and the events exactly as they happened. I will also document this with various exhibits so that all interested parties can be advised of the details.

I would like to preface my remarks by stating that I have been in coaching for nineteen seasons — six with the Mid-American Conference at Miami of Ohio, eight years in the Big Ten at Northwestern — and of course now this is going to be my fifth season here at the University of Notre Dame. During the entire time my recruiting policy has been very firm. Hopefully, I'm not too presumptuous in thinking that the decision to hire me here at Notre Dame was based on the clean record I had in the recruiting area. I have always lived by the NCAA rules regarding aid to student athletes and have instructed my coaching staff to do likewise.

You will note in the letter from [an exhibit, name withheld] that Michigan State had offered a Chrysler sponsorship — a car — an excellent job opportunity — round-trip transportation for the parents and also to pay the boy a monthly income. Now all of these things, with the exception of the summer job, are violations of NCAA rules, and let me assure you my position on illegal aid is well known. Staff members here at Notre Dame, after losing a prospect, have complained bitterly about added inducements taking place and, of course, I have always been the last one to accuse our competition of wrongdoing. I assume that for some reason the boy changed his mind and that we weren't going to get into a bidding contest.

My position has been well known for nineteen years of coaching at Miami, Northwestern and including the four and a half years at Notre Dame. However, I was greatly concerned because both boys being outstanding blue-chip prospects and highly sought-after had committed to attend Notre Dame at earlier dates and then subsequently changed their minds after having visited Michigan State. Add to this the letter indicating that one was receiving added inducements, and I decided to pursue this to find how valid the accusations were. I called [name withheld] and asked the source of his information. He told me that he had been very close to the family and that the dad had given him this information.

The outcomes after this incident were predictable. All but one. Fathers Hesburgh and Joyce had confidence that Ara had not acted in bad faith. By 1969, they knew their head coach too well to question his integrity. Yet, a complaint at the highest levels in academia had to be taken seriously, and answered. Ara's response was comprehensive, detailed, and altogether convincing. The response communicated to Michigan State's president isn't recorded in files accessible to this author. But the matter appears to have died quietly, and the NCAA appeared to be none the wiser. Were any other schools aware of the situation? If they were, they were also put on notice that attacks on Ara's character would not be persuasive or well-received by his superiors.

One of the young men involved in the recruiting conflict was ultimately convinced that Notre Dame was the better choice for his education and for his prospects in professional football. His career blossomed, and after starting three years at Notre Dame, he achieved All-American status.

The other young man did go to Michigan State and . . . had a successful professional football career.

CHAPTER 10

WINNING MINDSET

There was only one reason that Notre Dame began competing again for national recognition in football. The student body instinctively knew it the moment Ara Parseghian stepped onto the campus. Shortly after Ara's arrival, a spontaneous pep rally commenced on the steps of Sorin Hall on a cold and blustery evening in February of 1964. His brief, straightforward comments to the students resonated, "Football games are won by teams that are both physically and mentally alert; we will be at our peak for every game we play." A few days later the applause was thunderous at a varsity basketball game in the Old Fieldhouse when Ara was introduced between halves. It was love at first sight.

Allen Sack, a sophomore reserve player in 1964, a retired college professor, and author, summarized it beautifully in his 2008 book, *Counterfeit Amateurs*:

> Any misgivings I might have had about Ara Parseghian were quickly dispelled after his first meeting with the team. I had never met a person with Ara's ability to communicate and inspire. It is no exaggeration to say that the players sat spellbound as he laid out his strategy for how we would win the National Championship. I have often told people that after that

first meeting, Ara could have told us to jump off the top of Notre Dame Stadium, and many players might have seriously considered it. He had a clear vision of where the program was headed and the charisma to make the rest of us believe in it. In the weeks to come, he also demonstrated organizational skills that would have served him well in a military campaign. He left absolutely nothing to chance. Efficiency and time management were the hallmarks of Ara's system.[1]

Essentially, the same sentiments were echoed in *All Rise: The Remarkable Journey of Alan Page*, by Bill McGrane:

> Ara made a lasting impression on young Page. "I think it was his first meeting with the team," Alan said. "He drew a football field on the blackboard, then told us the game was really pretty simple; it was about position and possession. That was it."
> "I had never stopped to think about a plan for football before," Page said. "I just played. Now here was a coach, and he was making so much sense with this simple, basic theory. He turned a light on for me."[2]

Great teachers were at one time great students who themselves had great teachers. Parseghian credited the legendary Paul Brown with many of his successful coaching techniques. The enduring lesson that Ara took away from Brown was, "Never leave a game on the practice field on Thursday or Friday." The translation is, don't peak early or too soon in advance of the game. Prepare thoroughly, but don't burn the team out in the process. Save the optimal mental and physical performance for Saturday afternoon when it counts. The winning edge is to make sure that every player is mentally into the game and believes he is better prepared than his opponent. It is a hallmark of Ara's teams to a man. They believed that their coach was the smartest and best prepared person on the field. So, they had the edge going in. With that understanding, it made practicing during the week easier to endure and execution on game days more effective.

Well before he arrived in South Bend, Ara had made the transition from being a student of the coaching craft to becoming an innovator and a teacher himself. He had two personality traits working for him, and both had been obvious from his youth: intensity and leadership.

From Brown he learned organization and management and added these to his portfolio.

UNLIKELY FRIENDS

The moment you are named the head football coach at Notre Dame your popularity spikes, but so does your sense of isolation. Ara needed a confidant and a trusted friend to help him negotiate the tricky tides at Notre Dame. An outsider wouldn't know some of the stress points, like historical salaries, the condition of facilities and equipment, or how many scholarships were in play, who could influence scheduling, disciplinary concerns, and the rules for hiring assistants without the help of an "insider." Essentially, Joe Doyle, the sports editor at the *South Bend Tribune*, became that insider for Ara. The trust developed between Ara and Joe from the outset continued throughout Parseghian's coaching tenure. They made an odd couple to be sure; the head coach and the sportswriter could well have been antagonists. It happens.

But the two met for coffee quite often at Milt's Grill in downtown South Bend, around 5:30 a.m. before the coaches' meeting on campus at 7:00. Doyle's private counsel was invaluable to the new coach, especially when it came to understanding local South Bend customs or the Byzantine traditions of the Catholic Church as practiced on campus. Sometimes Joe simply offered friendly, practical advice. For example, Ara was quite concerned when halfback Nick Eddy wanted to get married during his junior season; Joe thought it might work out just fine, and it did. Joe claimed their friendship was built on one simple rule: "I never told Ara how to coach and he never told me what to write."

A PROVIDENTIAL ARRIVAL

In 1964, Notre Dame was desperate for a coach who could return to the tradition of winning football games, but doing that with a view toward maintaining high standards in the face of more confining rules that were emerging from the NCAA. Ara Parseghian's self-delivery to Notre Dame was nothing less than providential.

The highly respected sports information director at Notre Dame, Roger Valdiserri, who started in 1966, got to know the coach extremely well as he crafted the team's public information and simultaneously guarded the Notre Dame "dogma." He offered me this insightful reflection after sixty years of working closely with Ara, "When you are around Ara you feel like you're at a disadvantage. You might be driving the same make and model car, but through some strange quirk of fate, you figure his came off the assembly line with a bigger engine."

Jim Leahy was a player for Ara. His Notre Dame football roots run deep. He was the son of Notre Dame coaching legend Frank Leahy and later the father of two-time Notre Dame Football Captain Ryan Leahy. He left no room for doubt in his own reflection on Ara's arrival, "My father had tremendous respect for Ara. We all did."

THE INFAMOUS BUNKER

From 1964 to 1967, one of the most unassuming locations on campus was also one of the most important. We're not talking about Notre Dame Stadium. In fact, this location was about as physically removed from the stadium or the Cartier Field practice areas as it could be and still be on Notre Dame property.

Quaint personalized signs used to mark every reserved parking place on the Notre Dame campus. These were hand-lettered at the Notre Dame Sign Shop, with yellow letters painted over black boards and placed on stakes in front of the designated spaces. Parents delivering their young men to campus would have been confused when taking the exterior access road behind the Rockne Memorial Building and spotting the parking signs for "PARSEGHIAN" and all the other assistant coaches. The only more remote location was a temporary structure known as the ROTC Building across the street, a holdover from the Navy V-12 program in the 1940s. (It is still standing and in use.) Also across the street were the Notre Dame (Burke) Golf Course and open fields that extended to old Route 31, with Saint Mary's College "across the road" just a little further beyond.

The Football Office was on the ground floor of Rockne Memorial as one entered from the South Quad. This is where the strategies and plans for Ara's early teams were formulated. It is also where recruits would have been brought to meet with the head coach. It was the equivalent of Churchill's underground bunker in London during World War II, which today is referred to as the War Rooms.

As you entered "the Rock," on the first floor to the right of the foyer was a large high-ceiling room that was originally designed for formal physical education classes. This academic major was dropped in 1963, to the pleasure of Father Hesburgh. The Football Office had been itinerant over the years. It moved first from the Administration Building, where Rockne had a single office, to cramped quarters among two floors at the south end of dormitory Breen-Phillips Hall where the entire athletic department was housed, starting in the 1930s. Frank Leahy worked out of the Breen-Phillips offices and during football season was known to sleep in the Notre Dame Firehouse rather than make the tedious roundtrip to his family home in St. Joseph, Michigan. Terry Brennan's office was originally there as well. When space opened up in Rockne Memorial, football operations moved over. In 1968, the Football Office was moved again to the new Athletic and Convocation Center. Now football operations has its own palatial building, the Guglielmino Family Athletics Center, also known as "the Gug."

Within the confines of this former classroom-gym, there was a combination outer office and reception area. Coach Parseghian's secretary, Barb Nicholas, served as the gatekeeper. This area provided access to a single private office reserved for the head coach and an open "bull pen" workspace for the rest of the coaching staff. Ara's office was in the corner facing Lyons Hall. The remainder of the space was essentially open with desks partitioned by file cabinets that defined the assistant coaches' areas. Toward the rear was the conference room for watching film and conducting meetings; the room had a large table and was also where grad assistants were put. It was a crowded and noisy boiler room with desks, file cabinets, bookshelves, telephones, film viewing machines, tack boards, and blackboards. Except for the clutter, the space was almost military in its configuration and lack of creature comforts. For ten men on a mission, it was the perfect setup.

These were physically good-sized men, and the office space was quite crowded. The personalities and egos of the coaching staff were even bigger than their physical statures. Living together could have been disastrous. But their environs worked well for two reasons. First, with Ara in command, the focus was constantly on tangible team goals. No office politics were tolerated. Second, when there was steam to let off, it was no trouble to find a swimming pool, handball courts, weight rooms, basketball courts, or a place to hit some golf balls. The fact that this enclave was so far removed from both the Administration Building and the Athletic Department in Breen-Phillips Hall also created a welcomed buffer.

It was from this bare-bones outpost that football at Notre Dame was transformed and elevated to meet the expectations of high standards both on and off the field. It's a campus location that deserves a permanent historical marker.

THE FRATERNITY OF COACHES

Under NCAA guidelines, football programs could employ a maximum of eight assistant coaches and one graduate assistant. Ara got to hand-pick each of his assistants. There were no required holdovers from previous Notre Dame teams, one of the conditions that was undoubtedly negotiated before Parseghian accepted the job.

The names of Ara's initial coaching staff were: John Ray, Paul Shoults, Joe Yonto, Tom Pagna, George Sefcik, Jerry Wampfler, Wally Moore, and John Murphy. Brian Boulac, the original graduate assistant, served in the Air Force after graduation in 1964, but returned to the Notre Dame coaching staff in 1966.

Ara treated all his coaches as equals, although two were "more equal" than the others. John Ray ran the defense, and Ara gave him enormous latitude in doing so. Tom Pagna was Ara's right-hand man on the offensive side, and he also relieved Ara of the burden of attending to cumbersome internal administrative details, such as the paperwork.

Ara rationalized recruitment practices. He carved up the map of the United States so that each assistant had an area of recruiting responsibility and was expected to "mine" his area. This approach appeared novel at a time when only a few universities could claim to be truly national.

THE RUNNING OF THE STEPS

A team captain (or captains) elected by the team occupied an essential part of the organizational chart. Today, the designation of "captain" can be largely ceremonial and migrate among senior players from game to game. Ara made team leadership a real and essential part of the program. It started with student-run organized workouts at the beginning of the spring semester. These daily stadium workouts were strictly voluntary in keeping with NCAA rules. From time to time, assistant coaches could be spied in the press box — undoubtedly there to inspect the meticulous maintenance of the field turf, which was covered by a tarp and many inches of snow in February. From this perch, they could also observe the final group exercise every day, the infamous running of the steps. Led by the captain and followed by the juniors, the team would form a single line and run up one set of steps, cross over to the next set at the top row and then descend. Upon reaching the bottom, with another cross over, the process was repeated, over and over. Before the renovation, the original Notre Dame Stadium had sixty rows and thus sixty steps. The team wasn't in good enough shape to cover the entire stadium in this fashion on the first informal workout day in February. By a true spring practice in April, everyone had mastered the entire stadium circuit. These impressive workouts were universally despised.

THE SPRING GAME

The current format of the Spring Game is much different from what it was in 1964–1967. Today it is an intra-squad scrimmage where players actually vie for positions on the depth chart and hitting hard is semi-encouraged. The traditional Spring Game didn't mean much, though, except that it signaled the end of spring practices and raised scholarship money for the local Notre Dame Club in St. Joseph County. It was a game between a team of "old-timers" and the varsity, with second stringers added to the old-timers to fill out the roster. This tradition harkened back to the days of Knute Rockne when the graduating seniors and former players alike relished one more opportunity to play football on campus. The pro leagues were in their infancy and very few Notre Dame graduates selected professional football as an immediate career path in the 1920s. But by 1960, old-timers willing to play against the Notre Dame varsity were a vanishing breed. Pro players and seniors with a shot at the pros were reluctant to risk injury in an exhibition game. The last game nominally played in this format occurred in the spring of 1967, although the format had de facto already been changed. That last game was broadcast live on ABC's *Wide World of Sports*, and the old-timers (including former players like Johnny Lattner) merely roamed the sidelines and did media interviews.

SUMMER WORK

The prevailing NCAA rule was that football practices could commence twenty-one days before the first scheduled game. The custom at the time was for colleges to begin play in mid-September, approximately at the same time that college classes began at most institutions. While the same rule applies today, schools are now more likely to schedule games late in August. At present, all major schools have an official game by Labor Day weekend. The schedules have expanded from ten to eleven or even twelve games at Division 1-A colleges. The television appetite for college football is voracious.

While Notre Dame had an active summer academic semester back in the '60s, the predominant summer student profile was that of a priest, nun, or religious brother seeking an advanced degree with an emphasis on theology or philosophy and the intention of teaching. Athletes were not encouraged to take summer courses or to stay on campus for more "unofficial" workouts. The rank and file of the Notre Dame football squad returned home to work in steel mills, factories, farms, and family businesses. Some had less physical jobs, and many caught up with old friends where occasionally a beer or two was consumed, something they would never have admitted to the head coach at the time. A few even smoked cigarettes, something more commonplace at the time (before the Surgeon General provided clinical evidence to the dangers and mandated warnings on every pack). Since players spent the summers away from campus, the coaching staff had some anxiety about what could transpire to derail their best laid plans.

THE DEPTH CHART DECISIONS

Ara ran practices with military precision. Under his focused leadership, the other coaches and the players were able to approach their practice objectives with absolute clarity. Ara played his favorites in the games; everybody understood this. These favorites were the guys who gave everything they had in practice, the guys who proved they were better than the next guy on the depth chart. There was a constant sense of competition combined with an uncommon sense of fairness not found in many football programs. The guys who earned their spots played on Saturdays. It was that simple. It didn't matter if you were a highly recruited player with a scholarship or a determined walk-on.

To reinforce the point, Ara and the coaching staff reviewed the progress of every single player every day in morning sessions before practice. Some might call it overkill, but the discipline of doing this kept everyone alert and made for an even playing field. It was a business lesson that many players successfully carried with them beyond the confines of football. Brian Boulac recalled a particular session from when he was an assistant coach. Try as the coaching staff could, there was one seemingly talented player whom they just couldn't find the right spot for on the field. Finally in frustration Ara asked, "Why can't we find a place to play this guy?" Tom Pagna's memorable response was, "Because the kid has a pimple for a heart."

This element of Ara's coaching style, measuring a player's heart, combined with tireless preparation, became the cornerstones of his success. His approach meant that the best players, whether they were green sophomores or hardened fifth-year players, were on the field. They had all been tested in practice by some of the best football players they would ever face. The genius wasn't just in the plays or the schemes (which were also quite innovative), it was in the motivation of each player to survive, succeed, and contribute to the team. Ara understood that the only true motivation is self-motivation. He was a master at creating an atmosphere of incentives which challenged every player to reach his full potential.

When a player arrived daily at practice he could locate his spot on the depth chart since it was posted on the bulletin board for all to see. That chart, along with a schedule of where each player was expected to be and what was being drilled. It was simple and fair.

One way to move up on the chart was to be flexible and willing to play a new position if the coaches saw potential they wanted to develop or needed to fill a void. Players understood that and many embraced the chance to advance and finally get dressed or play on Saturday. Allen Sack arrived as a freshman quarterback recruit in 1963, one of six players vying for the position. At one point he was told by an assistant coach that he would never even dress for a Saturday game, and, that was that; sorry. But he eventually bulked up and played his way to success as a defensive lineman. Even better, while on the 1966 squad, Sack was drafted by an NFL team.

THE HOUSE THAT ROCK BUILT

Notre Dame Stadium was state of the art for college football stadiums in 1930, when it was constructed to Knute Rockne's specifications. Perhaps out of respect for "Rock," or more likely because there wasn't an extra nickel in the university's budget, the football facilities hadn't been upgraded by the time Parseghian began coaching at Notre Dame. The ghost of Rockne himself could have walked in and recognized every stick of furniture. The facilities that supported Ara's early teams were meager at best — a circa-1930 stadium locker room that lacked air conditioning and posed lots of plumbing problems.

The game of football had changed from the late 1920s in fundamental ways. Even the football itself became leaner with pointed ends, a design intended to make throwing it much easier than the "balloons" of the early 20s. The players' equipment became more sophisticated too, especially the composite plastic helmets with mandatory face guards. But the storied equipment manager was still right out of central casting for a 1930s movie. If a football player had a uniform or equipment problem, he would head across campus to the equipment room in the Old Fieldhouse and deal with Notre Dame's cantankerous equipment manager, Mac (Jack McAllister).

The players in Parseghian's era were much bigger as well, gargantuan by the standards of Rockne's days. And there were more of them to accommodate. There were always 120 scholarship players and as many as thirty walk-ons at every practice. Therefore, both the home and the visitors' locker rooms were used on practice days during the week. On Thursdays before home games players who weren't on the list to dress for the game were required to pack up their uniforms and gear and relocate it all to their dorm rooms. On Fridays, those players would have to dress in their dorm rooms and walk across campus to get to practice. Some freshmen and walk-ons were permanently relegated to dressing in the same antique facilities in the Old Fieldhouse used by the Four Horsemen. They had to walk across campus every day in full pads to practice. Ara inherited these conditions and they persisted until the fall of 1968, when the practice locker room for everyone was moved into the new Athletic and Convocation Center. After that, the Notre Dame Stadium locker rooms were used exclusively on game days.

THE REAL DEAL MONDAYS

During the season, Mondays were the most interesting days on Ara's practice field. They were especially important if you were a player attempting to work your way up the depth chart. The starters from the previous Saturday's game were given a light workout with minimal contact. The goals for them were to heal minor injuries and regain strength. All other players were inserted into live scrimmages to determine who wanted to earn, or keep, a spot on the roster for the following Saturday. These scrimmages were coined "Toilet Bowls," because everyone on the "shit squad" wanted to get in to the real action.

There is hardly a player from this generation who doesn't have a Monday practice story to tell. As defensive back Tom Reynolds later expressed it to me in a conversation, "It was the real deal. You knew you were playing against the best in the nation, and you had to give one hundred percent just to hold your position. There were no soft hits or easy yards during Toilet Bowls."

Larry Conjar was just one Toilet Bowl success story. He still remembers sitting on the top row of Notre Dame Stadium late on a Sunday after a home game in his sophomore year, having just run the steps before heading in for a shower. As he recalled to me by phone, "I looked over the field and just asked myself, what are you doing here? If you aren't going to go out and prove you belong in the games, what are you doing here? Right then I committed to give it my maximum effort on Monday." The coaches remember the results of this resolution well. Larry was asked to carry on four consecutive running plays and each time he delivered a punishing blow. His efforts prompted Coach Tom Pagna to say, "It's about time." Larry moved up the ranks that day and went on to have one of the most impressive careers at the fullback position in Notre Dame history. His succinct comment today: "Yeah, Monday was the real deal alright."

THE STRESS RELIEF RITUALS

Part of the culture of football is the liturgy of rituals that teams invoke to either get stoked up or to break the tension of anxiety over an upcoming game. Ara believed in such rituals as much as any other coach for a simple reason — they seemed to work. Unfortunately, it became harder to perpetuate these rituals in the future generations of more jaded high school athletes who prized NFL aspirations above their college careers.

The high priest of team rituals was Assistant Coach Tom Pagna. It was Pagna who composed and delivered the weekly messages from "the Phantom." It was Pagna who oversaw posting messages on the "clobber board," usually articles from the local newspaper of the next opposing team with an inflammatory statement highlighted. If Pagna couldn't find something juicy, he made something up. These traditions were the dose of fire and brimstone that offset Ara's consistently focused and businesslike demeanor.

Pagna concocted another little ritual to occur at the end of practice on Thursdays before games. Recall that Ara learned from Paul Brown not to leave your best game on the field during practices late in the week, but to save it for game day. To ease the mounting tension of constantly playing teams for which Notre Dame would be the biggest game of the year, sections of the team were assigned to compose poems or limericks about their positions (for example, the offensive line) in the context of the impending contest. Players were encouraged to expend time and creativity in advance of the exercise. The goal was to be the best, be the crudest, or just to get the biggest laugh. The rewards were meaningless — maybe receiving the first shot at hot water in the showers or being first in line at training table. None of these creative works seem to have survived. As star receiver Jim Seymour later stated to me, "You wouldn't be able to print them anyway." But the players all remember the ritual.

THE PLAYING TIME PARADOX

Playing major college football is a paradox. The participants work long and hard in practices to play for just seconds or minutes in the actual games. There are only about fifteen minutes of "real" action in a typical college game, and that amount of time is split fairly evenly between the offense and the defense. Even if starting players remain on the field constantly, they expend a maximum of seven or eight minutes of intense exertion. Some really talented players, especially at a place like Notre Dame, never get to play at all. Some players who religiously endure five days of grueling practice never even dress for a single game. They join the ranks of the other fans on Saturdays.

The paying fans on game days never get to see or feel the football that is played for hours and hours leading up to the game. The paradox is that fans see a condensed highlight reel of players' most intense efforts. It pits the best select few from one team against the best of another. But that doesn't really tell the story of "the team," at least not at a place like Notre Dame. When the Notre Dame "team" was practicing, the players knew they were playing against some of the best in the nation during the week — their teammates.

THE LUCKY SUIT SUPERSTITION

College football coaches tend to be a superstitious lot. The way the ball bounces may have a profound effect on the final score. But bouncing balls are difficult to prepare for in advance. Luck has a way of entering the picture. Thus, superstitions are a cosmic plea for good fortune. Although not entirely rational, coaches have their quirks to acknowledge the elements of chance. Ara Parseghian certainly did.

In Ara's first year at Miami University of Ohio, he would dress for games in a brown suit and tie (coaches often wore business attire on the sidelines in those days). After winning his first couple of games, Ara decided that this suit might be part of his formula for success. For every Miami game, home and away, Ara wore this same "lucky" suit — for five seasons. When he moved on to Northwestern, the brown suit started to show wear, and perhaps "shrink" a bit. But he didn't dare not have it around on game day. So, the suit was packed in a small suitcase and accompanied him into the locker room. With the suit close at hand Ara was able to select his actual game attire for more comfort and to accommodate variable weather conditions.

Katie Parseghian was confident that the brown suit didn't make the trip to South Bend. What became of it is unknown, but Notre Dame team managers were alert to Ara's precise dressing rituals on game days. All the elements of Ara's gameday ensemble had to be placed in his locker with precision, right down to the shoes with the name "ARA" written on the heels in all capital letters. Part of this was to relieve the tension of unknown surprises before a game. But the managers swear it became a superstitious exercise.

There is one enduring superstition that Ara Parseghian embraced from his first game coaching college football through his last. He had his lucky buckeye in his pants pocket, and it was the very same one for all twenty-four seasons. A buckeye is the nut of a common species of tree in Ohio. The nut is about one inch in diameter and has a warm brown shell highlighted by a beige "eye," which is so named because it resembles the eye of a deer: a *buck's eye*. Katie Parseghian was clueless as to where Ara initially acquired the lucky buckeye, but guessed that it came from the Miami University campus. Today this unique element of Ara's success is unassumingly ensconced in a trophy case at daughter Kriss Parseghian Humbert's home. Is it a priceless or a worthless keepsake? You decide.

CHAPTER 11

SIDELINES

All the preparation and practice before a college football game is meaningless unless there is a coherent plan and a framework to make in-game adjustments and decisions for maximum results. Ara Parseghian was among the first to utilize a systems approach to organizing data, formulating plans with options, streamlining communications from the sideline, and employing technologies that were new at the time. These components fueled his coaching genius. His peer coaches recognized (even if they were silently jealous) the innovations that were employed to provide strategic advantages for Ara's team on game days.

THE GAME CARDS

Ara Parseghian was not the first to use written crib notes from the sidelines while he coached, but he was among the first and most successful at it. Thankfully, these game cards survive and are among the true treasures of the Parseghian archives. These are approximately four-inch by eight-inch cards, slotted into a plastic sleeve, with the coach's tiny printing on both sides. The ensemble was designed to fit into a back pocket or under the belt and sweater. They were a part of the props used by Ara in his orchestrated sideline opera.

The significance of and respect for Ara's system was revealed many years after he resigned. In 1979, the head football coach at Indiana University, Lee Corso, made a personal appeal to be educated about how it was devised. This is the very same Lee Corso who has been a long-standing Saturday morning host on ESPN's *Gameday* broadcasts during the college football season. Ara's response below (unedited) is both generous and detailed. The average person might find it difficult to fully comprehend, and because there isn't evidence of follow-up questions, one wonders if Corso fully absorbed it.

> Dear Lee:
>
> Enclosed you will find a card that I used not only to brief me on the game plan that we had decided upon but also as a means of signaling to our quarterback.
>
> On one side you will see basic runs with capital letters going down the left side of the card of M, I, OT, SW. These indicate middle, inside, off tackle, and sweep. The initials adjacent to the areas are abbreviations. For example, BT under middle would be buck trap and PS under sweep would be power sweep and so on. Directly below that would be the Misdirection Run and Possessions Passes. Across from the run segment you find the title Basic Passes underlined in red. Run action, misdirection pass, and action pass. Underneath that you will find home runs and screens. These are obvious and self-explanatory. In other words, if I was looking for a misdirection run or a position pass on 3rd down, I would immediately focus on that category and the final game plan card would carry a numeral indicating which we liked best against the opponent. 1 and 2 being the ones that we would feature during the week and rehearse.
>
> And flipping the card over, you will note that we would operate out of two tight ends and also include cadence changes. This is marked on the card as a reminder. In other words, on short yardage situations, we would either go quick or extend our cadence in hopes of drawing our opponents outside. You will note, on the left side in black, short yardage runs, the category of middle and inside joined together, then off tackle and sweep. Again, in our final game plan card we would place a numeral beside the play that we liked best against our opponent.

On the right-hand side of the column, you see again the short yard-age passes as well as the misdirection passes. You will also note that we have both the 2-point run and 2-point pass depending on which we pre-fer to do and obviously the decision was made depending on the nature of the game. On Thursday and Friday, we would rehearse our entire game plan which included the 2-point run or pass. The last two things on the card indicate special plays or special formations.

Lee, the card that I've enclosed appears to be a Thursday rehearsal and we crystalized that down in our Friday meeting an assigned a nu-meral to indicate which plays we liked the best in each category.

I would appreciate your returning the card after you review it. Keep up the good work.

Sincerely,

Ara

Lee Corso returned a letter of thanks to Ara. In it Corso claimed to have tried the card system in a game against Michigan, and he declared he "was robbed" — the Hoosiers got 285 yards and twenty-one points in a losing effort. Still, Coach Corso seemed very appreciative of the help it provided in play calling.

THE SIGNALS

One of the many innovations that Ara perfected at Notre Dame was sending signals from the sideline to the team on the field. This added even more intellectual complexity to the positions of quarterback and defensive captain. The long-established NCAA rule at the time was that coaches couldn't communicate plays, especially offensive plays, from the sideline to the players. Ara Parseghian railed against what he called "a stupid rule." When he was at Northwestern he was even penalized once for a signal violation. As he retold it, one of his players was forced out of bounds in front of his bench. As the player was getting up, Par-seghian verbally gave him the next play to take back to the huddle. The official marking the ball dropped his flag (colored red instead of yellow in those days). Even a fleeting comment constituted a penalty. So col-lege coaches, including Ara, were forced to innovate. Every coach called plays from the sideline, but none did it better than Ara. In fact, his exact method was one of Ara's most closely guarded secrets.

Ara finally relented and cracked the code to a few close confidants, explaining to us the mechanics after so many years of keeping the closely guarded secret. It was amazing to watch. He had to stand upright in his home office to demonstrate it. The walls and shelves around him were cramped with plaques, trophies, books, photos, and assorted memorabilia — all silent witnesses to the demonstration. Both the coach and the viewers were transported back in time.

It wasn't a secret that there was a highly sophisticated series of signals, similar to what base coaches and managers use in baseball. But outsiders never claimed to know how it was done. A select few were in the know. Most of them had long careers working for Ara, so they were never in a position to take the code to another team. Those few that did move had too much respect for Ara to reveal his secret, although they probably used it themselves without attribution. Among the players, only defensive captains and quarterbacks were tutored on the signals.

Here's how it worked. From the coaches' position on the sideline at midfield the angles on forward progress are hard to read, especially near the end zones, where calling plays matters most. Team managers were assigned to each sideline to follow the progress of the ball down the field and immediately signal to the Notre Dame coaches the precise distance for a first down or a score. Speed of communication was critical to provide adequate decision time to plan the next play.

The team immediately retreated into its huddle with the signal receiver placed so that he could read the signals flashed from the bench. Quarterback Terry Hanratty remembers kneeling down and looking at the sideline from between the legs of the standing linemen. The other players in the huddle became in effect a human duck blind. The unsuspecting officials quit paying attention once they saw the huddle. Then the quarterback, or on defense, the captain, began translating signal language from Ara to the team.

Ara's signal language was simultaneously simple, elegant, and complex. It was based on subtle natural and normal gestures from Ara: how he held his play card (the side with the line facing out or the side without the line), which hand he used, and which quadrant of the clipboard held it. Was he standing or kneeling? Were his feet together or apart? If ever they thought an opponent might catch on, the signal calling was temporarily transferred to one of the assistant coaches using a key. All the gestures were completely natural: there were none of the gyrations one would expect (from watching baseball) that would attract unwanted attention from the officials.

Even the selection of the coach's attire was part of the program. Almost everyone from that era recalls Ara's custom wool sweater, navy blue with gold chenille letters applied in an arc to spell "NOTRE DAME." Ara proudly wore this sweater, as captured by the artist for Ara's cover of *Time* magazine in 1964. The convenient (albeit false) story at the time was that Katie Parseghian made this custom sweater as a gift to her husband. In fact, it was a well-considered prop so that the team's signal receivers could immediately pick out the coach on the sideline. Positioning was key; Ara virtually straddled the 50-yard line for the entire game. In later years, Ara put his hand or the play card over specific parts of the sweater.

Of course, making this complex code work with precision took incredible coordination. The head coach had to be entirely aware of and in control of his body language, lest a confusing or false signal be communicated. This fact goes a long way to explain two characteristics of Ara on the sideline: he never wore headsets (too distracting), and he rarely smiled or celebrated on the sideline. The intensity required to process information and plan the next moves wouldn't allow for either. He was always thinking one or more plays ahead.

Ara was the equivalent of a human football computer processing information, making decisions, and communicating them to the team on the field, all in fewer than fifteen seconds. At the time, there were only two physical computers on the Notre Dame campus, and the newest of those manufactured by IBM occupied practically an entire building called the Computing Center. Ara was the first "portable computer" at Notre Dame on football Saturdays, even if nobody appreciated it at the time.

This communication scheme also required smart and alert captains and quarterbacks. At a school with high academic standards like Notre Dame, players' level of intelligence didn't usually pose a problem. But sometimes not having acute vision did. Ara recalled that some defensive captains would squint in the direction of the bench during huddles, adding to the anxiety about what the player might think he saw, and thus alerting an official to drop a flag. Even today, quarterback Terry Hanratty takes special pride and boasts that he never missed an offensive signal. It is ironic that the most serious miscommunication during the 1966 season was on a play brought in from the sideline that resulted in Hanratty's separated shoulder at Michigan State.

The genius of the system was that the play calling was specific about formation or play sequence but allowed for multiple variations to be determined based on "formation keys" provided by the opposing team (and then processed and reinforced by verbal communication at the line of scrimmage). In a sense, every play was an "audible" as we understand the term today but with simple commands in the count. The playbooks were thick and detailed. Players had to reflect the coach's intensity and intelligence to play at Notre Dame. Communicating clearly was the necessary first step. All the players were expected to memorize the plays, their assignments and all the options, and then know how to execute instinctively.

Eventually, rule changes allowed more open substitutions during a game, and signals from the bench have been standard operating procedure for all college teams for over fifty years.

THE BOX

Another innovation Ara brought to the sideline was "the box." This was a small, portable, black and white television monitor that was connected to a dedicated TV camera on the roof of the Press Box. Notre Dame was the owner and licensee of a television station in South Bend, WNDU, and television equipment was readily available. Assistant Coach Brian Boulac was assigned to strap on a harness and carry the heavy piece of equipment around at Parseghian's side during the home games. This responsibility took incredible strength and stamina to do this for an entire game, even for the former lineman. As Brian said, "It was worth it. I had the best seat in the house."

Before every play the cameraman would be instructed by headset where to focus the camera. The action was only available in real time, with no video replay capability. Then Boulac would communicate what he saw to Ara, especially highlighting the down and remaining distance. This feedback all entered the coach's mental data bank, either for immediate use or to be retained for a future play call when it was important. Video contraptions like the box were outlawed by the Big Ten in 1965. And for important away games in 1966, at Northwestern and Michigan State, Notre Dame was without this tool.

The use of video and replay assistance on college sidelines was banned entirely by the NCAA after the 1966 season and that restriction remains in place. Professional football has no such restriction. Professional football technology includes direct radio links to quarterback helmets, printed screen shots of gameday plays and formations, and portable laptop computers in use during games — all commonplace.

THE BRAINTRUST

Of course, Ara had a full complement of coaches on the sideline, each one trained to collect data that was judiciously communicated to the head coach. John Ray ran the defense. Tom Pagna became the thoughtful "back-up computer" for Ara on offense. He processed much of the same information as Ara and performed a check on the decisions that were being made. This was quite important in the area of game management, especially as it pertained to time on the clock. Pagna knew what they could do with time remaining, or how to "milk the clock" to keep the ball out of the opponent's hands. On average, there are fourteen offensive possessions for each team in a college game. When play calling is benchmarked against statistical probabilities, the decisions become easier, or at least theoretically better. Pagna was in charge of monitoring this for Ara and providing just enough data to help Ara's mental computer function.

Speed in data collection was essential in addition to accuracy and immediacy. One could argue that Ara's brain processed information better and faster than any contemporary college football coach in America. So good was the system that Ara's 1968 team set an NCAA record by averaging just over ninety offensive plays per game over the course of a ten-game season. That record may still stand (although it isn't officially listed), even in the current era of no huddle and hurry-up offenses. Today it is rare for teams to have over seventy offensive plays.

Rapid and stealthy communication during games was the mysterious secret weapon at Notre Dame. But the Notre Dame players knew, even though most of them were only semi-aware of the intricacies of how it all happened.

CHAPTER 12

STRATEGY

Genius in college football coaching isn't just something a person is born with. Parts of a coach's talent may be acquired only through experience (success or failure), or through thoughtful observation of successful mentors and practitioners. Eventually all great football coaches must develop an overarching coaching philosophy that provides the bedrock for making their game decisions with clarity and conviction. Ara Parseghian wasn't an exception to this rule. Quite the opposite, he could be considered the poster boy for explaining his success on the field. No doubt he had strong influences from being coached in high school by Frank Wargo and thereafter, most notably, being coached by Paul Brown and working with Woody Hayes. But one of the coaching influences that could easily be overlooked is Ara's playing experience itself. Recall that he played at all levels — high school, college and professional — in a single-platoon format. Guys on the field had to know and execute plays on both offense and defense. This experience guided his coaching philosophy throughout his career, and his approach to the underlying rudiments of the game didn't evolve much, even as he observed the game late into his life. He would admit that tactics were constantly changing in the sport of football, but he believed a sound strategy withstood the test of time. Whether his philosophy could be implemented today is a matter for spirited debate. Without getting too technical, the summary that follows is an attempt to translate Ara's strategy into layman's terms.

Football is a game with only two fundamental variables: possession (of the ball) and position (on the field). Everything is built around these two concepts. A third variable is imposed by the rules of the game, a finite amount of time on the game clock. Sometimes possession should be sacrificed for position. Sometimes position must be ignored to retain possession. Every coach's game decision requires a calculus regarding what is lost and what is gained relative to possession and position.

Of the two, possession is preeminent in the decision calculus. The justification is simple. Your team usually can't score without possession. And similarly, your opponent usually can't score without possession. Teams that can successfully manage possessions have a higher probability of winning.

Mistakes on the field that unnecessarily and negatively alter a team's possession or position must be strictly avoided. This means the elimination of penalties, fumbles, interceptions, poor special team plays, and busted plays. The worst culprit is a penalty that is called due to a single player's lack of concentration — one person's inattention can hurt the entire team.

There are two opposing units on the field during play, the offense and the defense. It is generally agreed that defense is much harder to play well. The defense can't know what the offense is planning, so it must react. It takes much more physical energy to play defense, and this factors into game results, especially factoring in players' fatigue in the fourth quarter.

The offense has three goals when they are on the field: (a) they should aim to score; (b) they should aim to advance the ball — or improve position; and (c) they should manage play such that by incrementally improving position and by expending time on the play clock they are diminishing their opponents' opportunities to score. Importantly, the offense should keep the defense off the field as much as possible so that when the defense is called upon, they are mentally and athletically fresh. Mistakes can be made when (c) is ignored in favor of a quick score (a).

Following these three essential rules during game situations isn't as straightforward for a football coach as the casual observer might suppose. They are even harder to embrace if critical comments overheard in the crowd are the measure of success. When you are relying on teenagers to execute plays and your job is on the line, personal stress increases. Experience and situational statistics inform coaching decisions from the sidelines that optimize possession and position. However, it is exceedingly difficult to ignore the impact of emotion, crowd response, officiating, time pressures, the element of surprise, gambler instincts, and reinforcement bias (a common human struggle: we think we know more than we actually know) in making good decisions.

Ara's agile mind played a key role in helping him make good decisions quickly (over 150 times in each game he coached). If he couldn't sleep after a loss, especially one with a close score, he would lie awake to mentally evaluate each of the in-game decisions' adherence to the three fundamentals of his coaching strategy: maintaining possession, improving position, and managing time on the game clock. If the outcome was decided by factors beyond his control, it was easier for him to move on and rest his overactive mind.

One wonders if Ara's philosophy would have evolved and changed if he had coached under contemporary game conditions. Or, would he have retained his strategy and concentrated on adapting game tactics only?

For example, today the kicking game plays a central role in game outcomes. College teams, even those with smaller roster limits, recruit specialists, especially field goal kickers. It isn't unusual for talented high school kids to make 30- and 40-yard kicks with regularity and make 50-yarders on occasion. This kind of accuracy is a big change in the game and makes the playing field smaller in effect, since the zone for scoring has expanded farther from the end zone.

What about the effectiveness of the long pass, the bomb? It seems that every college team has a quarterback with the arm strength to be dangerous. Defending against such a throw requires more speed and more defensive backfield players ready to engage. Ara's teams typically played a 4-4-3 (line-linebackers-backs) defense oriented against the run. It was rare to have a team throw more than twenty-five times in a game. Now the usual defensive configurations are 3-4-4, 4-3-4, and even 3-3-5 (still line-linebackers-backs). Defensive backfield speed is a premium commodity in college players.

Even the evolution of stadium clocks could have factored into a change in Ara's approach. For over half of Ara's career, he coached with mechanical clocks that had sweep hands for minutes and seconds. In 1964, the clocks of the Los Angeles Coliseum were of this type, which made using timeouts at the end of the game imprecise. With digital readouts of exact minutes and seconds, the game can be managed with more precision, and better decisions can be made.

Capturing a short list of Ara's coaching pet peeves as he observed football later in his life demonstrates his thoughtful consideration of new variables. However, they still illuminate a strong adherence to his fundamentals. Here are some examples (most of which highlight his preference to have the offense run the ball instead of pass).

Inside the 5-yard line, why would a shotgun exchange be used? Every yard, in fact every foot, is hard-earned position. So why hike the ball five yards in reverse, momentarily changing the team's position and lower the probability for a clean exchange, thus jeopardizing possession? Does it make sense?

Using a shotgun formation inside the 10-yard line without having a single player in the backfield (also called an empty backfield) seemed like a statistical mistake to Ara. Even assuming a clean exchange, the advantage shifts to the defense. The run is not a good option and the quarterback is exposed to injury. Usually, a pass is being telegraphed to the defense when a team lines up this way. This makes it harder to create open passing lanes with less playing field to use. Ara believed the old coaching chestnut: "With a pass only three things can happen, and two of them are bad."

The fade pass into the end zone is also statistically challenged. To score requires a perfect pass and catch. However, the defense now has two additional invisible defenders involved with the out-of-bounds lines on the side and back. This is the equivalent of passing to or being trapped with a basketball in the corner of the court. It should be easier to throw into the front of the end zone while the defender is backpedaling.

The so-called hurry-up offense is a misnomer. Having the entire team of eleven players capture and process signals from the sidelines tends to result in unnecessary miscues and penalties. It is preferable to call a play in the huddle where miscommunication can be minimized and then check off at the line with an alternate play if necessary.

This last coaching pet peeve has some statistical relevance to success. Ara's teams consistently averaged over eighty offensive plays per game in each of his ten-game regular seasons. Today it is rare when any team completes even seventy plays per game, and most are using some form of the spread offense with the perception of a hurry-up personality. More plays, including time of possession, means more chances to score, fewer chances for the opponent to score, and a fresher defensive unit late in the game. It's not complicated — in theory.

Ara and a number of his former players were collected at the wake of his former assistant coach Wally Moore in 2014. Congregating in the hallway at the funeral home, Ara held court. Frank Criniti (halfback, 1966–1968) asked his former coach if he watched Notre Dame games on television. Ara replied, "Yes, and I find myself always yelling the same thing at the TV." Frank inquired, "What are you yelling, Coach?" Ara answered, "Run the damn ball."

CHAPTER 13

THE PLAYBOOK

One of the cruelest stereotypes is that college athletes, especially football players, aren't smart. Consider this quote from *LOOK* magazine's
September 20, 1966, edition: "Not long ago, Red Smith recalled a college football hero who was brave, fast as light and violent as a crime of
passion, but not pretentiously intellectual. 'In fact,' his coach said, 'if his
IQ were any lower, he'd be a plant.'" The data fail to support the stereo-
type. But sometimes incidental observations, especially raucous social
behaviors off the field, contribute to the misconception. One only has
to understand the demands of being an athlete in a major college football program to conclude that the intellectual challenges are substantial. Football is like taking another academic course in the classroom,
which is then followed by real-world daily quizzes (practices) and
weekly tests (games). The grading is much tougher than that for classroom subjects, often resulting in physical pain and injury, not to mention potential embarrassment in front of thousands of fans in the stadium and perhaps a TV audience in the millions.

You are never more aware of the mental rigor until you have studied an actual college playbook. As might be expected, the playbooks
devised by Ara Parseghian and his staff were extensive, detailed, and
innovative — many would argue they were all well ahead of their time.

For over half of a century, the few playbooks that escaped confiscation at the end of a season have been guarded like military secrets. To the lay person, the secrets remain largely obtuse. But the playbook continues to be worthy of high security clearance because in the hands of people with the right minds, the playbook might be effectively adopted and successfully used today with some minor adjustments.

The eloquent first page of the playbook is presented below in its entirety.

YOU'VE JOINED THE TEAM!!

1966 WILL ASK A LOT OF NOTRE DAME TEAM MEMBERS. IT WILL ASK YOU TO PLAY WITH A "FULL HEART," TO NEVER HAVE A "BREAKING POINT," TO GO FOR "60 MINUTES." IT WILL FURTHER ASK THAT YOUR DRESS, YOUR MANNER, YOUR APPEARANCE, YOUR BEHAVIOR BE THAT OF YOUNG MEN NOBLY PRIVILEGED TO REPRESENT NOTRE DAME.

PHYSICALLY YOU WILL TIRE. MENTALLY YOU WILL FEEL GREAT PRESSURE AND STUDYING WILL BE TOUGH. EMOTIONALLY YOU WILL BECOME HIGHLY SENSITIVE — FRAYED — UPSET AND CONFUSED. YOU WILL BE IDOLIZED BY ALL YOUNGSTERS, LOOKED DOWN UPON BY PSEUDO-SCHOLARS, PRAISED BY PARENTS, TORN BY THE WANTS AND PRESSURES OF OUTSIDE GROUPS, GUIDED & DISCUSSED BY COACHES — BUT MOST IMPORTANT YOU WILL HAVE BEEN A PART OF A GROUP OF MEN THAT WILL GIVE YOU AN EQUAL RETURN.

WITH YOUR COMMITMENT AND THAT OF ALL OTHER TEAM MEMBERS, WE WILL BE AN INSEPARABLE — STRONG — UNITED FORCE — READY TO FIGHT ONLY THE GOOD FIGHT — WINNING IF WE CAN, LOSING ONLY WHEN DESTINEY SAYS WE MUST. BRING ON THE OPPONENETS! NOTRE DAME IS READY! IF "NO ARMY IS AS POWERFUL AS AN IDEA WHOSE TIME HAS COME," IT IS TIME WE ALL COMMIT TO THE ACCEPTANCE OF "TEAM IDEA" — THIS IS THE COMMITMENT THAT WE CAN NEVER HAVE CAUSE TO REGRET — FURTHER, WE WILL ONLY PROSPER FROM THE GREAT FORCE THAT UNITY IGNITES! IT CAN MAKE OUR 1966 SEASON A BRILLIANT PAGE IN THE BOOK OF YOUR LIFE.

NOTRE DAME COACHING STAFF

Ara divided the playbook into twenty-five sections, chapters of sorts, each with a separate, colored tab. All of this is thoughtfully inserted into a fat, three-ringed binder. It is a comprehensive piece of work.

No detail is too large or too small to be incorporated. For example, is it really necessary to include the 1966 football schedule? Never mind; it's there, as is the daily schedule for preseason practices, prescribed in half-hour blocks, beginning with "Wake Up" at 6:30 a.m. and ending with "Lights Out" at 10:30 p.m. There's a map of the Cartier Field practice areas to prevent players from getting lost at practice.

The administrative rules are instructive. "Section I, Player's Book Responsibility" lays out clear expectations: "The Book will be returned at conclusion of season, before U.S.C. game." This is followed by a caution not to lose the playbook, since doing so "can hurt entire team if wrong person has access."

Training regulations are similarly no-nonsense. "No smoking or drinking (that's a twelve-month proposition). . . . All bars are off limits. . . . We will police." Then the most interesting paragraph reinforces page 1: "Your complete cooperation is expected, and insubordination will not be tolerated. High morale is essential to team success. You will have gripes, but you must set them aside in the interest of loyalty to team and coaching staff. The team is bigger than any individual connected with it. This game is not compulsory, but those who play must abide by regulations. No days off."

The "Training Hints" are equally detailed and direct. A practical example: "Watch your blisters (important)." Slightly more serious: "We will not tolerate stealing of equipment or practical joking with equipment. Your body protection is too valuable to be a toy." The approach is very adult for actions and consequences. "Discipline action for being late to practice and training room (5 laps). Continual lateness will cost you your uniform."

The playbook addresses personal hygiene. After each practice, players are instructed to do the following: "Expose feet to sun and air. Elevate and bathe with warm saltwater solution." It would be interesting to know how religiously players followed this advice.

Similarly, the preseason dormitory regulations have this admonition: "Please keep card playing at an absolute minimum (or it will be abolished)." There is no clarity about what "an absolute minimum" is. The unwritten subtext throughout is that this is Notre Dame; don't mess up.

The daily practices are broken down and orchestrated with precision. Each action — jogging, calisthenics, stretching, and sprinting — is listed and put into a thoughtfully designed sequence. It wouldn't be an exaggeration to believe that some players could instinctively walk through a complete practice sixty years after the fact without many prompts. That was probably the point of the regimented schedule: less thinking and more time for actually practicing.

The drills by position were well-known and purposeful — ball exchange drills, blocking drills, and an anti-fumble drill. Some had names too colorful to recall here. (But what exactly were "distraction" drills?)

The offensive line spent lots of time on the training sleds. The "1/2 line drill on sacks over guard, tackle and end" prepared players for what are now called "blitzes." You don't see or hear that term back in 1966. The defensive line had a "shed drill," a "spin drill," and a "peek-a-boo drill." (One can only imagine the talented Alan Page playing peek-a-boo!) The intended outcome of each drill would be for an opposing player to be "drilled." Other entertaining drill titles for the defensive backs: tip, angle tip, flag, combat, wave, and squeeze.

The playbook exposes and addresses what are known as offensive critical situations. These are the same at every level from pee-wee to pro, but they are thoroughly addressed nonetheless for clarity. For example: "KICK OFF: You must watch the ball kicked off the tee;" "PUNT: Block until sound of the ball;" "BEAT CLOCK: Be sure you get out of bounds;" "SAFETY: Offense can never be tackled in own end zone;" and "FUMBLE: A fumble is the greatest sin an offensive player can commit. Be aware of the ball and our trust in your proper carry."

Reading the playbook in sequence is surprisingly seductive. It's like listening to Einstein explain the theory of relativity, but for the first time, it starts to make sense. The real gem in the book is written directly by Ara and comes as close to expressing the heart of his coaching philosophy as a single sheet of paper can capture. Again, it is presented in its entirety:

THE INTERVAL THAT CAUSES GREATNESS

Three things comprise the "GREAT INTERVAL"

EFFORT +

EXECUTION +

ENDURANCE = INTERVAL

The longest play in football, a long kick-off return, is approximately twelve seconds in length.

The shortest is a no gain direct line dive. Its duration about 2.5 seconds in length.

The average play is near to four seconds.

When we say INTERVAL, we are talking about that time period from the ball snap that ignites us, to four seconds later. Nothing else really matters in a game.

On average, offense runs eighty or so plays. Defense runs nearly the same.

We are talking about 4 x 80 or 320 seconds, or about five minutes.

When we say INTERVAL, we are asking if you will give EFFORT, EXECUTION, AND ENDURANCE for Notre Dame — just five minutes' worth a game. A four second interval by every player on every play will make us a GREAT TEAM!!

Listen and watch for the word throughout practice.

WE WILL BECOME WHAT WE DO!

DO THE INTERVAL!

ARA PARSEGHIAN

So far, only a single tab out of twenty-five in the binder has been highlighted. The remaining twenty-four tabs are filled with all the diagrams you could imagine, with pages full of geometric shapes, Xs, Os, boxes, arrows, lines, dotted lines, and numbers. This is about what you'd expect. But the level of detail is impressive, actually overwhelming, when gathered in its entirety in a single binder.

Ara explains stances by position with specifics by situation. No one could possibly memorize this content; it had to be absorbed and then become habitual. The base split is two feet between players. An example, going position by position:

CENTER: Feet parallel and shoulder width, knees turned out.

GUARDS, TACKLES, ENDS: Feet arm pit width, straight upfield — stagger — heal, toe — weight on balls of feet.

HALFBACKS: Feet — inside leg back shoulder width. Inside hand down, Stagger — heal toe.

FULLBACKS: Feet parallel (right or left hand down) don't tip off play by weight shift.

TAILBACK: Feet parallel, hands on knees.

Every position has five or more directives just about stance. So far, the ball hasn't even been snapped.

There are step-by-step techniques for thirteen different types of blocks. For example, the "Downfield Block" is laid out as follows:

Hit out with count.

Cutoff release when necessary.

Get close to opponent, step on his toes.

Throw high — through and beyond opponent.

Roll with opponent. Get up and throw again.

Don't spend yourself too early.

Get close enough to make contact.

There are forty-two different defensive alignments to recognize, each with its own code name. Another example from the playbook:

To apply our Blocking System, one must understand the terms used for communication purposes. Our blocking strategy is based on the following:

The play call

Defensive alignment

Ratio of blockers to defenders

Tendencies of the defense

Tendencies of the individual defender

We arrive at various blocking combinations through the use of:

Base rule — for a particular play

Master calls — intra-line communication used to control full line or 1/2 line (example — Reach — Seal — 6)

Individual calls — intra line. Communication between two
   individuals (example — S-X-R)
Individual calls may be used within a master call.

This is tedious stuff, and this is only information under the second
tab of the book. It takes a high degree of intelligence to understand the
specifics and to recognize and apply rules as a team in real time with
game pressure. This is not *Football for Dummies*.

On the offense there are thirty-nine different running plays, all
with variations. There are thirty-two different passing plays, again with
variations. Then there are special teams plays, such as punts with at
least ten different variations. All of them are fully diagrammed.

The defense is equally complex. An effective defensive philosophy
is explained:

Defensive Objectives
   The major objective of defensive football is to keep your opponent
   from scoring. Every member of the defensive team should keep this
   fact uppermost in his mind at all times. To repeat, the first and only
   mission of the defense is to prevent a score. Strong as it may seem,
   defensive players often lose sight of this vital fact.
TEN BASIC "MUSTS" IF OUR DEFENSE IS TO BE SOUND:
   Do not allow the long pass for an easy TD.
   Do not allow the long run for an easy TD.
   Do not allow the offense to score inside our five-yard line
      by running.
   Do not allow a kick-off return for a TD.
   Cut down on kick-off return, so as to allow no more than
      5 yards per kick.
   The defense must intercept 3 out of every 14 passes attempted.
   The defense must average 20 yards per interception.
   During the season we must return 3 interceptions for TD's.
   The defense must make our opponents fumble at least 3 times
      a game.
   We must recover at least 2 fumbles of our opponents every
      game.

Defensive Theory
The theory of defensive football is based on three objectives.
Prevent your opponent from scoring.
Gain possession of the football.
Score ourselves.

The "Defensive Suggestions" list is filled with helpful nuggets that every player should embrace, such as:

Gang tackle, Gang tackle, Gang tackle.
Love body contact. Be a competitor.
Keep your feet moving.
Rush the passer with hands high.
Be hitters, not "catchers."

There are twenty of these helpful reminders. The most interesting is Number 17: "Any player lying on the ground watching the play and not attempting to give a second effort will get a better seat next week — ON THE BENCH."

After multiple pages of schemes and diagrams there is a page for "Terms We Should Know." The list is designed to summarize and simplify the complexity that goes before it.

Strong Side — Strong side of off. [offensive] formation.
Weak Side — Weak side of off. formation.
Fan or Sprint — No run action threat inside.
Run Action — Has threat of run inside.
Red — No switch in man coverage (HB & S).
Green — Switch if necessary in man coverage (HB & S).
Field Balance — lateral position on the ball.
Field Position — vertical position on the ball.
The closer the ball gets to our goal line, the tighter we play, Man or Zone.
Don't defend the end zone. Defend the goal line.
Use the side lines as an extra man.
Talk to one another on coverage & routes.
Know the down & distance.

Play the ball tough. The offense wins all ties.
You must read your keys.
Camouflage or hide the defense.

The entire playbook is over three hundred pages and includes over fifteen hundred diagrams. If this book was studied as part of a required course for the general college population, there would be very few A grades and a significant failure rate. Being a football player at a major college program is intellectually demanding, more so than academic purists might ever admit. Playing at Notre Dame for Ara Parseghian was even harder.

Ara Parseghian wasn't the only person at Notre Dame with a playbook. Father Ted and Father Ned had an invisible one of their own. The two playbooks merged effectively and with game-changing results. It was the goal of Father Hesburgh (president) and Father Joyce (executive vice president) to combine excellence on the football field with excellence in the classroom through direct university engagement. They put this vision into motion when they asked Mike DeCicco, a professor of engineering, to take on the role of advisor to the student-athletes at Notre Dame in 1964.

Professor DeCicco was the coach of the highly successful Irish fencing team and already an advocate for his athletes. As he recalled the chain of events, Father Hesburgh called him to a meeting to ask DeCicco to take on this new task. The role of advisor to the student-athletes wasn't just new to Notre Dame; it was new to college athletics. DeCicco listened to the university president and then asked for some time to think about it. He went home and discussed the offer with his wife, Polly. Her reaction was very straightforward, "When the bosses ask you to do something, you do it." That's how Mike DeCicco became the first to fill the novel role at Notre Dame.

Unfortunately, there was no established playbook for the new role, and often it required administering tough love to this special category of undergraduates. But DeCicco always started with the student's best interests, became an advocate for the athletes at Notre Dame, and made their college experiences focused and more rewarding. They have never forgotten that.

The NCAA took notice of the groundbreaking efforts of Fathers Hesburgh and Joyce in combination with the seemingly limitless energy of the gregarious Mike DeCicco. In 1966, the NCAA established a national committee on the topic of athletic advising. The goal was to improve the overall well-being of college athletes. Today, virtually all universities with national prominence provide this important resource for their student-athletes. Remarkably, it all started at Notre Dame.

CHAPTER 14

GAMES THAT MATTERED, 1964–1966

If you asked Ara Parseghian which games in his career mattered, he would have probably cocked his head, given you The Look, and then forcefully proclaimed that *all* the games mattered. That is how seriously he approached his job and the weight that he carried prior to every contest. When you are coaching at Notre Dame, you must assume that every opponent will expend maximum effort to earn lifetime bragging rights if they prevail with a win against the legendary Irish. Ara knew this all too well as he prepared his Northwestern teams to play Notre Dame with this very same motivational psychology. Ara didn't believe in gimmes on the golf course or on the football schedule.

It would be impractical and overwhelming to summarize every single game in Ara's career at Notre Dame, all 116, with an overall record of 95–17–4. Moreover, that task has already been ably addressed by authors Tom Pagna and Bob Best in their 1976 book titled *Notre Dame's Era of Ara*. It would be impossible to improve on this excellent resource, which was confidently relied upon to prepare this work. Both authors were on the scene and knew the coach well, especially Pagna as Ara's trusted assistant coach. The entirety of their book was thoroughly reviewed by both Ara and Katie prior to publication for content and accuracy. Thus the litmus test used throughout this volume is that if the coach agreed to Pagna and Best's version of what happened and Ara's own words, then that remains a fact worthy to repeat.

As a practical matter, through the lens of history, not all the games coached by Ara over eleven seasons at Notre Dame were in fact equal. Some were very important to the coach and to the fortunes of the University of Notre Dame. Others had personal significance, perhaps something learned or decided as a result. After thoughtful review by Katie Parseghian and others knowledgeable about the relevant timeframe, twelve important games were identified. They will be linked by connective historical commentary for continuity in two separate chapters, this one and chapter 19. The overviews will attempt to distill what happened, but more importantly to explain its significance.

GAME ONE, SEPTEMBER 26, 1964
Notre Dame at the University of Wisconsin
(Camp Randall Stadium), Won 31-7

First games of any season are important, but especially so for a new head football coach with a new team. All of the best efforts by Ara, his coaching staff, and a completely realigned team would be tested by an established Big Ten opponent on the road. Wisconsin had eked out a 17–14 win against Ara's Northwestern team at home in 1963, so this game was doubly important to him as a chance for coaching redemption. Game day conditions added to the pressure, with players required to contend with a steady light rain and sloppy field conditions. John Huarte debuted playing at quarterback in this game. It would be a test of his physical health and mental stamina after what was almost a career-ending shoulder injury in the previous spring.

At halftime the score favored the Irish 13–0, a lead established by two field goals and a touchdown pass from Huarte to Jack Snow. But the Badgers scored in their first drive of the second half, suddenly making it Notre Dame 13, Wisconsin 7. After three more scoring drives, highlighted by a final touchdown pass from Huarte to Snow, the Irish left Madison with their first win under Coach Parseghian. Ara's personal record held. He didn't lose his first game as head coach at Miami, Northwestern, or Notre Dame.

The Old Fieldhouse

The second game of the season was scheduled against Purdue at home. It was preceded by Ara's first pep rally in the Old Fieldhouse. These were traditionally raucous events that occurred on Friday nights before home games. If possible, with only a single victory, the brimming enthusiasm for the new head coach had just increased.

The lore of student pep rallies in the Old Fieldhouse (built in 1899) before home games in the 1960s provides a spectrum of insights into Notre Dame culture before the campus became coeducational. Pep rallies are remembered fondly as volcanic events, and those who were in gritty attendance now retain fewer of the details with passing years; their memories are generously selective as they cling to their youth. The current versions of the Friday evening rituals on campus contain very few elements of the forerunners.

During the 1960s, Saturday morning classes were still very common. Even so, the football game wasn't just the centerpiece of the weekend, it was the only thing. The many ancillary events that have since been added into the total weekend package hadn't yet been imagined. However, there was a longstanding tradition dating back to the days of Knute Rockne that took place on the Friday before a game at Notre Dame — the pep rally.

At about 6:00 p.m. on Friday, something quite unusual and distinct from any contemporary college campus morphed into being. This could best be observed from the grassy area just north of the Huddle, south of Cavanaugh Hall, and west of the Fieldhouse. There was a paved area outside of what was known as the Band Annex. The same building was once a campus epicenter as the first Huddle before LaFortune became the Student Center. Today this location is occupied by picnic tables and trees. After an early dinner, bandsmen arrived from the dining halls and filtered into their practice room under Washington Hall. As they began tuning, an alternative band of barbarians known as the "Meat Squad" formed outside. This was a drunken collection of campus ruffians that relished completing a specific, self-assigned task: to protect the marching band as they coursed through the campus on their way to the pep rally. (The band never requested this honor guard.)

By 6:30 p.m., the marching band was ready outside Washington Hall. The Notre Dame Marching Band has always been a big deal. Notre Dame claims to have the first university band in America and to be the first to perform during a football halftime. No other institution has disputed the claim. In 1964, the band numbered about 125 musicians. The band had a unique role in the evolution of Notre Dame Football pregame rituals. The logistical theory from a long-past era was for the band to play and thus summon the students out of their dorms and into a makeshift parade. So, the band marched deeply into the South Quad, past Badin, Howard, Morrissey, Lyons, Pangborn, and Fisher Halls before curling back past Dillon and Alumni Halls toward the North Quad. Some students religiously followed the band out of tradition; nobody got in their way. The Irish Guard, officially part of the band, would march out front to protect the horns and the dental work of anyone, including stumbling members of the Meat Squad, who tried to impede the determined marchers. They moved quite swiftly.

The parade eventually made its way into the Old Fieldhouse. The band announced their presence to the assembled crowd by playing the "Notre Dame Victory March," arguably the greatest of all university fight songs. The first few steps into the building were hazardous because of the slight embankment of the dirt track around the outside walls of the structure near the double-wide, utility side door. But for the band, and for everyone inside the poorly lit, dusty haze, uneven steps were the least of the dangers.

Students concerned with securing prime locations for the festivities filtered into the building well ahead of the band. Daring parents and adult fans did as well, but they tended to retreat to the furthest reaches of the place, settling at the edge of or onto the basketball floor at the eastern end of the building. The maximum capacity of the building strained at about six thousand people, although today that estimate is nostalgically exaggerated by a factor of at least three. The inside of the Fieldhouse quickly became a warming oven, and the aromas weren't pleasant. (Think of putting dirty, wet sneakers into a clothes dryer.)

By the time the band arrived, the adventuresome students, some as self-medicated as the Meat Squad, had become well-practiced in the art of building human pyramids. The goal was to build one high enough so that a single person could climb onto the tie-rods that crossed over the space and held the iron structural arches together. This required three human layers before the last lunatic was deployed. Eventually the human structures collapsed onto the tightly packed crowd below, a danger for all nearby. If you weren't watching out for a tumbling mass of sweaty drunken humanity there was always the prospect of a roll of toilet paper (commonly thrown about as streamers) hitting you in the head from any direction.

Cheerleaders (all male) warmed up the crowd with simple and familiar cheers. Officially, the rally began from the balcony on the west end of the building as a suited student government official introduced the team. The players, all wearing jackets and ties, carefully made their way up the rickety stairs at the front (west side) of the building to sit in the tiny, tiered, second-story balcony. Ara attended these events more often than not in the early years. He reported that the reverberating sound of the crowd combined with the band was deafening.

Players were induced to say a few words, interspersed with the band playing the unique repertoire of Notre Dame songs. When Ara was there, he'd roust the crowd one last time. The playing of the alma mater, "Notre Dame Our Mother," would signal that the event was almost over. The players filed down the stairs to the repetitive strains of the "Notre Dame Victory March" and out to school buses that took them across the lake to Moreau Seminary for an overnight stay away from campus. A few children camped out at the base of the stairs to collect autographs.

It didn't take long before the freshmen were rudely introduced to a new challenge. They discovered there was no toilet paper to be had in their dorms' common bathrooms. It was all draped over the girders or scattered on the dirt floor of the now-locked Old Fieldhouse.

The 34–15 win over Purdue, Ara's first home victory at Notre Dame, was followed in succession by wins over Air Force, UCLA, Stanford University, Navy, the University of Pittsburgh, Michigan State University, and University of Iowa. When Notre Dame "escaped" with a win over Pittsburgh, 17–15, they moved into the No. 1 ranking for the first time in a decade. The football fever on campus became intense and distracting to everyone, now including the faculty, staff, and administration. By midseason the national media caught on to what was happening with the Irish. Without much warning, Ara was featured in a *Time* magazine cover story with a banner that read "The Fighting Irish Fight Again." The drama of a Notre Dame return to glory was now being hyped from coast to coast.

GAME TWO, NOVEMBER 28, 1964
Notre Dame at the University of Southern California
(Los Angeles Coliseum), Lost 17-20

This is one of the three most-discussed games of Ara's tenure at Notre Dame. The Irish entered the Los Angeles Coliseum undefeated, No. 1 and with more national media following them since the hey-days of Frank Leahy's dominant teams. The Irish were the favorites going in, and for a couple of reasons could or should have won the game. Up to this point in the season, the Irish were scoring an average of twenty-six points per game, while allowing an average of only 5.7 points per game.

The hype of anticipation accelerated the week before the game. *LIFE* magazine correspondent Joe Bride, an alum who had worked for Charlie Callahan in the Notre Dame Sports Information Office as a student, offered this written, firsthand account:

> *LIFE* wanted to do something special for the game. We convinced Ara that he should let us have special access. On the team bus, in the locker room, close to everyone on the sideline. After a lot of thought he agreed.
>
> We had buttons made. "We like Ara." They were takeoffs of the 1952 presidential campaign buttons of Dwight Eisenhower, "We Like Ike." We

gave the buttons to priests to wear and to the families of John Huarte and Jack Snow, and took pictures. It was raucous and successful.

Notre Dame owned the first half and the third quarter. Then we scored a touchdown to give us a 24–13 lead, but it was called back by a questionable holding call that no one ever saw when it happened or later on film. Unfortunately, there was a history of questionable calls at the Coliseum that benefitted the home team. This was one. SC drove down the field. In the closing seconds Craig Fertig threw a pass to Rod Sherman. SC won 20–17. National Championship gone.

I've still got a picture of me kneeling just beyond the end zone taken from about the 20-yard line. I look helpless as Sherman catches the pass. I was still in that end zone ten minutes later when Rev. Glen Boarman came up to me and said, "Well Joe I knew that you finally had grown up when that touchdown pass was caught. You didn't run on the field and tackle Sherman." Father Boarman was a highly visible and likeable priest during my time at Notre Dame.

LIFE had a great story. We had Ara telling the team at the half, "only 30 minutes to go." Quotes and comments that no one else had. We had lots of pictures, particularly of the players, Ara, and the Snow and Huarte families both in joy and sadness. It was a good story. We packaged up the pictures and sent big albums to Ara and the Huarte and Snow families.

Ara did keep his sense of humor. "We dominated the game for more than three quarters. I like to think our record in 1964 is 9 and 3/4 and 1/4." He didn't have a lot of humor when he talked to me at the hotel after the game. "Bride, that's the last time any blankety blank reporter and photographer get any special consideration from me. Got it. The last time."

But he didn't hold a grudge. Fifteen months later on a cold and snowy February evening, when I was waiting in Baltimore for Catsy [wife] and our one-year-old son Cres to emerge from a flight from Louisville, Ara was first off the plane with a big grin on his face. He was carrying Cres.[1]

The fourth quarter "phantom" holding call against Bob Meeker on the 1-yard line negated an Irish touchdown. If the score had counted, the Irish lead would have been extended to 24–13, which would have been considered by most observers of the game to be insurmountable. The penalty also changed the field position and cost the Irish ten yards. They failed to score with three more attempts (including two incomplete passes).

It is interesting to speculate what could have been if Notre Dame had attempted a field goal at this point in the game. A miss would have kept the final game score the same. But three more points may have been enough to keep the game tied at the final whistle. Perhaps USC could have attempted a two-point play, which would have been decisive either way it turned out. Would the Irish have been named undisputed national champions with a tie? Maybe.

Partisan officiating had been considered the norm on recent trips to LA, and this day reiterated the point. There was an invisible fourth quarter holding call against the Irish on a punt play that resulted in an improved USC field position of thirty-nine yards after the penalty and the repeat kick. Then, there was a defensive play that would have backed the Trojans up on an obvious quarterback sack. The play was ruled an incomplete pass because a feeble effort was made to push the ball forward to the ground by Trojan quarterback Craig Fertig. Today, this would be called an intentional grounding penalty. The officiating crew was entirely from the new Pacific Athletic Conference (1964), later renamed the Pac-8, Pac-10, and Pac-12. The surviving video is illuminating and seriously calls into question either the officials' competence or their bias. Take your pick.

A lesser-known postgame story about Ara showcases his character. Anticipating a continuation of the return to glory narrative, a local Los Angeles television talk show host and Notre Dame graduate, Regis Philbin, had arranged to interview Ara on the Sunday morning after the game. Much to Philbin's surprise, given the game's disappointing outcome, Ara arrived at the Coliseum promptly at 9:00 a.m. for the interview as planned. Ara's professionalism and respect for the media was on full display. His remarks are thoughtful and magnanimous: "They were knocked down out here yesterday. They were knocked down physically and mentally. But you can't feel sorry for yourself because you have another problem coming up tomorrow. And I think this is one of the things football teaches us." Regis Philbin was fond of telling this story, especially to young broadcasters, throughout his historic career in television. Ara and Regis remained lifetime friends.

Prior to the ND–USC game, local Los Angeles media postured that if by chance the Trojans could beat the Irish they would be voted as the Pacific Conference selection to the Rose Bowl. After the game USC

Head Coach John McKay had his team assembled at a restaurant awaiting word about the Rose Bowl. Early in the evening the selection committee announced that Washington (who had beaten USC in the regular season), not USC, would represent the conference. So, both teams on the field that afternoon ended the day profoundly disappointed.

While the pain and disappointment of losing the national championship to Southern Cal never disappeared, Ara remained concerned about another person caught in the unforgettable drama. The phantom holding call was made against offensive tackle Bob Meeker, a Notre Dame senior and a fellow lad from Akron, Ohio. Nearly sixty years later, he still sometimes has nightmares about it. In a phone conversation with the author, he shared the following:

> I was lined up to slant block on my left side, away from the side where the play was called. The defender did a slide over the guard and I completely missed my block. I'm flat on the ground, embarrassed, and never made any physical contact with anybody. I looked up and see that we scored. Then a few seconds after the whistle, an official away from the play throws a flag and points in my direction.

This is how Bob Meeker remembers his last day as an Irish football player. He and Ara stayed close over the years. In 1988, Parseghian sent a letter to Bob Meeker as he was being honored by Saint Vincent-Saint Mary High School, Meeker's alma mater, in Akron, Ohio. In that letter, Parseghian made reference to the controversial holding call against Meeker in the 1964 Notre Dame–Southern California game, writing, "We both know that the worst officiating call in the history of college football took place in Los Angeles in 1964. And through this letter, I document for you that Bob Meeker was the innocent victim of an incompetent official. I just thought I would put in writing, for posterity, the facts." The letter is framed and hangs in Meeker's law office.

There were coaching moments in that 1964 game that Ara internalized and would mentally refer to later in his career during championship situations. Why the team didn't attempt a field goal on fourth down after the phantom hold is a mystery, and there is no longer a living person to provide a reasoned explanation. If the Irish had been able to retain possession for a couple of minutes longer late in the fourth quarter with the score 17–13, there wouldn't have been enough time for USC to have scored what became the winning touchdown. Only one sustained offensive drive to eat enough time was needed to help the exhausted defense. Ara and his brain trust called all the plays from the sidelines evaluating possession and then position.

The 1964 season remains memorable and significant for many reasons. The new head coach turned things around quickly, and Notre Dame became part of the college football conversation for the first time in many years. For this, Ara was recognized by his peers as Coach of the Year, the only time in his career he was so honored. It was well deserved. John Huarte was awarded the Heisman Trophy, the only one of Ara's players to be so honored. Days later, after being feted by the Downtown Athletic Club, Huarte also received his first varsity monogram (letter) ND at the team's annual banquet.

The season's gridiron statistics were mind-boggling. Twenty-seven team records were broken and another two tied. Notre Dame finished ranked No. 4 behind the University of Alabama, the University of Arkansas, and the University of Texas. The final rankings were set prior to bowl games at the time. The 10–0–0 Crimson Tide lost to Texas in the Orange Bowl, but Alabama is still in the record books as the 1964 National Champions. Arkansas beat Nebraska in the Cotton Bowl. Only the National Football Foundation had the courage to name Notre Dame their national champions with the MacArthur Bowl, taking into account the questionable officiating in California and the fact that the Irish came within one minute, thirty-three seconds of retaining their No. 1 ranking. Today, NCAA official records show three teams as sharing national championship honors in 1964, including Notre Dame. This is relegated to a footnote, since Notre Dame has never attempted to claim a national title in 1964 among its official publicized list. Many would argue it should.

Religious Counsel

After the 1964 loss at Southern Cal, Notre Dame President Father Theodore Hesburgh was prompted to write an essay that was published in the student magazine, *Scholastic*. Commenting on a football game would be unexpected for a college president, but the erudite priest determined it was appropriate in this case and seized the teachable moment. Father Hesburgh's essay is a thoughtful treatise on the similarities between sports and life, and then between sports and everlasting life — something that could only have been written at a place like Notre Dame in 1964. The first paragraph is as follows: "It's dark and cold outside. I'm too old to cry and not old enough not to feel hurt . . . . We can never be sure of total victory, not even of eternal salvation, until we've won it. Life goes on, the challenge remains, and it will be a really dark day and cold place here if we ever lose the desire to be No. 1 in everything we do, or lack grace and style and humanity in doing it."[2]

In 2010, Father Ted was asked if he thought that Notre Dame was ever unfairly treated on the football field or in the press because of religious prejudice. He paused for a few moments before answering carefully, "As a priest, I'd like to believe that didn't happen." After another significant pause, he apparently felt the need to complete his answer, "But I do think that it was easy to be jealous of our success and that may have been a factor."

Fan Base in Wheeling

The top of West Virginia, known as the panhandle, is squeezed between the jaws of a vise by Pennsylvania to the east and Ohio to the west. Both states have massive college football egos. The home state West Virginia University Mountaineers are way far south, or so it seems, because the route to Morgantown is circuitous over hills and through hollows. Both Pittsburgh and Columbus are closer. So, in the northern tip of the state, the town of Wheeling maintains some independence when it comes to college football loyalties. In this once bustling river town, there are a significant number of disciples of Notre Dame Football and for them, public devotion is not forced underground.

Therefore, it wasn't at all surprising that Ara Parseghian would be invited to speak to a Wheeling audience early in 1965 or that he'd be warmly received. In fact, the reception was so memorable that it was vividly recorded in *From Rockne to Parseghian*, the Francis Wallace chronicle that was the preeminent Notre Dame "must read" when it was published just after the 1965 season.

The Wheeling Airport is located north of town. The landing area is a flattened mountain top. The terminal is an architectural gem sponsored by the Works Project Administration (part of Franklin Delano Roosevelt's New Deal), an art deco project constructed for regular airline service that never came. Ara arrived at the Wheeling Airport late in the afternoon on a private plane. He was surprised by the welcome. A police escort whisked him right into town and to the Elks Hall. Ara was the keynote speaker for a multiple sclerosis fundraiser (a local grocer paid his speaking fee). The local Notre Dame Club was part of the planning for the event. There was a cocktail reception before the dinner and pictures to be posed for and autographs to be signed after the event. The whole affair was over before 9 p.m.

A perennial question for the people of Wheeling always has been, what do you do after 9 p.m., with or without a visiting celebrity? A local couple, Pat and Harry Buch, spontaneously offered their home to Notre Dame insiders for a post-event reception and cup of coffee. Ara accepted the invitation to join this supposedly small gathering. Where else would he go on a weeknight in Wheeling? The Buchs lived in a modest two-story, three-bedroom home. The word got out that Ara would be there and eventually many fans were stuffed into the crowded first floor.

Ara was called upon to say a few words to the adoring Notre Dame crowd. Harry distinctly remembers what followed. Standing in front of the smallish fireplace with his shirt sleeves rolled up and necktie loosened, Ara started a stream-of-conscious narrative that drew everyone into his inner thoughts about the 1964 season, the crushing Southern Cal game, the officiating, and where the Irish were headed. This lasted a full thirty minutes and when he was finished there was no need for a Q and A session. Ara departed for Oglebay Lodge for a short night's sleep and departed early the next morning, off to another speaking engagement in Flint, Michigan.

When the evening concluded, Harry Buch says he knew two things for certain. First, he had to buy a bigger house. Second, as soon as he could afford to do so, he had to buy Notre Dame season tickets. Eventually, he did both.

What happened that night in Wheeling may not have been totally unique. To those in attendance the message was clear. In the mind of Coach Ara Parseghian, winning the national championship was no longer an idea, no longer a possibility, no longer a goal. It had become an obsession.

The impact of the surprising near national championship year of 1964 was immeasurable both to the university and to the football program. Without it, the present-day character and fortunes of Notre Dame might be hard to imagine. But they would have been significantly different from what has emerged, and what is now largely taken for granted.

After 1964, the accusatory yoke of de-emphasizing football was finally lifted from the backs of Father Ted and Father Ned, and it was never seriously referenced again. The collective psyches of the Notre Dame community were repaired, from the faculty and students to the janitorial staff. Pride in the football team was once again in fashion. The "brand" was back. The immediate tangible evidence was a spike in sales for licensed Notre Dame merchandise from the Hammes Bookstore, one of the first college bookstores to have its own mail-order catalog.

Perhaps the most important leap in stature came in the improved applicant pool for freshman admissions. Notre Dame had long been perceived as the best-known Catholic university in America. But other quality schools, especially those in attractive urban settings, were rapidly gaining ground as viable alternative choices for smart Catholic guys during the Period of Penance (the time between national championships for the Irish). The 1964 football season reversed the trend and restored Notre Dame to the head of the list of best potential schools.

This factor had a long-lasting and positive effect on the university. The overall high quality of admitted students improved even more. With the Baby Boom bulge and the installation of coeducation in 1972, the applicant pool more than doubled in size while the number of positions stayed practically fixed. The effect was that almost overnight the average SAT scores of applicants to Notre Dame jumped into the category of the elite academic schools. This student quality has been sustained ever since. Coeducation alone didn't improve Notre Dame rapidly. The combination of high demand along with coeducation catapulted Notre Dame up in the national rankings. Any haughty and skeptical professors on campus were proven wrong about the benefit of developing a stellar football program. Notre Dame didn't have to endure a substandard football program, like an Ivy League college, to compete for top students. It wasn't an either-or equation pitting academics against athletics after all. Credit the 1964 Notre Dame football team for a big assist in turning the tide.

Restocking Players

The increased visibility of Notre Dame Football also had a significant role in improving the long-term prospects of the team. In 1964, if you were a star football player at a Catholic high school, Notre Dame was automatically part of the conversation. Very few Catholic colleges even had football as a varsity sport, and many of those that did eventually abandoned it for financial reasons. With rare exceptions, football lost money for a school. Boston College prevailed, just barely, and today is the only other Division 1-A football program among Catholic colleges.

Under Ara recruiting became much more disciplined. Each assistant coach was assigned a geographic region to cover. The goal was to get a prime candidate to campus, especially on a football Saturday. Parseghian described his 1965 recruiting this way, "We view over one thousand high school films each year in order to end up with a working list of about seventy boys, which usually dwindles down to between thirty and thirty-five youngsters who are vitally interested in Notre Dame and who are academically acceptable."

The 1965 Notre Dame football season is often described today as "transitional." The implication is that in historical perspective the Irish were in motion, coming from somewhere and going to somewhere. We know the context. It was the bridge year from a near national championship win in 1964, after a decade of near obscurity, to an undisputed national championship in 1966. The Irish went from heartbreak at the Los Angeles Coliseum to elation two years later at the Los Angeles Coliseum.

Because of the drama in both 1964 and 1966, the quality of the 1965 Notre Dame football team is often overlooked. It ultimately finished ranked No. 8. By any measure, then or now, this was pretty darned good. But in Notre Dame lore, remembrances of the 1965 season lack the clarity or the fondness of either '64 or '66 because of its awkward juxtaposition between "exceptional" and "extraordinary."

Ara's job suddenly became much harder as he walked off the turf in Los Angeles in 1964. For one, the expectations were now higher across the board among the Notre Dame family. A record of 6–4 wouldn't be considered progress ever again in South Bend. There would be no sneaking up on opponents who may have underestimated the Irish in 1964. For another, they were graduating a surprisingly good group of seniors that played over their heads, especially on offense. It is challenging to replace a Heisman Trophy quarterback, John Huarte, and an All-American receiver, Jack Snow, who finished fifth in the same balloting. That, in a nutshell, became the most daunting challenge in 1965.

The emphasis in early 1965 was to restock the talent pool. It was an extraordinarily successful effort, one that may have given the coaching staff moments of confidence as they prepared the team for the 1965 campaign. But this potential bonanza was a year away from maturation and players' eligibility. With the considerable talent still remaining, the strategy for winning had to be more specifically targeted. The defense, largely intact, would have to be even stingier with yardage and scoring and constantly wrestle for every inch of field position. The offense would have to be run oriented with an untried quarterback. But the credentials of running backs Bill Wolski, Nick Eddy, and Larry Conjar were well-established, along with a promising sophomore, Robert "Rocky" Bleier. Defensive and offensive line play would be the critical battleground for success.

Enthusiasm Runneth Over

In September 1965, the season started with sky-high expectations. Even if the coaches had concerns, the students and the pollsters were blindly enthusiastic. The Irish were good enough to almost win the national championship in 1964, and with better officiating or a faster time clock in Los Angeles, they likely would have. So, Notre Dame was installed as a preseason favorite. Undoubtedly, this decision to feature the Irish on magazine covers across the nation was also good for circulation. Like 'em or hate 'em, Notre Dame Football always makes good copy.

Students' enthusiasm going into the new season overflowed. An unfortunate and ill-advised tradition was renewed prior to the first game, an away contest at the University of California at Berkeley. A bedsheet banner reading "Beat CAL" was attached with a rope and hung from the venerated Golden Dome, at the feet of Our Lady. This didn't happen very often and in the minds of most, it shouldn't ever happen. The feat required serious lock-picking and then climbing a tightly enclosed set of rickety stairs that is sandwiched between the exterior dome structure and the plaster ceiling visible underneath from the rotunda of the Administration Building. This act would be the first indication that spirit at Notre Dame had perhaps gone too far and degenerated into thoughtlessness. Setting the insensitivity to religious symbolism aside, the possible damage to the expensive 18-karat gold leaf on the Dome was unconscionable, along with the danger involved. But it hung there briefly and although it didn't stay in place very long, photographs have survived as evidence.

Tame by comparison, but just as interesting, is a photo appearing in the *South Bend Tribune*. It was taken at the South Bend airport as the players were climbing the portable stairs to board the plane for the season opener at UC Berkeley. For historical perspective, the American Airlines charter was a four-prop and not a jet. A 20-foot banner is being held by Coach Parseghian and local civic officials and reads: "GOOD LUCK IRISH, South Bend-Mishawaka Chamber of Commerce." South Bend realized where its bread was buttered after the sudden Studebaker automobile plant closing in 1963.

Notre Dame easily beat Cal by a 48–6 score. After the game the Berkeley Coach Ray Willsey was terse. "They had the ball for eighty-eight offensive plays and after a while that begins to tell on your defense." Ara's teams would consistently aim for over eighty offensive plays per game for the remainder of his career. This gave his defense a chance to rest, regroup, and dominate. In what would emerge as a 7–2–1 record in 1965, Notre Dame only allowed an average of 7.3 points per game, third lowest in Ara's career (to 3.8 in 1966 and 6.6 in 1973, both national championship years).

As another historical note, the National Broadcasting Network (NBC) broadcast the Cal game regionally. Lindsey Nelson and former Irish Head Coach Terry Brennan formed the announcing team. This would be the last year that NBC would broadcast regular season college games until 1990, when it signed an exclusive contract with Notre Dame to broadcast all Irish home games. (This contract has continued uninterrupted.)

Retaining its preseason No. 1 ranking for a week, the Irish traveled to West Lafayette, Indiana, for its then-traditional game with Purdue. Harsh reality filled the bus ride back to South Bend after a 21–25 loss. The national press made it sound worse than it was, such as the *Sports Illustrated* article by Dan Jenkins, "Boilermakers Shatter an Ambitious Dream."

Back in 1965, without sports-talk radio or cable TV, magazines were the media where facts and commentary were woven together by design, into clever, often sarcastic fare that would spawn controversy and become the talk around water coolers and coffee machines at work. As a writer, Jenkins could jab at someone or something with the best of them, especially where there was no incentive to economize on words. In long-form pieces, days were spent writing in advance and much of an article was virtually complete before a sporting event. Truth could be irrelevant to making the final edit, especially if it was uninteresting. To illuminate the point, contrast Jenkin's headline with one from a respected newspaper man, a writer with time pressure to tell a story that would comport with the facts witnessed by thousands of fans.

Joe Doyle of the *South Bend Tribune* offered this description on September 26, 1965: "Fantastic Bob Griese, throwing the ball as if he invented the forward pass, picked Notre Dame's defenses to pieces and Purdue knocked the never-quit Irish out of the nation's top ranking Saturday afternoon. A record-breaking Purdue crowd watched the magnificent battle of Griese's passes against the power-running of the Irish and agreed it had to be an all-time classic."

The Notre Dame–Purdue game in 1965 was one heck of a game. In the end, the incredible play by junior quarterback Bob Griese was the difference. He made nineteen of twenty-two passes and threw for 283 yards and three touchdowns. He ran nine times for forty-five yards. He punted three times. He set four Purdue records. Most importantly, he led the Boilermakers back from a late deficit with less than four minutes on the clock.

The Irish felt bitter disappointment and plummeted from No. 1 to No. 9 in the polls. The loss foreshadowed a season of constant struggle as opponents discovered that the Notre Dame offense was essentially one-dimensional — run only.

Ara responded to defeat with respectful graciousness in comments to the press after the game. "I don't have to see the statistic sheets to tell you what happened. That was the most fantastic passing performance I've ever seen. Why, that's hard to do even in practice let alone in a game. Can you imagine a passer hitting nineteen out of twenty-two?"

His disappointment was only mildly tempered by what he observed on his own practice fields. As he reflected on the 1965 season later in his life, he shared, "We [coaches] were frustrated. We were watching the freshman at practice and these kids were flinging the ball all over the field." The 1–1 and no longer No. 1–ranked Irish returned home to play their first home game of the season against Northwestern. This was the first meeting between Ara and his former team, now coached by his closest friend, Alex Agase. The game was surprisingly close, closer than the final score indicates.

In his article on October 3, 1965, Joe Doyle of the *South Bend Tribune* trumpeted: "Defense! That was the name of the game all week on Notre Dame's Cartier Field practice grounds. And it was the big difference Saturday when the Irish broke open a tense low scoring duel to beat Northwestern, 38–7." Northwestern's Agase summed it up well, as reported by Doyle in the same article, "When you make a mistake against Notre Dame it shows up on the scoreboard." Buried in the box score, the Notre Dame defense held the Wildcats to minus two yards rushing. Brutal effort.

Notre Dame stayed on track with successive wins against Army (17–0), Southern California (28–7), Navy (29–3), Pittsburgh (69–13), and the University of North Carolina (17–0). A home loss against Michigan State (3–12) put the final chill on any hopes of a restored No. 1 ranking. The exhausted Irish played Miami away, at night, finishing in a 0–0 tie.

If revenge is sweet, beating USC in South Bend was a sugar high for the students, although eleven months too late. Southern Cal had a fine running back, Mike Garrett, the eventual Heisman Award winner. He was averaging 170 yards rushing per game. The determined Irish defensive unit held him to forty-three yards. One particular offensive player, Larry Conjar, will always remember that day as well. He scored all four touchdowns with heaps of help from the offensive line. His personal total of 116 yards would be forty-two more than the entire USC offense made all afternoon. All the starting Notre Dame backs had more yardage than Garrett — Eddy (65), Wolski (64), and as Ara could still correctly recall forty-five years later, quarterback Bill Zloch (50).

As of 1965, USC had won only three games in the Midwest (two were played at Soldier Field in Chicago) in a series going back to 1926, and had not won at Notre Dame Stadium since 1939. After the game about half the Irish student body poured out onto the damp playing field to celebrate the emotionally important victory on national television.

When the polls were announced prior to the Michigan State game, the 7–1 Irish were ranked fourth behind Michigan State, Arkansas, and Nebraska, all three at 9–0. Purdue had dropped to No. 10 with a 6–2–1 record. It was a long shot, but the Irish could still be in contention for the National Championship Trophy. Beating Michigan State was required.

Warning Shot

The 1964 Michigan State game, also in South Bend, was marred by an inexcusable incident where a few students threw objects at the passing Spartan Band when they marched from the stadium to their busses. This bald disrespect was too much for Father Hesburgh to tolerate. In an open letter to the student body, he wrote: "Spirit is more than noise. It should not be confused with rowdiness, buffoonery, or inhospitality to opponents. Those responsible here — students, faculty and administration — are increasingly unwilling to continue on this course, even if it means eliminating what can be a very good and wholesome activity. It (football) is, after all only a game, and this place is first and foremost a university."[3]

The implied threat to abandon football was a hollow one. The university needed the influx of revenue and in fact depended on it. The veiled threat to severely punish anyone who would put that in jeopardy, however, was quite real.

GAME THREE, NOVEMBER 20, 1965
Michigan State University at Notre Dame
(Notre Dame Stadium), Lost 3-12

Historically, this remains the second most important game ever played between Michigan State University and Notre Dame. No. 1–ranked MSU was already Big Ten Champion and bound for the Rose Bowl.

Going into the contest, it seemed almost incredible that Notre Dame was tied for first place in the nation in scoring. This record was impressive for a team with only one offensive dimension yet had found ways to win, often after halftime. The Spartan defense held the Irish to minus rushing yards. Lack of gain was the story of the game. The Irish passing game was held to twenty-four yards on two completions.

But the Notre Dame defense kept the game close and provided three critical turnovers in MSU territory that created opportunities to score: a recovered fumble on the 19, an intercepted pass on the 25, and another fumble recovery on the 18. In the end, all that could be mustered was a 32-yard field goal by Ken Ivan. That was good enough to keep the Irish ahead through the first half, 3–0. But on that day, it would take more than three points to win, and the Irish were thwarted at every attempt to score. While the Spartans had a meager ninety-one yards on the ground and twenty-one yards passing in the second half, it was enough for twelve points on two touchdowns. Thankfully, nothing was thrown by students in the direction of the Spartan Band.

This game was Ara's first loss in Notre Dame Stadium, one of only six in eleven seasons. The Spartans finished their season ranked No. 1 and tied with Alabama. The table was set for the 1966 game of the century scheduled at Spartan Stadium.

When players are asked about the final game of the 1965 season, with Miami, they simply groan. Notre Dame had run out of gas. The environment at the Orange Bowl in Miami was memorable because it was so wretched. The battle in the trenches reached the sidelines. All the players on the bench were instructed to wear their helmets throughout the game to fend off debris tossed from the stands. It was hot and humid. The roster was so depleted that George Goeddeke was called into action only two weeks after having his appendix removed. He was still bandaged and stitched up.

Give the Irish defense credit. Under terrible conditions they held the Hurricanes to zero points. But Miami had seen the films, knew how to defend against Notre Dame, and had the players to execute the plan. No points were scored against them either. Ara later lamented in conversation: "When your passing attack isn't really strong, people catch up with you. But they stormed. They stacked up on us. Half the time we were running against virtually a nine-man line."

This studio photo, circa 1927, displays Ara (*left*) standing next to his brother, Jerry (*right*). (Photograph courtesy of Katie Parseghian.)

This studio photo, circa 1929, shows the entire Parseghian family: Ara's father, Michael; mother, Amelia; the eldest son, Gerard (Jerry); the middle child, Ara; and the youngest child, Isabelle (Zabell). (Photograph courtesy of Katie Parseghian.)

Ara's mother, Amelia, took her three children (Gerard, Ara, and Isabelle) to France to visit her relatives in 1926. While most written accounts highlight Ara's Armenian descent, he was in fact half French thanks to his mother. French was Ara's first language until he attended school. (Photograph courtesy of Katie Parseghian.)

Church record of Ara Parseghian's baptism, June 9, 1934, St. Peter's Catholic Church, Akron, Ohio. (Image courtesy of the Archives of the Diocese of Cleveland.)

REGISTRATION CARD—(Men born on or after January 1, 1922 and on or before June 30, 1924)

Draft card of Ara Raoul Parseghian, 1943, Registration Form 1, D.S.S. This is the oldest known autograph of Ara's. (Image courtesy of the Archives of the Diocese of Cleveland.)

(*opposite*)
Photo of Ara Parseghian in his United States Navy uniform, circa 1944. This was probably taken on a photo set since there is no record of Ara serving on a ship. (Photograph courtesy of Katie Parseghian.)

Photo of the 1941 Akron South High School Football Team. Ara Parseghian is in the back row, standing next to his teammate Conwell Findley, the only Black player on the team. (Photograph courtesy of Notre Dame Athletics.)

(*opposite*)
Stock photo of Ara Parseghian as a football player at Miami University in 1947.
(Photograph courtesy of the Miami University Archives.)

Katie and Ara were married at the First Presbyterian Church in Greenfield, Ohio, on December 30, 1948. Their reception was held in the church basement, a common custom in the Midwest at that time. (Photograph courtesy of Katie Parseghian.)

This portrait of the Parseghian family was taken during the Northwestern years. Katie and Ara stand behind Michael, Karan, and Kristan (*left to right*). (Photograph courtesy of Katie Parseghian.)

Robert Patrick "Rocky" Bleier returned to Notre Dame for the October 18, 1969, game with the University of Southern California. Bleier had been severely injured in Vietnam and was invited by Father Ted Hesburgh to be introduced at halftime. The sold-out crowd now had a name and a face to attach to the increasingly unpopular war, the former Irish team captain from 1967. (Photograph courtesy of the University of Notre Dame Archives.)

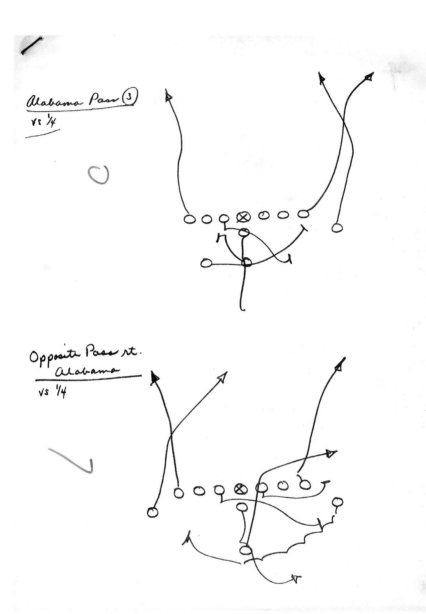

This play was hand-drawn by Ara Parseghian for insertion into the official 1974 play-book, and designated as "Alabama 73." It captures the most memorable play in Coach Parseghian's career: the pass from quarterback Tom Clements to tight end Robin Weber in the 1973 Sugar Bowl, sealing a win that resulted in the National Championship title. The original play was not in the 1973 playbook because it was an effective improvisation by the quarterback. (Source: Ara Parseghian's personal files, courtesy of Katie Parseghian.)

Ara surrounded by his four grandchildren (*clockwise from top right*): Ara, Marcia, Krista, and Michael (the children of Cindy and Mike Parseghian), circa 1995. (Photograph courtesy of Katie Parseghian.)

When Ara sat at his home office desk after retirement, surrounded by awards and memorabilia, this photo of his family was the centerpiece, directly across the room in his view. It was taken for his seventy-fifth birthday and shows all living children and grandchildren at that time. Katie Parseghian lovingly pasted in the image of Ara and Katie's grandson Michael, who succumbed to Niemann-Pick disease type C before the photo occurred. (Photograph courtesy of Mark Hubbard.)

Ara Parseghian was honored by the University of Notre Dame with a life-sized bronze statue outside the stadium's aptly named "Ara Parseghian Gate." The statue was dedicated on September 22, 2007. The inspiration for sculptor Jerry McKenna was a photo of Ara being carried off the field after the 24–11 win against Texas in the 1970 Cotton Bowl. (Photograph credited to Matt Cashore, university photographer. Used with permission.)

Miami University has a "Cradle of Coaches" arcade on campus outside of Yager Stadium. The bronze statue of Ara Parseghian by artist Kristen Visbal was dedicated on October 3, 2009, with Katie and Ara in attendance. Even though Ara coached at Miami, the statue depicts him as the head coach at Notre Dame. (Photograph courtesy of the Miami University Archives.)

To raise funds for the Ara Parseghian Medical Research Foundation, Notre Dame Dean of Science Greg Crawford and his wife, Renata, once biked across the country, starting in California. This is a photo of Ara welcoming Greg and Renata home to South Bend. Greg was later named president of Miami University and maintained a close friendship with Coach Parseghian. (Photograph credited to Matt Cashore, university photographer. Used with permission.)

The season finished with a tidbit of historically interesting trivia. Ara Parseghian's Notre Dame teams were only shut out (meaning they did not score any points) one time. But it wasn't in a losing cause. The final game score resulted in a tie, Notre Dame 0, Miami 0.

The grueling 1965 season finally ended with a dull thud, no touchdowns and no wins in the final two games. But the team would hold on to a national Top Ten ranking.

With the long perspective of almost sixty years, it isn't a wild exaggeration to speculate that Notre Dame could have won national championships in Ara's first two seasons. They were only one play away in 1964, and only one player away (a passing quarterback) in 1965. The best was yet to come.

Shifts in Summer 1966

By the end of spring practice, Ara and his coaches were finally able to exhale. They were feeling pretty good about the personnel they had assembled and the prospects for the coming 1966 campaign. The "bunker" became the epicenter for the strategic planning that would be required to outwit opponents and advance the football program beyond a 7–2–1 record and a No. 8 ranking in 1965. If everyone returned from summer break in good health and in good shape, the coaching staff knew they would be ready.

But plans changed. On a summer's evening in Kirkland, Washington, sophomore receiver Curt Heneghan was playing what he described as "grab-ass football" with some of his buddies. Running full speed up the field with spikes, he planted his right foot, but it didn't release cleanly. Right away he knew it was a serious knee injury and sought local medical attention. The next day he was on a plane to South Bend for examination by the Notre Dame orthopedic doctors. They advised against surgery and opted for him to complete rehabilitation instead. That effectively rendered him unavailable for the 1966 season.

With two great sophomore receivers on the roster, Curt Heneghan and Jim Seymour, the coaches hadn't contemplated preferring one over the other. Their plan was a shift in the backfield, from three backs to two, while adding a flanker. That approach had to be abandoned with the injury to Heneghan. The most surprised player who returned in August was Rocky Bleier. He figured he would be the odd man out in the new configuration. Sitting out either Eddy or Conjar was unthinkable. So, he was reinstated into the familiar three-back set and went on to contribute in ways he never would have imagined as he worked out privately over the summer in Appleton, Wisconsin.

Historical Benchmarks

There are specific dates in Notre Dame Football history that are benchmarks. The dates may be significant because of the opponent or the score of a game, but that's not always necessary. Fans and sportswriters tend to view events with this short-term perspective. Historians take a different view. The benchmark dates are defined by one simple rule; after that particular date, there was a fundamental change in the course of history from which there was no reversal.

For example, there would be universal agreement that college football changed forever after the Army–Notre Dame game on November 1, 1913. This game effectively legitimized the forward pass as an offensive weapon. There was no turning back the clock after the Gus Dorais to Knute Rockne combination was heralded in the New York papers having beat the Cadets 35–13.

Much the same can be said about the 1924 season, the first national championship awarded when Rockne's Four Horsemen won in the Rose Bowl on January 1, 1925, against Stanford and the legendary Ernie Nevers, 27–10. The national attention, based largely on having star players crafted into media personalities during the 1920s, advanced the spectator appeal of college football and then encouraged a wave of college stadium projects that were intended to capture enormous paydays. This attention and growth have continued unabated. The phenomenon turned the likes of Babe Ruth, Red Grange, Bobby Jones, and Jack Dempsey into household names. (This happened almost exclusively in newsprint since radio wasn't used commercially until 1927.)

The 1936 Notre Dame game at Ohio State University merits consideration because it went right down to the final play in Columbus: a pass from Bill Shakespeare to Wayne Millner for the Irish win, 18–13.

Katie Parseghian remembers attending this game with her father. This was a radio event, probably the first landmark one for Notre Dame Football. Likewise, fans would consider the 1946 tie with Army (0–0) to be another landmark because of the long-standing rivalry. It was No. 1 Army versus No. 2 Notre Dame, and the array of four Heisman Award winners in uniform that day: Doc Blanchard, Glenn Davis, Johnny Lujack, and Leon Hart.

December 3, 1949 may be the absolute pinnacle of Notre Dame Football. That day the Irish beat Southern Methodist University and finished four consecutive seasons undefeated under Frank Leahy. It's hard to imagine that feat ever being repeated. Knocking off Oklahoma on November 16, 1957 with a 7–0 win in Norman (thus ending the longest winning streak in NCAA history at forty-seven) was significant enough to keep the pilot light lit for Notre Dame Football tradition during the Period of Penance. Oddly, the win against the best in the nation may have accelerated the demise of Notre Dame Head Coach Terry Brennan. Why couldn't his teams perform like that every week? The arrival of Ara Parseghian on campus in January, 1964 stoked hot, blue flames in the Notre Dame burners.

GAME FOUR, SEPTEMBER 24, 1966
Purdue University at Notre Dame
(Notre Dame Stadium), Won 26-14

In 1966, there are two authentic benchmark dates. One is easy to guess and will be addressed in detail. The other was the first game of the season, September 24, at home versus Purdue. This game marked the beginning of the first season of exclusive NCAA-controlled football coverage on a television network (ABC), the brainchild of broadcast innovator Roone Arledge. College football was about to become a Saturday staple on television, and since then there has been no looking back. The network was giddy over the prospect of having a national audience that showcased college football's most storied program.

The season opener against Purdue also marked the first game of the first season when all Notre Dame home games were sold out. In fact, they were sold out in the preseason. This high-water mark was a huge fiscal accomplishment after thirty-six years; for the initial home game at Notre Dame Stadium in 1930, only about fifteen thousand seats were actually sold. During the Depression, South Bend businesses were flogged with regularity to purchase season tickets to help the team and the local economy. Otherwise, visiting teams wouldn't come to South Bend and the entire aura of Notre Dame Football would have become pedestrian. Even so, until 1966, there were very few sold-out games on campus. Since 1966, tickets to home games have been difficult to obtain, and this revenue stream has been as predictable as September rain in South Bend.

While September 24, 1966, may not jump off the page as a benchmark event in Notre Dame Football history, Father Joyce would have certainly agreed with the designation. With $112,000 of television revenue paid to the university and a sold-out crowd at $6.00 per ticket (before parking, concessions, programs, and bookstore sales), this was the single largest revenue day in Notre Dame history. Therefore, September 24, 1966, set the benchmark criteria; there was a fundamental change from which there has been no reversal. Mark the day in history as the day that Notre Dame Football became the undisputed most valuable economic franchise in collegiate sports. It has held one of the top positions ever since.

Lastly, there was the importance of the game itself as a barometer, the predictor of the football climate to come. Was success in 1964 temporary, or was the "Era of Ara" legitimate? The 1965 Purdue game had been a defeat very few had seen coming, and it was a rude interruption to the hoped-for story of redemption. In 1964, the team really believed it was beaten by the officials in Los Angeles instead of the other team. In 1965, the Irish knew their first defeat was at the hands of a superior opponent in West Lafayette, no matter how close the score was. With no touchdowns and no wins in the final two games of 1965, the faithful may have wondered where things were headed.

Breakfast

After a quiet Friday evening at Moreau Seminary watching John Wayne movies, the Irish football team moved back onto campus and their highly structured game-day schedule. There was Mass at Sacred Heart

Church, celebrated by Team Chaplain Father James Riehle, C.S.C. After that the team ate the private pregame meal at the North Dining Hall, well after breakfast had been served to the regular students and well before the normal lunch meal. After breakfast was a team meeting before going to the stadium to dress and warm-up.

It had been announced that three sophomores would start the game: Terry Hanratty at quarterback, Jim Seymour at receiver, and George Kunz at offensive tackle. In the dining hall, the upper classmen were keeping an eye on these three, hoping that pregame jitters wouldn't become a factor.

Fireworks

If you were one of the fortunate 59,075 ticket holders to the sold-out Notre Dame Stadium and arrived late for the Purdue game on September 24, you didn't miss much. It was halfway through the first quarter before the fireworks began. Then you saw quite a show, especially if you were an Irish fan. You got your money's worth.

The pregame stories tended to focus on the quarterbacks. Purdue had a great one, All-American Bob Griese playing in his senior year. He was "the man" for Purdue Coach Jack Mollenkopf, his face adorning the "1966 Purdue Media Guide." Notre Dame was well aware of his abilities. It was Griese who guided the Boilermakers to a late score in 1965, to beat them 25–21. That day he set a Notre Dame record for opposing quarterbacks, going nineteen of twenty-two, which stood until 1981.

For a different reason, stories about Notre Dame also focused on the quarterback position. Here the slant tended to be one of curious uncertainty. It was obvious from the 1965 season that the Irish needed a player to replace the graduating Bill Zloch, the stalwart and steady performer who was drafted into playing the position out of sheer necessity.

The preseason table from which the ravenous press had been noshing was the decision Ara would make on opening day between two attractive sophomores, Terry Hanratty and Coley O'Brien. The eighteen-year-old Hanratty was 6 feet 1 inch and 190 pounds, from Butler, Pennsylvania. The slightly smaller O'Brien, 5 feet 11 inches and 173 pounds, hailed from the Washington, DC area, specifically Arlington, Virginia. Both were right out of central casting for a Notre Dame quarterback: polite, articulate, handsome, and had Irish surnames. For Ara it was an overdue bounty of talent. Either one could have started at any college in America needing a quarterback. Had either one been eligible in 1965, the season may have ended with a national championship. It was a close call, but late in the week Parseghian finally decided that Terry Hanratty would start. Both quarterbacks would be called upon for heroics before the season ended.

The preseason polls had Notre Dame at No. 6 and Purdue at No. 7. The Irish were five-point favorites going into the game. With a matchup like this, ABC Sports was eager to have this contest open its very first season of NCAA football under the new contract. The decision would become troublesome later on when the network coveted coast-to-coast coverage for the historic ND–MSU game. NCAA rules prohibited two national games for a single school in the same year. Chris Schenkel, a Purdue grad who still lived in Indiana, and former Oklahoma coaching legend Bud Wilkinson were the announcing team for that game and for the key game each week throughout the season.

The opening kickoff went to Purdue. The Boilermakers had three plays and a punt. One of those was a savage quarterback sack by Alan Page, one that stands out in a season of few signature tackles. Griese was wobbly after that. When Griese finally completed his first pass it was for a 3-yard loss. That prompted another Purdue punt.

On this possession Notre Dame opened with a 42-yard pass over the middle, with Terry Hanratty finding Jim Seymour, who was just barely caught from behind on the Purdue 15-yard line. Nobody knew it at the time, but history was unfolding. Two plays later Rocky Bleier fumbled an errant halfback pitch on the 6-yard line. Running parallel to Hanratty at quarterback, the ball bounced off Bleier's shoulder pads as he turned to catch it. It hit the ground and bounced straight into the arms of Purdue defensive back Leroy Keyes. He sprinted ninety-four yards, untouched, into the end zone. Early advantage, Purdue.

On the ensuing kickoff, Notre Dame's All-American halfback, Nick Eddy, returned the favor and the football ninety-six yards for an Irish touchdown. Two touchdowns in under twenty seconds led to a tie ball game.

There's a story behind that play. Tom Pagna had the team practicing a new "center wedge" alignment for kickoffs that week in practice. It worked pretty well against the prep team and so it was decided to try it under game conditions. The key players in the center of the formation were Bob Gladieux, Don Gmitter, Jim Seymour, Larry Conjar, and Rocky Bleier. After fifty-five years, the players on the field who are still living can still remember making their blocks and watching the back of Eddy's uniform (number 47) coast into the end zone. One Purdue player sustained a broken leg on the play. On the sideline, student trainer Tom Feske remembered it this way, as he shared with me in conversation:

> Larry Conjar was the great fullback on that team and was a key blocker on the kickoff team. After Eddy returned the kick for a touchdown and they returned to the bench I still remember Larry saying to Nick with this huge smile: "Hey, I was looking to knock somebody on their butt, but the hole was so big there was nobody left. I had to lay back just so I could hit somebody (trailing the play) at about the 25."

The Eddy runback was electric. Looking in the rearview mirror of nearly sixty years, it may have been the most important play of the entire season. The 1966 Irish team would be built on a stingy defense combined with an opportunistic offense. But ten minutes into their first game, neither the offense nor the defense knew their personality or their potential. Being able to take a football mulligan was important for the team's psyche.

Thereafter, the momentum of the game favored Notre Dame. The game ended Notre Dame 26, Purdue 14. Take away the mulligans by both teams and it would have been Notre Dame 19, Purdue 7. The fourteen points scored by Purdue would be the most scored against the Irish all season, and seven of only seventeen scored against the first-team defense.

Respect

Today the game is remembered as a mild blowout, although it was far from being one. Purdue moved the ball for a total 293 yards. Bob Griese made fourteen of twenty-six passes for 178 of those. This was a pretty fair afternoon against what was to become the toughest defense in the nation. Griese eventually came in second in the Heisman balloting (Nick Eddy came in third and Hanratty eighth). Florida's Steve Spurrier finished first. The way the Heisman voting works (points given for first, second, and third by each voter), one has to wonder if Griese would have won the 1966 Heisman had not so much talent been located in the Midwest, specifically in Indiana. Purdue ultimately finished second in the Big Ten, losing only to Michigan State (41–20). The Boilermakers took their first trip ever to the Rose Bowl and played against Southern California, winning 14–13, and finishing a respectable No. 6 in the polls.

In his first game, sophomore Jim Seymour broke two Notre Dame single-game records, for number of receptions with thirteen and number of yards receiving with 276. He tied a third school record with three touchdown receptions in a single game, and he almost had number four on his first catch. Seymour was completely unaware of the dimensions of his afternoon's work. In his polite manner he was later quoted as saying in the press conference: "Honest sir, I don't know how many I caught. How many was it?"

Hanratty had an excellent day in his debut at quarterback. He was sixteen of twenty-four, for 304 yards, only twenty-nine yards short of setting a Notre Dame single-game passing record. His three touchdowns to Seymour went for eighty-four, thirty-nine, and seven yards, respectively. A strong running game made everything work. Eddy had fifty-two yards rushing, Conjar forty-eight, and Bleier thirty. Years later, everyone involved is quick to give most of the credit to the offensive line: George Goeddeke (center), Dick Swatland and Tom Regner (guards), Paul Seiler and George Kunz (tackles), and Don Gmitter (tight end). In truth, everyone had a day they would remember.

The postgame comments by a disappointed Coach Mollenkopf were both gracious and prophetic. "We weren't prepared for Seymour," was his first statement to the press. "We had no idea how great he is. Man-to-man he is impossible to cover." He later stated: "This might be the best Notre Dame team in twenty or twenty-five years."

Mollenkopf and the Boilers, led by quarterback Mike Phipps and Leroy Keyes (converted to halfback), would beat Notre Dame the following year with a score of 28–21. Jim Seymour played against double coverage for the entire game.

Ara's take on the game was succinct: "I was afraid to say how good I thought these kids were." He was named UPI Coach of the Week.

The Purdue Marching Band (then the nation's largest band with three hundred members) played on the field at halftime doing a tribute show to the 150th Anniversary of Indiana statehood. The band moved seamlessly from formation to formation — from a birthday cake to an Indy race car to two spacecraft linking. At that point the announcer intoned the following over the stadium public address system: "Indiana is the land of the astronaut, with many spacemen being Purdue University graduates. The first Gemini Rocket docking attempt was piloted by Astronaut Neil Armstrong, Purdue bandsman. The space link-up — another first for the United States."

On September 21, 1966, the only link-ups that Purdue would remember would be between the Notre Dame Geminis on the field, sophomores Terry Hanratty and Jim Seymour. Neil Armstrong would go on to be remembered for something much more significant.

After the Purdue game the Irish dominated opponents for the next seven games: Northwestern (35–7), Army (35–0), the University of North Carolina (32–0), the University of Oklahoma (38–0), Navy (31–7), the University of Pittsburgh (40–0), and Duke University (64–0). No one scored on the first-team defensive unit.

Thank You, Woody Hayes

It is convenient — often too convenient — for sportswriters to lob "luck of the Irish" moments into game accounts. With reluctance, one such event must be inserted into this particular narrative because it is the turning point for the entire Notre Dame season in 1966.

The Irish were having their way with North Carolina during an adverse weather day, largely because Notre Dame's team and playbook were designed to deal with weather contingencies in the Midwest.

But in Columbus, Ohio, quite another scenario was being played out in essentially the same weather conditions, with perhaps an added dose of rain. Both the visiting MSU Spartans and the hometown Buckeyes were prepared to play in the mud on offense and on defense. The result was a very close game that Michigan State eventually won by a slim margin (11–8) and thanks to a trick play by the Spartans in the fourth quarter.

Fortunately, the pollsters, sitting in dry offices without the benefit of instantaneous game highlights on TV, simply compared the Notre Dame score with the Michigan State score and then flipped the rankings of the two teams. Notre Dame became the new No. 1, and Michigan State the new No. 2. This advantage sustained the Irish through a difficult November, both on the field and off. It was on this day that becoming the undisputed national champions became a possibility and the Irish became masters of their own destiny.

In 2010, when I asked Ara if he ever thanked Coach Woody Hayes and the Buckeyes for their assistance in the rankings, he rolled his eyes with an expression that signaled "You've got to be kidding." But he understood that behind the question was a legitimate historical inquiry. So, he crafted a thoughtful response. "You know, when you are in the middle of a season all you can think about is winning your games. If you lose once at a place like Notre Dame your season is finished, because all we ever had to play for was the national championship. Even when we were named No. 1 the coaches never paid much attention. We always knew we had to win the next game."

Kiddie Corps

One of the most enduring visual images from Notre Dame's 1966 football season is the cover of *Time* magazine on October 28 depicting head shots of sophomores Terry Hanratty and Jim Seymour in a composition, as if in a huddle, that includes fragments of other uniforms (the back of number 75 is Bob Kuechenberg). It is noteworthy for a number of reasons.

It is among the first *Time* covers to feature college students, and all of those are football notable names like Red Grange, Dick Kazmaier, Johnny Lattner, and Roger Staubach. It is believed to be the first cover depicting teenagers. Only covers depicting Shirley Temple and Princess Elizabeth (later Queen Elizabeth II) as a child have verifiable younger subjects (unlike military action photos). Since Hanratty is younger than Seymour, this could make him the youngest male to be on a *Time* cover up to that point in time. This was pretty heady stuff. Later in the 1960s, as protests against the Vietnam War combusted, images of college students became more prevalent but for very different reasons.

Sports Information Director Roger Valdiserri provided an interesting backstory to this cover. *Time* officials called his office looking for photographs of the two sophomores to use. Valdiserri thought putting two underclassmen on the cover of a national news magazine was a terrible idea, and for good reasons. First, the two had played in only a few games. The team had a group of seasoned veterans; some had played in 1964 when a national championship was almost realized. A case could easily be made that they were all more deserving of national recognition. But Roger was most worried about internal team chemistry. He took his concerns up the chain of command, from Ara to Moose Krause, and then to Father Edmund Joyce. All agreed that two boys with a few games under their belts should not be on the cover of *Time*. Therefore, the request for photographs was denied.

Then magazine officials informed the university that they were going to proceed nonetheless, using original art if necessary. Notre Dame held its ground and so did *Time*, and the cover was published. The team was informed of the sequence of events and the cover became a symbol of unity, not a divisive force. Captain Jim Lynch reflected, "Hanratty and Seymour were key to our success, along with a great sophomore class." Terry and Jim took their share of ribbing, mostly good natured, thanks to advanced warnings by Valdiserri.

Imagine, when the magazine ran with the cover story, Hanratty and Seymour had only played in four games at Notre Dame. This speaks loudly to the power of Notre Dame Football as being part of the American consciousness in 1966.

The cover also prompts an interesting trivia question. How many people associated with Notre Dame have ever been on the cover of *Time*? The answer is eight, on seven covers. The names, in order are: Knute Rockne (1927), Frank Leahy (1946), Johnny Lattner (1953), Rev. Theodore M. Hesburgh (1962), Ara Parseghian (1964), Terry Hanratty and Jim Seymour (1966), and Joe Montana (1982). Reading the list above, the contention that football is a core strand of Notre Dame identity is blatantly obvious.

It is interesting to note that Notre Dame graduate Condoleezza Rice (Master of Arts, 1975) never featured on the cover of *Time* as the United States Secretary of State, an unfortunate oversight. Recently, *Time* elected not to dedicate a cover to Justice Amy Coney Barrett when she was confirmed on the US Supreme Court, perhaps the greatest public office achievement by a Notre Dame graduate (Law School) to date. For all three seasons Hanratty played for the Irish he was among the top vote getters for the Heisman Trophy, finishing third in 1968. He won the Sammy Baugh Trophy in 1967.

Jim Seymour had no burning desire to attend Notre Dame. His older brother John had played halfback for Army for three years. In fact, Jim had committed to the University of Michigan and Head Coach Bump Elliott. But one day during his senior year, he was called out of class and ushered into an office to meet Notre Dame Assistant Coach Paul Shoults. At the end of that session, he was invited to visit Notre Dame. As he told it, he still had no interest in going to South Bend. But he selfishly accepted an invitation to visit the campus to see a high school buddy, Dan Saracino, who had moved to nearby Mishawaka. Saracino eventually became the admissions director at Notre Dame and held that position until 2011. In Jim's words, "As soon as I met Ara, I knew I wanted to play football for him." Jim thought of Ara as a second father figure, saying, "I'd like to be remembered as one of his favorite sons."

There are often-recounted stories that Hanratty and Seymour would practice together in the Old Fieldhouse during the 1965 offseason. Some believe it was just a legend. But the stories are true. Someone provided a key and the two worked out together on the poorly-lit dirt floor while the winter winds blew outside. The passes from Hanratty had to be hard and flat to avoid getting entangled in the structure's overhead tie rods. Seymour had great hands and became comfortable catching the "heavy ball" (a ball thrown hard and fast). The two guys got to know each other's moves and tendencies pretty well. They remained close.

The *Time* cover was immediately followed by the November 7, 1966, cover of *Sports Illustrated*, with a story "That Legend Is Loose Again," by Dan Jenkins. The university's policy of not supplying photographs continued. A young Walter Iooss Jr. was assigned to visit campus for the North Carolina game and capture a suitable cover shot. This cover would make Hanratty the first identified athlete to be on the cover of

both *Time* and *Sports Illustrated* in the same week. (As an unappreci-
ated historical note, Ara Parseghian never appeared on the cover of
Sports Illustrated.)

The sports media machines were now in full gear, working over-
time toward what was looming as the purported game of the year in East
Lansing. Many different names were floated for the new Notre Dame
passing combination: "Dynamic Duo," "Baby Bombers," "Torrid Two-
some," and "Mr. Fling and Mr. Cling." The one that is most historically
appropriate comes from the *Chicago Sun-Times*, the "Kiddie Corps,"
because it allows for the inclusion of the entire sophomore class of
Notre Dame gridders. Names like Winegardner, Stenger, Kunz, Norri,
Lauck, Kuechenberg, McKinley, Monty, Belden, O'Brien, Criniti, Dushney, Gladieux, Landolfi, Lavin, Quinn, Skoglund, and Vuillemin had
important roles in 1966 and played many downs of football for Notre
Dame over their three-year careers.

The boys — and that's what they were — just wanted to play football. That and to be respected by the upperclassmen on the team. Hanratty reflected, "We got a lot of ribbing from our teammates, but everybody was great about it. Jim and I didn't wear it on our sleeves. We were
probably more embarrassed about it than anything else, that out of all
these guys, they pick two youngsters. There were many guys much
more deserving than we were at the time."

Ara tried to manage the situation as best he could.

> Well, they're great kids. They're handling it real good. That's the thing, they're
> such great kids. But, geez, the stuff going on. Everybody wants 'em to pose
> for a magazine cover, everybody wants a private interview. I'm tripping over
> television cable right here on my own practice field. . . . A lot of pros think
> Seymour could start for them right now. Well, he's a good one, all right.
> We knew he was good. We knew Hanratty was good, too. But we were
> afraid to think how good. I'll tell you, I still don't know how good they are.[4]

Surprise Diagnosis

Coley O'Brien thought he was just a little under the weather because
of a stressful near-emergency landing in Chicago and then the overall

discomfort as the trip resumed to Norman, Oklahoma. He didn't sleep much that night. His roommate, Terry Hanratty, finally asked him what was wrong as he kept going to the bathroom to urinate. O'Brien didn't know, but figured it would pass.

The continued experience of feeling sick prompted O'Brien to seek medical attention as soon as he returned to South Bend. It didn't take long for the doctors to diagnose diabetes in this otherwise totally fit young athlete. He returned to action after missing two games; his medical condition would later play a role late in the game against Michigan State.

We're No. 1

The away win against No. 10–ranked Oklahoma (38–0) was particularly rewarding for the Irish. In the locker room after the game the Notre Dame players were uncharacteristically boisterous. Team chants of "We're No. 1" erupted spontaneously, but died down quickly when the press was invited in.

Asked if the Irish should be rated No. 1, Sooners Coach Jim MacKenzie is reported to have answered: "If they're not No. 1, it's just because enough people who cast ballots haven't seen them." Said Oklahoma Guard Ron Winfrey, "They're No. 1 in the country as far as I'm concerned, unless it's the Green Bay Packers."

According to Ara:

> We didn't expect this. I don't know what made the difference. I thought it would be a hard-fought defensive battle. You never know if the breaks are going to go for you or against you. But I never expected that score. Hanratty hit some clutch passes, and that opened them up for our running game. I'm proud of the way halfback Nick Eddy performed, too. And halfback Bob Bleier — he's been a very steady player and outstanding runner all year.[5]

Drumbeat

For the interested scoreboard watchers, Michigan State beat Purdue 41–20 at West Lafayette. Those were the two best teams in the Big Ten in

1966. It wasn't as big a mismatch as the score might imply. In the *New York Times* on October 23, the respected sportswriter Red Smith (also a Notre Dame grad) wrote, "At a conservative estimate, Purdue contributed twenty-one points to Michigan State and subtracted seven from its own score." By Smith's accounting, Purdue should have won the game 27–20.

The follow-up Associated Press story on October 23 officially started the drumbeat toward November 19 in East Lansing: "Notre Dame and Michigan State have at least three things in common — a top ranked football team, a perfect record and a problem. On November 19, the Irish and Spartans meet in a game that could quite possibly decide the National Championship."

GAME FIVE, NOVEMBER 19, 1966
Notre Dame at Michigan State University
(Spartan Stadium), Tied 10-10

Excitement about the Irish built nationally as well. One example from an Associated Press report in Plainville, Connecticut, on November 14 demonstrates this nicely:

> The priests at Our Lady of Mercy Roman Catholic Church asked a favor of the parishioners. "We're sure you'll understand," the four priests said in a letter read at Mass Sunday, requesting that the parishioners come to confession a half hour later Saturday. They explained that the regular 4 p.m. confessions time would be right in the closing minutes of the Notre Dame–Michigan State football game. The request came from Fathers Gerald Corrigan, James O'Connell and John O'Mara — whose Irish origins are evident from their names — and Father Franklin, who says, "Put me down as mostly Irish."

On that very same Sunday morning the Notre Dame coaching staff had already convened in their cramped offices on the first floor of the Rockne Memorial Building. The task at hand was preparing for Michigan State. The film of their Duke game wasn't really of significant help. Film from MSU would be essential. That, and the scouting report by Assistant Coach John Murphy who was in Bloomington, Indiana, for the MSU–Indiana game on Saturday (which the Spartans handily won 37–19). Sunday would be the last "quiet" day the Notre Dame coaches would have to prepare. By Monday the media feeding frenzy had exploded.

Thus began the most intense week in Ara Parseghian's coaching tenure. In one of our conversations, Parseghian recalled: "It was like going to a bowl game, only worse. I'd never been to a bowl game as a coach. And at Notre Dame we didn't start going to bowls until 1969. So, I had no inkling of what to expect before the Michigan State game. But the game was for the national championship. Everyone understood that. So, the press onslaught was like nothing I've ever experienced. It made it much harder to prepare for the game."

Not Iowa

Undoubtedly, at some point in the season leading up to the Michigan State game, Ara had a private conversation with Athletic Director Moose Krause pondering what the season would have looked like had they been playing Iowa. In 1960, that's how the Notre Dame schedule read: November 19, 1966 would be an away game at Iowa. But the Iowa Athletic Administration opted out of their contract with the Irish in December 1960. Instead, they eventually scheduled a game in Miami against the Hurricanes on the same date. The reasons for the change are unclear and the participants have long since passed.

Looking to fill the unexpectedly open 1966 date, Krause called his friend Biggie Munn, the athletic director at Michigan State. The Spartans also had an open date on November 19, and at the time they were quite satisfied to play just a nine-game schedule. The appeal made to State was an opportunity to schedule the additional game, along with all the additional revenue, in East Lansing. So, the deal was struck. Notre Dame would play at Michigan State on November 19. Largely as a result of this scheduling addition and the unhappy fallout from con-ference teams who played their final home games, the Big Ten Con-ference instituted rules that essentially prohibited future out-of-confer-ence games so late in the season.

For the record, the Iowa Hawkeyes had a miserable 2–8 season in 1966. Michigan State clobbered them 56–7. They lost the game at Miami 44–0. At some point it must have occurred to both Krause and Parseghian that Iowa would have been a much easier opponent than Michigan State in 1966. Thus a scheduling oddity forever adds to the lore of the game of the century.

Hate State Week

It was hardly a secret on the Notre Dame campus that the scheduled contest at Michigan State was the Irish's biggest game of the season, not just for their football team, but for all of college football. While the game would be played 150 miles away, nonetheless it would become the greatest distraction from campus normalcy in the history of Notre Dame. Professors who had scheduled midterm exams would later lament that they hadn't fully comprehended the degree of distraction. Many would be forced to throw out test results and reschedule exams later in the semester. The role of football in the psyche of the campus was somewhat better understood and tolerated in the 1960s. No event since has ever tested this tolerance to the same degree.

On Monday, Tuesday, and Wednesday evenings there were impromptu pep rallies held at selected dorms. Key Irish players would stop by after having dinner at the training table and be asked to speak over bull horns to excite the student crowds. Enough of the Marching Band would show up informally to provide the musical glue that has bound the Notre Dame population for ages. The crowd would disperse and retire to the highly agitated state of studying which permeated the typically laconic campus before an away football game. But this wasn't just any away football game. Everyone knew the stakes, the national championship.

As if the campus needed additional pregame fever, more was provided quite unexpectedly. Midweek, an airplane flew over the campus and dropped thousands of leaflets disparaging the Irish and echoing some variant of "Kill Bubba, Kill." This phrase would appear on virtually everything associated with fan support in East Lansing. The leaflets were supposed to be a distraction to the players and student fanatics. They had just the opposite effect. The campus focus became sharper, and the team's determination became even more intense. If the Notre Dame Alumni Association had paid for this stunt, it couldn't have been more effective. Nothing quite like this had happened before or has happened since.

Thursday was the official pep rally in the Old Fieldhouse, complete with Ara and the team. Recollections of this event still give chills to those who were there, players and students alike. Except for a hoard of press people wandering around campus, the event was strictly a family affair; filled to capacity at 4,500 (this is the only capacity figure that has survived Fieldhouse legends). Accounts of the event followed the script for a typical pep rally full of crazed excitement. Ara was quoted as saying, "We respect the Spartans, but we are not going to Lansing to lose." The usually quiet and understated Alan Page added, "I think our defense is better than theirs."

No detail was too small for the voracious press, which at one point was generously estimated as numbering seven hundred on the Notre Dame campus prior to the game. One newspaperman reportedly wrote that Ara "stabbed" a roll of toilet paper out of the air with his left hand. The final speaker at the Thursday pep rally was Team Captain Jim Lynch who declared, "Speaking on behalf of the No. 1 football team in the nation, Notre Dame will beat Michigan State."

Betting Line

Early in the week Notre Dame was installed as four-point favorites by those who made their living making predictions of that sort. A *Detroit Free Press* article on November 17 quoted a friendly bookie, "In 25 years of business, I've never seen so much action on any proposition. Most of the big money is on Notre Dame. Nationally some $30–50 million will be wagered on the game." He added, "This does not include the 'creeps' who bet among each other rather than with bookies."

The mathematical rationale for the spread is hard to reconcile, even years later. Professional oddsmakers try to balance the anticipated action on both sides of a bet — thus making their money as the middlemen.

This means that the organized betting on Michigan State to beat the Irish was also quite heavy, but not heavy enough to offset the generally irrational behavior of Notre Dame subway alumni. In the minds of most, the game was a toss-up, especially among the "creeps."

Predictions about the game appeared from every corner. Even Notre Dame Athletic Director Moose Krause proffered, "The winner will score at least four touchdowns."

Looking back, only one prediction could be found that correctly slotted the final score. Dennis Kraft of the *Elkhart Truth* wrote on November 17, "Now football fans have their eyes focused on Nov. 19, 1966. Saturday's clash brings together again two unbeatens and the 'possibility' exists of a stalemate. . . . 'It could turn out to be a dull game for the fans, unless they like solid defensive play,' Irish Coach Ara Parseghian said. The Spartans downed the Irish a year ago, 12–3 with 'perfect' defense. 'In all my years of coaching, I have never seen a more perfect defense than the one State used against us last season,' Ara unsmilingly remarked."

In a *Chicago Sun-Times* article the Wednesday before the game, Michigan State Head Coach Duffy Daugherty also thoughtfully attempted to diffuse the media hype, "This won't be a wide-open scoring battle. A break could decide the game. And it could all come down to a field goal. I think the honest feeling of both myself and Parseghian is that there is greatness on both teams involved."

Friday Frenzy

The Notre Dame team had a final practice early on a chilly Friday morning in South Bend. With just enough time to pack gear and have a hasty lunch the team boarded the regularly scheduled Grand Trunk train from South Bend's Union Station at noon. It would be the next-to-last time a Notre Dame football team would ever board a train for travel to an away game. Apart from the game itself, this train trip was a memorable experience for the team members. All were in good spirits. The trip felt like a throwback in time. At crossings and station stops along the way, crowds greeted the team and waved signs of encouragement, especially before the train crossed the state line into Michigan.

At one stop, nuns stood with their uniformed grammar school classes and waved and cheered wildly for the Irish. It felt like something out of the Rockne Era of the 1920s.

Arriving in Lansing, the cheers quickly turned to jeers and the signs were distinctly less friendly. For the duration of the visitors' stay at the Jack Tar Hotel there was a white Cadillac parked outside with "Kill Bubba, Kill" painted on it in black letters. That phrase became the predominant MSU chant of the weekend. The Notre Dame players diffused the effect of the message once it was determined that the slogan lacked proper sentence construction — it lacked either a subject or an object. They started to make fun of it after that.

The biggest sports story of the day unexpectedly occurred at the Lansing train station. Future All-American halfback Nick Eddy had been carefully nursing an aching shoulder all week, but it was feeling much better. He expected to play on Saturday. As Nick tells the story, he had a new pair of wingtip dress shoes which he wore on the trip. The Notre Dame tradition of professionally dressed travel squads (jackets and ties) was enforced by Parseghian. The new leather soles weren't scuffed up, so they were quite slippery. As Nick stepped down the expanded metal steps from the railroad car to the station siding his footing slipped. He instinctively grabbed the metal handrail and in so doing wrenched his already tender shoulder. On the step just below him was the diminutive Sports Information Director, Roger Valdiserri, who narrowly escaped injury himself from the tumbling Eddy. Even constant therapy overnight proved fruitless. A disappointed Eddy stayed confined to the sideline the following day, the biggest game of the season, and perhaps the biggest game of the twentieth century.

Fifty Thousand Letters

The biggest off-the-field controversy the week before the game surrounded who would be able to watch it on television. In the new contract between the NCAA and ABC it was stipulated that no single team could be on a national broadcast more than once every two years or on a regional broadcast more than twice in any two-year period. Notre Dame had already been on a national broadcast in 1966 during their home opener against Purdue. The NCAA was responding to the fears of many member schools that paid attendance at college games would decline if there were a key national game on the tube every single week.

The math was rigged so that Notre Dame and many of the power-house football schools couldn't be on television more than three times in any two-year period. It made preseason game selections by ABC quite difficult because some of the important games weren't even evident until the season unfolded, like Notre Dame at Michigan State. Traditional rivalries were considered safe choices: Harvard–Yale, Army–Navy, Michigan–Ohio State. But even those games couldn't be shown in two consecutive years under the guidelines, except to regional audiences. It was a mathematical mess.

The rule didn't last long. The Notre Dame–Michigan State contest was the first to put the NCAA on the ropes. Allegedly, over fifty thousand letters were sent to ABC network headquarters in New York demanding to see the game. The veracity of this claim is suspicious because ABC was itself seeking relief to broadcast, what had emerged as the biggest college game in many years. By midweek a compromise had been worked out, a "bending" of the rules. The game would go on air before the regularly scheduled "national game," between traditional rivals UCLA and USC. The game would be shown to almost the entire nation, thus effectively creating the first college football double header. But a small sliver of geography would be held out so a regional game in the South could be broadcast. Thus, the big game was technically a regional telecast to about 95 percent of the nation. According to a press release made by the ABC publicist at the time, Beano Cook, "We're putting out enough material to make *Gone with the Wind* look like a short story." The *Wall Street Journal* even put a preview article about the big game on the front page of its Friday edition — something it rarely did for a sporting event.

Nonplussed Preparation

The Notre Dame team followed the normal pregame schedule for an away contest. They walked to 9:00 a.m. Mass at the nearby St. Mary's Cathedral and returned to have a 9:45 pregame meal and meeting at the hotel. At 11:30 a.m., two police escorts accompanied the team busses to the stadium. Except for the extra tension, the morning before the 1:30 kickoff went normally.

Pregame warm-ups by special teams occur before the entire team takes the field for calisthenics. It's a time for a handful of players and specialty coaches to have the full range of the playing field to practice kickoffs, punts, and field goals. While placekicker, Joe Azzaro, was warming up, a scruffy older gentleman with white hair and dressed in Spartan green approached him and started a casual conversation about kicking. He was very personable and Azzaro initially took him for a groundskeeper. Only when the fellow walked away did the light go on. The unassuming man was Duffy Daugherty, the Spartans' head coach. Why was he on the field? Perhaps to get into the head of Azzaro, thus providing a preview of the role kicking would eventually play in the game. Perhaps it was just to assess field conditions, which were adverse for kicking: windy, cold, and a hard frozen field. Azzaro was nonplussed. It was his twenty-first birthday.

Ticket Holders

The ten thousand tickets in the hands of Notre Dame fans created enough vocal presence to be heard on the field. But the folks from South Bend had mixed color loyalties. Some wore the traditional blue and gold; others were decked out in kelly green, and they got lost in the crowd that was already filled with Spartan green. Popular buttons were: "Ara's Army," and "Ara's Lynch Mob" — both with white letters on a green background. (The wording of the latter would have seemed clever at the time because of Team Captain Jim Lynch's name, although it is egregious to our modern sensibilities.)

The State crowd was in a frenzy. There was a scarecrow-like figure of a Notre Dame football player hung in effigy from the smokestack of the MSU power plant. Other than the ubiquitous "Kill Bubba Kill," there were other messages on banners in the stadium designed to irritate the Catholics from South Bend, "Hail Mary, full of grace, Notre Dame's in second place," and "Bubba for Pope."

Guy with the Cigar

The face value of a ticket to the ND–MSU game was $5.00. They were a precious commodity! Scalpers were easily getting $100 per ducat before the game. If you were from Notre Dame and had a ticket, it couldn't be had at any price. The ticket allotment to the visitors was limited under contract to one-seventh of capacity, rounded to ten thousand. This included members of the team who made the trip but didn't dress, players' families (two tickets per family), favored alumni, season ticket holders, and the official University of Notre Dame traveling party. The Notre Dame Marching Band did not make the trip. A student lottery was held on campus for the remainder of the ticket allocation, exactly five hundred.

Coach Parseghian had one indelible memory from before the game. Just before kickoff the teams were on their respective sidelines. A gentleman wearing a topcoat, fedora hat, and smoking a cigar stood next to Ara. This wasn't a face familiar to the head coach, so Ara challenged him, "What are you doing here?" The man responded, "Watching the game, same as you." The unknown fellow was ushered away by security. Ara claimed that Duffy packed the stadium with his friends and found ways to get everyone in, even if it meant crowding the visitors' bench. The guy standing with the team on the sideline was a clear reminder to Parseghian that his coaching counterpart would pull out all the stops to win the game. Before the opening kickoff, the Irish head coach was already fit to be tied.

Ara Doesn't Do Dumb Things

The Notre Dame–Michigan State game, as it was played on November 19, 1966, may be accurately summarized in just five simple sentences. The hitting was ferocious. There was no winner. Nobody played to tie. Those involved left the stadium unsatisfied. Players and coaches are still remembered for, if not haunted by, the experience.

After all that has been written about this contest, and that has been considerable — perhaps more than any other college football game in history, it is worth the time and effort to seek truth by relying only on primary sources. The most accurate are: 1) the official written game record, play-by-play, as recorded by official scorers and submitted to the NCAA, 2) video tape of the game that remains from the ABC television broadcast, and 3) the firsthand accounts of the actual players and coaches. All other commentary, especially by third-party accounts from people not intimate with the game, is unfortunately replete with misinformation, prejudice, and baseless opinion.

The need for primary sources drove the early research on this subject. Notre Dame Assistant Coach Brian Boulac generously agreed to share his memories of this game to help the cause of building an accurate record so many years after the fact. Then he was shown the videotape of the game. Frequently he would shake his head and comment, "I just don't remember it that way." He reviewed the tape multiple times; in fact, it was left at his home so he could review it in private. One frequent television image shown is that of Ara Parseghian on the sideline and there is Brian standing right next to him. While "the box" had been banned, Brian nonetheless had one of the best vantage points in the house, and Brian's memory remained very sharp. He is considered a primary source, albeit not infallible. Thus, the conclusion is that other observers who were not directly involved with the game just aren't that reliable. After over fifty-five years they remember what they "think" they saw, or more dangerously, what they "wished" had happened.

For the record, Michigan State didn't lose their bid for the national championship on November 19. Yes, they could have been permanently installed at No. 1 if they had beaten Notre Dame, but that didn't happen. Given the perspective of history, they actually lost their claim for a portion of the No. 1 ranking at Columbus, Ohio, on October 15, when they barely eked out an 11–8 victory against a mediocre Buckeye team. In the course of a ten-game season, the Spartans only played three teams with winning records — Purdue, Michigan, and Notre Dame. And in what is historically considered a weak schedule, including conference games, Michigan State allowed ninety-nine points.

Also, for the record, Notre Dame didn't retain their No. 1 ranking on November 19. The two major polls were divided between the two teams after the game. The Irish didn't even win the game "on points" as many have tried to suggest over the years, as if this were a boxing match. The two teams played to a tie. The Irish only regained undisputed claim to No. 1 the following week. The National Championship Trophy was awarded for a "body of work" over the course of the entire season. Notre Dame clearly had the superior record.

But comparisons of this game to a heavyweight title fight have merit. A detailed play by play account of the game is presented in my earlier book *Undisputed: Notre Dame, National Champions 1966 (A Football Family and the Game of the Century)*. And while certain accounts and memories vary, everybody who was there at Spartan Stadium is in one hundred percent agreement on this singular point. It *was* a brutal game.

First Quarter

Notre Dame won the toss and chose to receive, meaning Michigan State would kick and defend the south goal. Kenney kicked off to Conjar at 12, downed by Waters after a 15-yard return.

That's how the game began, as officially recorded in the press box. The NCAA sent carbon copies of the official reports to the participating schools. These copies still exist in the Notre Dame Archives and are reproduced below throughout the chapter by permission.

Michigan State was obviously tense when they started their first possession on their own 11-yard line. Notre Dame's John Horney stopped MSU quarterback Jimmy Raye for a 2-yard loss. On the next play Raye fumbled and Regis Cavender recovered for another loss of five yards. The third play, a 6-yard run by Raye, was short of a first down and forced a punt from the MSU 8-yard line. Dick Kenney blasted a 54-yard kick that set up the Irish on their own 38-yard line. Looking back, this impressive defensive stand by the Irish could be viewed as a lost scoring opportunity should they have recovered the fumble or blocked the punt from the end zone. It would be a day of defensive dominance. That and strange luck — good and bad — that affected both teams.

The next Notre Dame series is central to the outcome of the game and unfolds as follows:

1-10	ND 38	Hanratty's pass for Bleier, incomplete.
2-10	38	Hanratty's pass for Bleier, incomplete.
3-10	38	Hanratty passed complete to Gladieux, downed by Phillips after 26 yards.
1-10	MSU 36	Gladieux, downed by Thornhill, gained 1.
2-9	36	Hanratty rolled out right and was stopped by Smith and Thornhill after 2.
3-7	33	Hanratty pass for Bleier incomplete, broken up by Phillips.
4-7	33	Hardy, back to punt got a bad pass from center and passed incomplete.

Even though the Spartans only got the ball on their own 33-yard line after that disappointing sequence, significant damage had been done to the fortunes of the Irish. The rollout by Hanratty was actually a quarterback draw play brought in from the sideline. It was called as a halfback draw, but miscommunicated in the huddle. The tackle, a grab by Spartans Charlie Thornhill and a finish by Bubba Smith, was fierce. Smith landed on Terry Hanratty as he was falling. Terry insists, even today, that it was "clean." The contact separated his shoulder, but Hanratty didn't immediately know the extent of the injury. On the next play he threw a weak and errant pass toward Rocky Bleier as his shoulder screamed in pain. He grabbed his arm and trotted off the field, done for the day and for the remainder of the season. That day at Michigan State, Hanratty only attempted four passes and had a single completion.

Just as unfortunate was the punt play. The punter, Kevin Hardy (kicking for his first time in college competition), tried to recover from a bad snap. Unable to get the kick off, he spotted his outside contain man George Goeddeke, wide open. The athletic Hardy instinctively threw a pass. Goeddeke was normally the offensive center, except on long snaps. He was inserted for Jim Seymour who was held out of punt coverage to preserve his sore ankle from open-field shots. Not hearing the ball kicked, Goeddeke turned just in time to see the ball in the air headed his way. He lunged, but missed it. Michigan State defender Jess Phillips leveled him as he came down. Goeddeke severely sprained his ankle, and he was forced to leave the game for good. Notre Dame lost their starting quarterback and starting center within seconds and without a score for either team. Three future All-Americans were now on the bench (Eddy, Hanratty, and Goeddeke), and there were over three quarters left to play. That was a punch to the gut on the sidelines. Sophomores Coley O'Brien at quarterback and Tim Monty at center, were thrown into the melee for the remainder of the afternoon.

The Spartans were frustrated on offense. Running the ball was virtually impossible, especially up the middle against the Notre Dame front four. Their bruising backfield of Dwight Lee, Clinton Jones, and Regis Cavender only netted sixty-three net yards all afternoon. Duffy Daugherty started to call plays for his quarterback to roll to one side or the other with the option of passing. No matter the call, Raye always rolled right, away from Notre Dame's fierce Alan Page. At the end of the game, Jimmy Raye would have twenty-one running attempts and seventy-five net yards. He also attempted twenty passes, completing only seven, with three interceptions. The QB option would be the Spartan's stock-in-trade play for the remainder of the game.

The two teams traded hard-hitting possessions. Just before the end of the first quarter MSU got the ball back on their 27-yard line after another Irish punt. The very next snap yielded one of the defining plays of the game. Raye hit talented receiver Gene Washington for a 42-yard passing gain, the longest pass completion of the afternoon. This gave the Spartans the ball on the Notre Dame 31-yard line. The play triggered a successful drive for State's only touchdown. After that drive, it would also be the best field position the Spartans would enjoy for an offensive series for the remainder of the game. Nine consecutive running plays featuring Jones, Cavender, and Raye followed.

Second Quarter

The Irish starting defense was scored upon for the first time since the Purdue game. On a third and goal play Regis Cavender ran over right tackle for a touchdown. Kenny kicked the extra point.

Michigan State 7   Notre Dame 0

Later in the quarter Jim Lynch intercepted a Raye pass. But when he was tackled midair and flipped to the ground, MSU recovered his fumble. State was able to move the ball to the 37-yard line where Kenny connected again for a 47-yard field goal. Dick Kenny was considered by many to be the best kicker in college football. Ara now knew that anything inside thirty yards could result in a Michigan State score. Indeed, it did.

Michigan State   10   Notre Dame   0

This would be the last time Michigan State would score in the game. They would not get beyond the Notre Dame 46-yard line for the remainder of the contest. But it is clear from the video and from the record that State started this drive with momentum. Notre Dame gave up some large chunks of real estate before the Jim Lynch interception-fumble.

That play by the Notre Dame captain was a momentum changer for the Irish. The interception was one of those that a linebacker dreams about, and the tackle of Lynch on the play was equally memorable. This play is one that fans have and will talk about for as long as football is played between the two schools. Lynch had his feet taken out from under him as he was unsuccessfully attempting to jump the tackler. That flipped him midair, so he landed directly on his head. A photo of the moment of impact appeared in *Sports Illustrated*. (Some would argue that it should have been on the cover.)

Notre Dame was on the edge. The team couldn't tolerate losing another future All-American. That play by Lynch further toughened up the defense. Holding the Spartans to a field goal felt like a victory of sorts. Probably no other college team in America at the time could attempt a 47-yard field goal and believe they could make it, even with wind surging at 20 mph behind them. The barefoot Hawaiian kicker, Dick Kenney, was that good. The kick established a line in the sand for the Irish defense. Any MSU field position inside the Notre Dame 35-yard line would likely mean points for them. They never got that far again.

The game turned to favor the Irish after that. With 10 minutes, 30 seconds left in the quarter, Coley O'Brien engineered a four-play drive of fifty-four yards, capped by a 34-yard pass to Bob Gladieux, who caught the ball on the goal line and took strides into the end zone. This was one of the biggest touchdown plays in Ara's career and matched the Nick Eddy run against Purdue in significance. Joe Azzaro kicked the extra point.

Michigan State   10   Notre Dame   7

There was still time to be played in the first half. Michigan State would have the ball twice and Notre Dame once. Both teams failed to make a first down for the remainder of the half. The collisions on the lines were extraordinary. They could be heard in the stadium's upper deck. The first half statistics were quite equal, as would be expected.

Premonition

The last sequence of the first half merits serious scrutiny, something very few observers have deigned to do. After a Notre Dame punt by Kevin Hardy, the ball was downed by Jim Seymour at the MSU 1-yard line. Seymour had returned in the game to replace George Goeddeke, who was injured while replacing him on punt coverage earlier in the game.

Backed up deep in his own territory, MSU Head Coach Duffy Daugherty called three safe running plays to quarterback Jimmy Raye. He didn't dare call a pass play that could have been intercepted for a possible run back and score by Notre Dame. He knew that punting the ball might create a miscue which could result in a Notre Dame score. So, he elected to run out the clock as best he could. He did what every experienced coach would do in the same situation and it was the right thing to do under the circumstances. In effect, he played to keep the scoreboard frozen at 10–7. No one has ever criticized him for doing this. Keep that in mind as the final plays of the second half unfold.

There are a couple oddities to this sequence. The timekeeper on the sidelines allowed the time to run out when the clock should have been stopped. The referees didn't catch this oversight as the teams ran into the locker room. There was no television camera synchronized between the clock and the field action, and also no provision for review. If there had been, this would have given Notre Dame a few additional seconds to run a couple of plays before the end of the first half. More curious: Notre Dame did not call a time out and try to get the ball back with decent field position. Yet this possibility is simply never mentioned.

Third Quarter

The quarter started with fireworks, which ultimately didn't factor into the game.

Azzaro kicked off to Waters who carried it from the 10 to the 30, Pergine tackled.
1-10 MSU 30   Raye fumbled and Horney recovered for ND on the 31.
1-10 MSU 31   O'Brien's pass for Bleier intercepted by Phillips on the 2 and was tackled there by Bleier.

Looking back, that interception may have ended one of Notre Dame's two best shots at winning the game. After that each team had the ball twice before the final quarter.

Notre Dame's second drive started at their 20-yard line. Coley O'Brien had completions to Rocky Bleier, Larry Conjar, Bob Gladieux, and Dave Haley. Runs followed by Haley, Bleier, and Conjar. Unfortunately, another Irish halfback was forced out of the game in this sequence, Bob Gladieux. In 1991, he recounted it to me this way, "I was going out for a pass against the grain and MSU's Jess Phillips was going with the grain. He hit me when I was midair. It was a clean hit. My quadriceps [muscle] was splattered. In fact, my thigh pad was shattered. That leg still bothers me a little when one of my kids sits on my lap."

As the quarter ended O'Brien went back to pass, found no one open, and then ran for no gain. The ball rested on the MSU 10-yard line.

Michigan State   10   Notre Dame   7

Fourth Quarter

Opening the quarter, with fourth down and three yards to go, Joe Azzaro kicked a 28-yard field goal into the wind. Thus ended Notre Dame's second opportunity to take the lead in the game. The tie was tallied.

Michigan State   10   Notre Dame   10

Each team had the ball five times in the final stanza. There were only three first downs, two by the Spartans and one by the Irish. A desperate fight was underway. It had everything to do with winning and nothing to do with not losing. The defensive units played with abandon. For most of the season neither team had used first-stringers this late into a game. They were at the brink of exhaustion. Fortunately, Notre Dame defensive back Tom Schoen intercepted two of Jimmy Raye's passes. Michigan State never got closer than the ND 46-yard line. After the second Schoen interception the score sheet reads as follows:

1-10	MSU 18	Conjar downed by Thornhill and Richardson, gained 2.
2-8	16	Haley downed by Hoag and Smith for 8-yard loss.
3-16	24	O'Brien passed incomplete to Bleier.
4-16	24	Azzaro's kick for a field goal was long enough but wide to the right and no good.
1-10	MSU 20	Jones downed by Duranko for 6-yard loss.
2-16	14	Raye's pass for Washington, incomplete.
3-16	14	Cavendar up the middle, downed by Pergine after 15 inches short of 1 down.
4-1	29	Raye sneaked for the first down with inches to spare.
1-10	30	Jones met Lynch and Horney trying left end for 2-yard loss.
2-12	28	Brenner caught Raye's pass for 8-yard gain, Schoen tackled.
3-4	36	Raye's pass for Brenner incomplete.
4-4	36	Schoen called for fair catch but fumbled, and recovered on the ND 30.
ND		
1-10	ND 30	O'Brien downed by Thornhill after making 4.
2-6	34	Bleier downed by Webster and Hoag on the draw after 3-yard gain.
3-3	37	Conjar downed by Thornhill, made 2 yards but short of 1 down.
4-1	39	O'Brien sneaked for first down with 2-yard gain.

1-10	41	Smith downed O'Brien going back to pass for a 7-yard loss.
2-17	34	O'Brien sneaked for five yards as the game ended.

Michigan State 10   Notre Dame 10

It all sounds pretty straightforward when you read it over a half century later. But interesting details need to be inserted. First, the Azzaro field goal attempt was into the stiff and swirling 20 mph wind, making it a long forty-one yards, a tough kick for the steady Notre Dame place kicker. Azzaro remembers, "The ball came off my foot cleanly and I thought it was going to be good. Then the wind took it." Witnesses claim it was wide by about a foot. That's how close Notre Dame came to winning the game — twelve inches, or thereabouts.

When State got the ball back after three plays, they were confronted with a fourth and one. They went for it and got it. The ABC announcing team of Chris Shenkel and Bud Wilkinson heralded this as a courageous and daring move by MSU Coach Duffy Daugherty. After three more plays against the Irish defense the Spartans were forced to punt.

This was where Notre Dame came close to losing the ball — and the game. The pigskin fluttered in the variable wind and Tom Schoen fumbled a fair catch on his own 30-yard line. This was well within the kicking range of Kenney, especially with the wind mostly blowing behind him. Fortunately, Schoen recovered his own fumble. This ruling was controversial at the time, as State was scrounging for the loose ball. Years later, Ara identified this recovery as one of the best plays of the game.

The sequence of six Notre Dame plays with only 1 minute, 36 seconds on the clock will probably be debated by football fans for the remainder of time. If you recall Alan Page's observation from the very first team meeting with Ara, the coach's moves all make perfect sense. Think "possession and position." Parseghian was not about to give the Spartans another chance on offense, especially when the Irish were within Kenny's kicking range. The first order of business was to maintain possession.

The only way for the Irish to score from the field position it had was to maneuver for a field goal. They had to get to at least the MSU 25-yard line to do this. The Spartan coaching staff had this figured out as well. So, State positioned seven defenders back in a "prevent" configuration through the entire sequence, in effect creating a picket fence with a theoretical goal line at the 25. Ara's challenge became how to achieve position and keep possession.

Coley O'Brien was zero for six passing to that point in the fourth quarter. Ara suspected something was wrong. Brian Boulac remembers Tom Schoen (the backup QB in 1965) being instructed to warm up on the sideline, which he did. Running was the only sensible option to maintain possession, hoping to find a seam in the four-man front.

With fourth down and one, Ara made the most courageous call of the entire game. He decided to go for it. Practically nobody remembers this, especially Spartan fans. If they made it, Notre Dame would have retained possession. If they didn't, MSU probably would have won the game. The broadcast announcers weren't nearly as effusive about the courage of Parseghian's decision as they were only moments earlier when Duffy made a similar decision. This singular call receives little play in the debate and yet it permanently defines Ara's credentials as a winner. Quarterback Coley O'Brien rushed for two yards to the right behind guard Dick Swatland and tackle Bob Kuechenberg and made the first down.

On the second to last play of the game, Ara called for a rollout option pass — hoping to get close enough for another play or two and a field goal attempt. He had judiciously saved his timeouts. Again, this call is generally forgotten; some have mistakenly called it a run. O'Brien was dropped for a 7-yard loss by a charging Bubba Smith who grabbed him from behind. This changed the team's position and put the ball back in Kenney's field goal range yet again. Ara believed that Coley O'Brien holding onto the ball after the savage Bubba Smith blind side tackle was another key play of the game.

If the game had ended on this play, probably so would have the unfortunate controversy about playing for a tie. With a field position of second and seventeen and only six seconds remaining on the clock, the game was effectively over. O'Brien didn't have the arm strength for one last Hail Mary pass. So, Ara called a quarterback sneak. Remove that play or have O'Brien throw the ball into the tenth row of seats instead, and the historical controversy is moot. That one play, a quarterback sneak (on second and seventeen, no less!), turned all the hype about the game of the century into a reality.

One persistent question still lingers. Why did Duffy Daugherty elect to punt on the second Michigan State fourth down when he had to know his team probably wouldn't have the ball again on offense? He traded possession for position, a logical strategy with Kenney's leg in mind. He was hoping for a mistake by the Irish, and it almost happened on the fumbled punt. Defensive lineman Tom Rhoads summed up the MSU strategy and the Notre Dame response in their final possession, "Michigan State wanted Ara to do something dumb. Ara doesn't do dumb things."

Statistics

The statistic that jumps off the pages years later is that there were sixteen punts in the game, eight by each team. That correctly signals a defensive struggle. The tackle leaders for Notre Dame were: Jim Lynch (13), John Pergine (12), John Horney (11), Tom O'Leary (9), and Kevin Hardy (7). Alan Page had zero tackles in the game, primarily because State was afraid to run to his side of the field. The tackle leaders for MSU were: Charlie Thornhill (16), Jeff Richardson (13) and George Webster (10). Bubba Smith had only two solo tackles and was contributed to four more. But all of them seemed to come at important times in the game.

Lost in the fog over the years is the fact that Notre Dame attempted more passes than Michigan State, twenty-four (four by Terry Hanratty and twenty by backup Coley O'Brien) versus twenty for Jimmy Raye. It was a dicey weather day for passing; there were only fifteen completions (ND had eight and MSU had seven). Michigan State had more first downs overall, thirteen compared to Notre Dame's ten, and they led in net rushing yards 142 to 91.

There were no complaints about the officiating after the game. There were just six penalties called, and only one of those was against Notre Dame for five yards.

Of the fifty-player Notre Dame travel squad to Michigan State, thirty-two saw game action. Ten were sophomores. The official game record as submitted to the NCAA reads:

Left End: Seymour, Rhoads
Left Tackle: Sieler, Duranko
Left Guard: Regner, Hardy
Center: Goeddeke, Monty, Kelly, Page
Right Guard: Swatland, Pergine
Right Tackle: Kuechenberg, Lynch
Right End: Gmitter, Stenger, Horney
Quarterback: Hanratty, O'Brien, Martin, Azzaro
Left Halfback: Gladieux, O'Leary, Burgener, Criniti
Right Halfback: Bleier, Smithberger, Quinn, Haley
Fullback: Conjar, Schoen, Dushney

Postgame Reflections

An examination of Notre Dame's scoring at Michigan State provides an interesting insight into the makeup and character of the team. On the only Irish touchdown, Tim Monty hiked the ball to Coley O'Brien. Monty was just a sophomore. Weighing about 215 pounds, he was supposed to snap the ball and then block the guy lined up over his helmet, Bubba Smith, who weighed about 275 pounds. Despite the size mismatch against his direct opponent, Monty made the touchdown pass possible. Coley O'Brien, another sophomore who had been called in to replace starter Terry Hanratty, was playing in only his third week after returning from the hospitalization resulting in his diabetes diagnosis. He had a personal physician on the sideline in case of emergency. O'Brien threw the ball over the middle to sophomore Bob Gladieux, who had been slotted into Nick Eddy's vacant position at the last minute. O'Brien was involved in all of the scoring plays as a quarterback and kick holder, a detail that is rarely mentioned. Gladieux scored six points, although later in the game, he was hit so hard that his swollen thigh removed him from the game and also finish his season. It's fair to say the sophomore standouts were responsible for the Irish holding their own on the field.

As previously stated, the Notre Dame–Michigan State game, as it was played on November 19, 1966, may be accurately summarized with just five simple sentences. The hitting was ferocious. There was no winner. Nobody played to tie. Those involved left the stadium unsatisfied. Players and coaches are still remembered for, if not haunted by, the experience.

Applesauce and Sour Grapes

When the game finally ended there was a momentary, eerie silence in the stadium. Multiple players, coaches, and fans who were there described the atmosphere as eerie. "That is how I remember it playing out. I was there on the 40-yard line behind ND bench just fifteen rows up. And yes, it was 'eerie' afterwards. We just sat there staring at the scoreboard. I think the fans were exhausted by what they saw and heard on the field, something that could not come through on television." This is how Mike Collins (Notre Dame '67) remembers it. He knew and lived with many of the players and was sports director of the student radio station WSND. Collins is well known for his many years as the public address announcer at Notre Dame Stadium.

Everyone in the confines of Spartan Stadium recognized that it had been a brutal game. Later, much later for some, they would reflect that they had witnessed something historically significant. Ticket stubs and programs became highly collectible. At the time it was hard to absorb the result. Everyone was exhausted. And everyone wearing green and white was especially frustrated because their season was now over. That frustration started to leak out once the eerie silence was broken.

Forty-four years after the fact, Ara clearly recalled exiting the Spartan Stadium field on November 19, 1966. He was running toward the locker room through the crowd of players, coaches, and bystanders when he started to hear the taunts. "You chickens!" "Hey Coach, why did you play for a tie?" There were many variations on the theme, most of them unprintable. The person often identified on the MSU side as a prime instigator was an assistant coach.

But frustration is a powerful force. Walking off the field, Michigan State insiders instinctively knew that they had not landed the knockout punch. In fact, theirs was a rather weak showing in the second half, especially on offense. In the absence of "Ara doing something stupid," they were now probably out of the running for any standalone claim on the national championship, especially if Notre Dame were to beat Southern Cal. Even if Notre Dame lost to USC, the best they could have done would be a shared award, probably with Alabama (again).

Ara wasn't immune from the catcalling as he tried to jog off the field. He was fuming when he finally got to the visitors' locker room. As he told me later, "When I got inside the coaches' room, I saw an apple on the table. I took that apple and threw it as hard as I could into the shower room, smashing it against the wall." Did he mind that story being retold, I wondered? "Hell no, I was damn mad. The kids on the field, on both sides, had played their hearts out. They all deserved credit for what they had done. Nobody played for any tie, I can tell you that." It's a real shame that this definitive message from Ara was drowned out by the ongoing discussion of playing for a tie.

The head coach collected himself and addressed the team in the locker room before allowing the press to come in. He recalled telling the players how proud he was of their effort and their comeback against adversity. Then he explained that they still had a chance to be national champions if they went to Southern California and won convincingly. The coach had already assessed the postgame situation and turned the page to the challenge for the coming week.

Serious Injuries

After such a brutal game, consider the challenges for the Notre Dame medical team and trainers while the team showered and collected their equipment. Carnivorous reporters squeezed into the crowded locker room. Attending to the "casualties" sustained by the Irish players became difficult at best, although certain priorities became clear.

Rocky Bleier unexpectedly needed immediate attention after he urinated blood in the locker room. The considered decision was made that he was well enough to make the trip back home. He was immediately hospitalized when he returned to South Bend and received the diagnosis of a lacerated kidney — a serious injury. Bleier would still be in the hospital a week later. Terry Hanratty had his arm in a sling. He felt excruciating pain to move any part of his upper body; the painkillers did not help much. Removing his remaining football pads and pants required delicate help. Bob Gladieux's thigh had ballooned up and was packed with ice. None of these players, Bleier, Hanratty, or Gladieux, played another down of football in 1966.

Jim Seymour passed out in the locker room, exhausted. George Goeddeke hobbled around with crutches to keep the weight off of his severely sprained ankle. For all practical purposes his injury also finished his season, although he would hobble to play one charity down the following week. Coley O'Brien went through the motions to act normally, still drinking orange juice as protection against diabetic shock. He would remember virtually nothing after the game and to this day, his friends all claim he was "out of it." Nick Eddy quietly changed into street clothes. His sore shoulder still throbbed, but he harbored a hope of playing the next week in California, his home state. The guys who sported simple cuts, scratches, and bruises — and there were many — had to fend for themselves.

Mike Collins further remembers, "We [Notre Dame students] waited outside the locker room. Even players I knew as classmates were not talking afterwards, it was if they had spent everything they had, and many were hurting. At that point I don't think a one of them had it figured out that a win the next week would give them the championship. I always have thought that Jim Lynch got a concussion on that hit he took after the interception. He seemed like a zombie outside the locker room and stared at me like he did not know who I was — which he did." Getting back to Notre Dame's campus became the immediate goal for the weary Irish. There was a private train waiting for them on a siding within view of the stadium, the last train to ever transport an Irish team.

Aftershocks

The immediate reaction of the press, at least by those who actually witnessed the game in person, was relatively balanced. If you were there and then checked the stat sheets, it was obvious that you had witnessed one heck of a college football game. After that, partisanship would spin the stories to appease the home market readership. One exception was written on November 20, 1966, by Joe Falls, the sports editor for the *Detroit Free Press*.

> Bless me, Father for I have sinned . . . I rooted for Michigan State. But now I would like to repent. The winner, and it hurts me to say it, was Notre Dame. . . . Make no mistake about it — the two best teams in the land were on display here Saturday and our grudging admiration goes to the Fighting Irish. . . . They were up against everything and still managed to pull off a tie in the most nerve-wracking football game that could possibly be played. It was a classic in the truest sense of the word. . . . It was regrettable that the game ended in a chorus of boos from the highly partisan crowd as Ara Parseghian chose to settle for the tie instead of trying for a bolt of lightning in the last minute.

This is an honest account from a writer who admits his bias and had every reason to slant the story to provide solace to Michigan State loyalists. Recall that Ara had also made "the boldest move any coach could make," going for it on fourth down with the game on the line. The irony is that he has never been properly credited for this. To the contrary, the second wave of media coverage starting on the Monday after the game was highly critical of Ara, unfairly so, and borderline vitriolic to a large extent.

The pinnacle of negativity was achieved in the *Sports Illustrated* cover story on November 28. The prosaic cover photograph of tangled players in the final play of the game had been taken by an emerging young photographer, Neil Leifer. The heading was, "Notre Dame Runs Out the Clock Against Michigan State." The bold banner insert in orange read: "Furor over No. 1." The accompanying article was formatted next to a full-page color photograph of Jim Lynch landing precariously on his head in one of the major turning points of the game. The trite title, "An Upside-Down Game," was designed to complement this amazing photo. Reporter Dan Jenkins opened his piece with the following: "College football awaited an epic that was supposed to decide the national championship. But it all fell apart when Michigan State faltered after a fast start, and Notre Dame took the easy way out. Old Notre

Dame will tie over all. Sing it out, guys. That is not exactly what the march says, of course, but that is how the big game ends every time you replay it. And that is how millions of cranky college football fans will remember it."[6]

With this singular article, the news cycle for the 1966 Notre Dame–Michigan State game extended from one week to . . . well, forever. The writer deserves no literary credit for this. The article may have been a stylistic success, creating controversy and selling magazines. But it was equally a factual fantasy that didn't match up with the action that millions of people had witnessed for themselves.

The Notre Dame players and coaches had no idea how their season would ultimately conclude as they began practice for the upcoming game against USC. The polls had been announced on Tuesday morning. Associated Press writers ranked Notre Dame No. 1. But UPI coaches had Michigan State at No. 1, probably a tip of the cap to Duffy by his fellow coaches. Most of the evaluators hadn't witnessed a single play from the game. There was no video tape of the game to be distributed. This support for MSU was unexpected. The Irish had many reasons to be concerned when they looked at the depth chart Monday afternoon, especially after the loss of so many key players. With a short week of practices and a cross-country trip ahead of them, the task at hand was daunting.

GAME SIX, NOVEMBER 26, 1966
Notre Dame at the University of Southern California
(Los Angeles Coliseum), Won 51-0

Ara Parseghian had two years to prepare for walking onto the turf again at the Los Angeles Coliseum. The memories of 1964 had to come flooding back. The coach was returning with another No. 1–ranked Notre Dame team, and this group of guys was probably even more talented than the team that came within 1 minute, 33 seconds of winning the national championship. Parseghian thought he was robbed by inept (perhaps biased) officiating in 1964, a claim supported by the filmed visual evidence. So, the coach prepared his team for every possible contingency, except one. He knew he couldn't predict how the refs would call the game.

A total of 88,520 people would sit in typical sunny southern California weather to watch the matchup, including almost all of the 18,623 USC student body (three times the size of Notre Dame's enrollment at the time). It would be the largest crowd to watch a football game that year, college or professional. For Notre Dame, would it be another upset by the Trojans or a national championship and football immortality? Either way, history would be made that afternoon. If you weren't in attendance, the radio was the only way to keep track of the game action. There was no over-the-air television, as ABC had already worn out its welcome at the NCAA when it came to airing Notre Dame games. Southern Cal had been on a national telecast the week before, so they were at their limit as well.

As Ara looked across the field during warm-ups, he might have spotted Craig Fertig, the former player who joined USC Head Coach John McKay as an assistant in February 1965, one week after graduation. It was then USC quarterback Fertig who threw to Rod Sherman on November 28, 1964, to beat the Irish 20–17. Ara would also have noticed Traveler, or as he referred to it, "that damned white horse," who was mounted by a half-naked, middle-aged man in a costume pretending to be a Trojan and who cantered up and down the sidelines every time USC scored. Parseghian hated that horse.

Southern California entered the game ranked No. 10. They had just been designated the Pacific Eight Conference representative to the Rose Bowl, a decision that stirred up some controversy from their crosstown rival, UCLA. The Bruins (3–1 in conference) had beaten the Trojans (4–1) the week before with a final score of 14–7, also at the Coliseum. Therefore, USC had motivation to prove their dubious bowl selection to the local media. A win against traditional rival Notre Dame always added incentive. Being able to knock off the No. 1 team in the land completed their motivational trifecta.

Battered and Bruised

After a morning workout on Thursday and then spending Thanksgiving lunch together in the South Dining Hall, the Irish departed South Bend by a United Airlines charter for California, battered and bruised. They would use Friday for a light workout and to acclimate to the time change.

Terry Hanratty was out for the season with a separated shoulder. Coley O'Brien would start his first game at quarterback (and as irony would have it, his last). Doctors were still trying to regulate his diabetes medications and diet to insure his optimal physical performance. Center George Goeddeke was dressing for the game, but still limping and not scheduled to see any game action. Halfback Rocky Bleier was also out for the season, as was his immediate replacement, Bob Gladieux. Gladieux made the trip on crutches. Bleier was back in South Bend in a hospital room. Rocky's roommate, second unit defensive back Dan Harshman, was getting his first start at offensive halfback. He had been converted to this position at Monday's practice and had spent the four intervening days learning the offensive playbook.

At the other halfback position, Nick Eddy was still nursing a sore shoulder, but he expected to see action. He was determined to play in his last Notre Dame football game, and he wanted to score at least once more in front of his California family and friends (he had scored in the Cal game in 1965 that had been played in Berkeley). Jim Seymour had been diagnosed with mononucleosis the Monday before the game and wasn't at one hundred percent strength, but felt good enough to play. The weakest team Notre Dame had suited up all season was being called upon to win the now-biggest game of the season for the national title, and everyone believed they could and would do it. All they had to do was look into Ara's eyes. He would find a way to lead them to victory. The banner draped over the back of the Notre Dame bench said it all: "To hell with UPI, we're No. 1."

Digging Deep

By now you know how it ended.

Notre Dame 51   Southern California 0

Not much needed to be said for motivation in the locker room at halftime. On the blackboard were the words: "We relaxed in 1964," which referenced when the Irish finished the first half ahead 17–0 and didn't score at all in the second half. In this 1966 game, the twenty additional points scored by the Irish in the second half weren't a matter of running up the score, as some later accused. The effort was a long overdue tribute to the head coach, proving that the team wouldn't let up and providing an insurance policy for the game's outcome.

On the first drive of the second half, Coley O'Brien found the newly converted halfback Dan Harshman with a 23-yard scoring pass. When Notre Dame got the ball back the next time, Nick Eddy fulfilled his dream, scoring his last touchdown for Notre Dame in California for his family to see, especially his mother.

A singular moment of sportsmanship had nearly been forgotten over the years, until George Goeddeke recalled it years later. Very late in the game, the injured center was inserted at tight end, just so he would have a memory of playing his last game at such a momentous time. Noticing that the hobbling Goeddeke was going in, USC Head Coach John McKay gestured from across the field to his defensive team not to hit him. It was a classy move by a legendary coach. Goeddeke was unaware of the gesture until after the game. If only he had known. This is the same guy who was called upon to play two weeks after an appendectomy in the final game of the 1965 season against Miami. The irrepressible center chased his would-be blocker across the line of scrimmage trying (unsuccessfully) to make a block and reinjured his swollen ankle in the process. Let the record show, though, that George played in his final college game.

At the end of the game the team carried a triumphant Ara Parseghian off the field on their shoulders. A UPI telephoto captured the moment and the image appeared on sports pages across the nation on Sunday morning.

Locker Room Moods

The highly quotable Coach John McKay is often cited as saying to his team after this game, "Go take your showers, those of you that need them." While that's the legend and it always gets a chuckle, nobody steps forward to confirm it. Making jokes after the defeat didn't really fit the situation or the character of the coach. The story is mentioned here because you'll likely read it elsewhere and may want to know the truth.

The truth is that a deeply disappointed Coach McKay had a good coach's sense of the moment in the press conference after the game. "I guess I've never seen a better team than Notre Dame was today." He went further, "Let me tell you one thing about Notre Dame — that the coaching is tremendous. If we played them a hundred times, we'd have trouble winning one or two." Eleven months later Southern Cal beat Notre Dame 24–7 in South Bend.

The mood in the visitors' locker room was obviously joyous and reinforced by an undercurrent of nervous relief. An emotional Ara Parseghian addressed his team, "Thank you. Thank you for today's victory, for the whole season, and for the past three years. And thank you especially for *this*." "This" was the game ball, which thereafter resided prominently in Parseghian's home office.

In front of the press, Coach Parseghian waxed, "This is by far the best football team I've ever coached. Not only that, but it is also the best-balanced college football team, offensively and defensively, I've ever seen in my life. They just gave me the ball and tossed me in the shower. I enjoyed it."

Also sensing the historical nature of the coaching moment Ara went further, "I want to pay tribute to the team for the determination it displayed, I want to pay tribute to our little 165-pound quarterback [Coley O'Brien] and I want to pay tribute to our medical team that got him ready." This comment exposed the silent fear Ara had coming out of East Lansing. His backup quarterback faced medical challenges, and the fortunes of his team depended on a one hundred percent effort from player number 3, which they got. In fact, O'Brien had played beyond everyone's expectations. The feisty quarterback completed twenty-one of thirty-one passes, for 255 yards and three touchdowns. He had more completions in this game than Terry Hanratty had in any of his previous nine starts, or any other Notre Dame quarterback had ever had in a single game prior.

With antibiotic assistance and still wearing high-top shoes, Jim Seymour had eleven receptions for 150 yards and two scores. In his final game, Larry Conjar carried nineteen times for 62 yards, a 3.26 yards per carry average. Nick Eddy had eleven rushes for fifty-five yards, a 5.0 yards per carry average, and a coveted final touchdown in California, with his mother and other family in the crowd.

Other statistics just further highlighted the separation between the two teams. Notre Dame had 31 first downs; USC had 13. Notre Dame had 82 total plays for 461 yards; USC had 69 plays for 188 yards.

At the time, a secondary story of the game received little attention: the Notre Dame defense registered its sixth shutout, and did so on the road and in front of the largest football crowd of the year (also against the No. 10 team in the nation). The strength of the Notre Dame defense had been underplayed by the media throughout the season, overwhelmed in print by offensive stats that were much easier to tally. But looking back, the team's consistent record of success leaves any spectator impressed. No other defensive team in modern college football history has allowed an average of a mere 2.4 points per game over an entire season. Not one.

Smoldering Aftermath

John Hall of the *Los Angeles Times* captured the aftermath as follows on November 27, 1966: "It was the end of the war. Name a war. Any war. Notre Dame won it. Notre Dame demanded unconditional surrender."

Comments after the game reflected on the contrast between the two teams who were obviously more equally matched than the final score indicated. Notre Dame had emerged a convincing winner by building on USC mistakes that kept compounding. The game was Ara Parseghian's one hundredth win as a college coach, making it doubly memorable. It was also the worst defeat of a Southern California football team in history. And it still is, nearly sixty years later.

Natural Rivals

As such, it would become the perennial bulletin board fodder for every remaining confrontation between Coach Parseghian and Coach McKay.

McKay is often quoted as saying that he'd never let Notre Dame and Ara beat him again — something he persistently denied saying until his death in 2001. In one of his final interviews, he clarified the comment, "I said that Notre Dame would never beat us 51–0 again." What was actually said is immaterial.

Both coaches always started their seasons knowing that winning the ND–USC game would be crucial to their success. Since the intersectional rivalry began in 1926, this had often been the case. During the Parseghian–McKay years the national championship in college football was determined as a direct or indirect consequence of this rivalry. But McKay's alleged vow developed some traction because none of Ara's teams beat the Trojans again until 1973 — the next time the Irish were named national champions. After 1966, John McKay's record against the Irish was 6–1–2. McKay left college coaching in 1976 to become the head coach of the expansion team Tampa Bay Buccaneers in the NFL, but he eventually returned to USC after his death; Coach McKay's ashes were spread over the turf at the Los Angeles Coliseum.

As mentioned above, the Trojans traveled to South Bend in 1967 and beat the Irish 24–7. For that game, McKay and the team brought reinforcements: their marching band (the USC Band has performed at every game against Notre Dame, home and away, since 1966) and a junior college transfer at tailback with unstoppable moves and speed. He had a career day — 160 yards on thirty-eight carries and all three USC touchdowns. The kid with a Hollywood smile would go on to win the Heisman Trophy in 1968. With O. J. Simpson, Southern California would be crowned national champions.

Notre Dame extracted some revenge in 1968 by securing a 21–21 tie with the No. 1–ranked Trojans in Los Angeles. The Irish defense held Simpson to fifty-five yards, his lowest output for the season. That game was the first to capture a larger television audience than the 1966 Notre Dame–Michigan State contest. And that tie so late in the season contributed to the final rankings. When Ohio State beat USC in the Rose Bowl, the Buckeyes were named standalone national champions. One could argue that the Irish debt to Woody Hayes and the Buckeyes for slowing down Michigan State in 1966 was repaid.

Scattered Celebrations

While his team celebrated in California, Rocky Bleier remained confined to a hospital room in South Bend, where he was still recovering from his lacerated kidney. I share below Bleier's recollection of the ND–SC game, which has never been told publicly.

> I listened to the game on the radio in my hospital room. That was the only way to get the immediate play-by-play. The game wasn't on TV, at least not in a way that I could see it from the hospital. I remember how great it was to score all those points in the first half. And when the team scored some more after halftime, I started to relax a bit — knowing that we were going to win. When the game ended, I was still all alone. After a few minutes a couple guys I knew from South Bend came to visit me. They had been listening to the game in a lounge somewhere. They had been playing a game where each would have a shot and a beer every time Notre Dame scored a touchdown. By the time they got to my room they were feeling no pain. That's when my celebration really began.

A good portion of the team (including most of those not of legal drinking age) went to a party held at the Los Angeles home of tight end Don Gmitter's friend from Notre Dame, Doug Simon, whose father was a local judge. Hollywood joined the mix at that party. Actor-singer-comedian Jimmy Durante showed up and entertained the boisterous group from the piano. Then he posed for pictures. Participants in one particular photo would love a copy of it today. Terry Hanratty, Frank Criniti, and Ron Jeziorski, all guys with distinctive noses, posed side by side in profile with the "Schnozzola" himself. Actor Scott Brady, who was a familiar character in many B-grade westerns, was also at the party. A year earlier he had passed on the opportunity to be in the initial cast of a low-budget TV show about space travel called *Star Trek*. Assistant Coach Brian Boulac remembers being at this party, probably the only official coach to attend. The players thought of him more as a friend.

By comparison, quarterback Coley O'Brien spent a rather subdued evening having dinner with his dad (a Navy admiral who had flown in to see the game) and extended family members. O'Brien remarked to me, "You know, we still didn't really know what the polls would do after that game. But we knew we had done all we could do."

Ara took the coaching staff out to dinner and made an early evening of it. He didn't want to horn in on the celebrations of his players. Moreover, because he conceded that the no-alcohol team rule was unenforceable and suspected it was being violated, he really didn't want to know where the players were.

Three players had no time to celebrate with the team at all. Together they departed immediately for the Los Angeles airport after the game. Jim Lynch, Tom Regner, and Nick Eddy were already scheduled on a Saturday evening flight to New York for a guest appearance on the Sunday evening *Ed Sullivan Show* with other members of the Associated Press Kodak All-American Team. There, they spent time with Michigan State All-Americans Clinton Jones, George Webster, and Bubba Smith. Eddy, who had been able to bring his wife, Tiny, with him, remembers, "Those were good guys, and we had a lot of respect for each other. We got along well and we all had a good time in New York City." This was only eight days after the game of the century!

Homecoming

On the Monday after the game, the full United Airlines chartered flight from Los Angeles to South Bend was diverted to Chicago's Midway Airport due to a snowstorm. Notre Dame students returning from the four-day Thanksgiving break confronted the same travel difficulties getting to campus for their first day of classes. The team loaded onto chartered buses, which carefully made their way across the Indiana Toll Road and eventually turned up Notre Dame Avenue at about 6:00 p.m. It was dark and there were no crowds lining the slick avenue amid the gusting wind and blowing snow. The team thought that the campus might still be deserted because of the storm, but then the buses pulled up right next to the Old Fieldhouse. The place was filled to bursting. The 1966 Notre Dame football team was finally home, undefeated.

Behind the scenes, sports editor Joe Doyle had been pressing his contacts at the Associated Press for an early release of the final football rankings, which were normally released late Monday evening for print on Tuesday mornings. He finally got word by telephone. The Notre Dame family reunion in the Fieldhouse heard the official announcement: "No. 1, Notre Dame." United Press International agreed. Undisputed national champions.

CHAPTER 15

FANS AND NUTS

Taken from the file cabinet portion of Ara's office desk was a bulging file marked in his own distinctive handwriting: "Fans and Nuts." Other multidrawer file cabinets in the Parseghian basement were similarly marked, chock full of paper that hasn't seen the light of day in many years. These files contain the letters mailed to Ara during his coaching tenure at Notre Dame. It wouldn't be an exaggeration to speculate that the total of this mail may exceed ten thousand pieces. That would only be a rate of about one thousand per year, or less than one hundred per month.

Buried in these vaults there is said to be a letter from an aspiring basketball coach circa 1965, Richard "Digger" Phelps. He would have been about twenty-four years old at the time he sent this letter. In it he claims to explain his aspiration to become like Ara as the future head coach of the Notre Dame basketball team. Although it did not happen in time for inclusion in this volume, Digger Phelps's letter may eventually be uncovered.

Each of Ara's transitions from head coach at Miami to Northwestern to Notre Dame came with new tasks and increased responsibilities. There would have been no way for an outsider to anticipate the extraordinary volume of mail coming to the Football Office at Notre Dame. Ignoring the mail altogether would have held unique perils for the new coach who was assigned to rebuild the spirit of the place along with the football team. He instinctively knew that coaching and communication with fans went hand in hand. But occasionally it took poise and self-control to submit to the unrelenting flow of correspondence.

It may surprise some readers to learn that Ara read almost all of the letters addressed to him. It would not surprise those who really knew him that he devised a system for answering the steady stream of missives. The centerpiece of this well-oiled process was his able administrative assistant, Football Office Manager Barbara Nicholas. She previewed each letter and coded it with a letter grade, ranging from A to G. The codes corresponded to predetermined answers relating to the subject matter of the letter. After submitting letters for the coach's perusal, Barb would type a standard answer and have it ready for Ara's signature. The coach would override the code on occasion and make notes for his assistant to incorporate.

There was one additional category that Ara reserved for his own designation, those he personally marked "nuts." One such letter is addressed to "Dear Chicken Liver." Letters in this category didn't receive a response since Ara believed none was deserved. Occasionally mixed into the pile were copies of letters sent to Father Hesburgh or the Development Office that required delicate treatment, but those were few.

A reader of hundreds of these letters — and there were thousands — soon picks up on the repeated themes.

For example, letters written on lined paper in large, careful printing, with simple sentences and dubious spelling, were deemed to be from children. (Those children would now be nearing retirement age.) These all received autographed photos in response, perhaps with a note attached to them. Ara kept the originals. One young admirer told "Mr. Parsigian" [sic] that "I like football and Notre Dame very much and hope you have a good year" and requested a signed picture of the team. Today, if a child's letter like this was paired with the personalized, autographed answer and then put into a frame, it would be a valued collectible.

There was a flurry of correspondence activity in 1964 and 1965. Almost without exception these are positive and complimentary.

A preponderance is written by Notre Dame alumni excited by the new spirit of success that Ara had engendered in the Notre Dame team and by extension, the broader Notre Dame family. A member of the 1917 graduating class wrote Ara thanking him for "the endless thrilling Saturday afternoons you have given me." Some of the most touching notes are written by nuns from various Catholic schools across the nation. They are fairly easy to authenticate with the "JMJ" (for Jesus, Mary, and Joseph) invariably included in the heading. One Sister congratulated the team on performing well despite a tough schedule and offered this blessing: "May God bless you and your labors and keep you at Notre Dame for many happy years to come." These are treasures because of the practiced handwriting produced using the Palmer Method, making them distinctive and near works of art.

A second spike of letter writing occurred during and after the 1971 football season. After a very good season in 1970, including a Cotton Bowl win and rankings of 2 and 5 (AP and UPI, respectively), expectations were high for the following year. But the most important offensive cog in that wheel, quarterback Joe Theismann, had graduated. The offense suffered without his level of talent and maturity. Some of the disappointment about the season unfairly targeted one of Theismann's replacements in 1971, Cliff Brown, who was Notre Dame's first Black quarterback. Reading those notes is embarrassing even fifty years later, especially since the team finished 8–2–0 and ranked 13 (AP) and 15 (UPI). Many of the Notre Dame coaches after Ara would have prayed for a season like this, especially since a couple of them may have retained their jobs with such a record.

Missives from fans and "nuts" were occasionally indistinguishable at first. The letters sometimes started with a sentence or paragraph intended to establish credentials. "I've been a fan since [pick any date since Noah's Ark], and I've never written to a Notre Dame coach before." Then came the praise, the advice, or the vitriol.

The nice letters were signed by the author and included return addresses. Some recalled fond memories: "My wife and I saw you beat Ohio State last year and we were yelling our heads off for Northwestern because you were the coach." Some offered sympathy for disappointing outcomes: "Even though being a Trojan, I was pulling for you to complete a perfect season. One injustice administered was the delayed call of the umpire." Other writers aspired to serve as assistant coaches. One amusing letter begins with the line, "First, let me admit that I know very little about the intricacies of football; I am only a dilettante," which is the followed by four paragraphs of detailed advice. Another fan's suggestion was "when the weather is wet or cold, spray deodorant in the players hands." Ara responded to this quirky letter with a personal note and said he might try it.

There is a pattern of the negative notes being postmarked from the towns with customary traditional rivals or jealous teams not on the ND schedule. One such letter asks, "Why did you have to cheat to keep Michigan State from scoring? I realize Notre Dame has nothing going for it but football — being a mediocre academic institution." Maybe the East Lansing postmark is just coincidental?

After they retired from coaching, Ara and his former assistant coach Tom Pagna concocted a plan to write a book for publication using the letters collected over the years. Unfortunately, this never materialized. There was just too much material to choose from. Simply transcribing each of the letters into bookworthy text would have been challenging.

Among the letters Ara saved in a special file were those from Father Hesburgh and Father Joyce. These are all highly personal notes regarding a holiday, a birthday, or general thanks for accepting the head coaching position at Notre Dame and representing the university in a positive way.

Enduring constant scrutiny, criticism, and praise delivered almost daily by the United States Post Office was a part of the head coach's job at Notre Dame. It is difficult to read a representative sample of the letters and not be impressed by the deeply personal feelings each communicated. During his tenure at Notre Dame, Ara embraced both the good and bad aspects of becoming a celebrity with thoughtfulness, humility, and an even temper. He was arguably the most prominent coach in college athletics and knew well the constituencies (fans of all ages, alumni, administrators, detractors, and admirers) who carefully watched his every move. Engaging these constituencies was a part of the job, and over eleven seasons, Ara never fumbled.

CHAPTER 16

HOME AND AWAY

The Parseghian household was managed much like a successful family business with clear responsibilities and decision powers. One of the hidden secrets of Ara's career success was the capability of Katie to see things clearly and get things done in the background without fanfare. They were in harmony on financial matters. As children of the Depression, they were thrifty and maintained a modest lifestyle throughout their married life. Ara was quick to acknowledge, when it came to matters at home, Katie was the head coach.

Against the background of what major colleges coaches can command as salaries now (into multiple millions of dollars annually), it is important to be reminded that it wasn't always that way. Ara's Notre Dame salary in his first year (1964) was $20,000, and his final salary (1974) was $35,000. This was on the lean side even when compared to other top college football powers at the time. The salaries for coaches at Notre Dame were theoretically pegged against faculty and administrator compensation standards and thus weren't allowed to balloon beyond reason. Winning was the most important internal metric for job security. To offset this acknowledged system of internal checks and balances, many college coaches, including Ara, were allowed and even encouraged to seek additional income in other venues, so long as they were performing their primary duties in line with NCAA guidelines.

When room, board, and tuition at Notre Dame was approximately $2,400 (the cost of a new Chevrolet) in 1964, the head football coach's salary indexed at 8.4 times that amount. If the same factor were applied today, wherein the average all-in cost to be a student at Notre Dame exceeds $72,000, the head football coaching position would be valued at around $600,000.

The jump from Northwestern to Notre Dame provided Ara with a much more lucrative platform to increase his compensation from side hustles. After leading the Irish in a surprising turnaround in 1964 and landing a *Time* magazine cover story, his outside earning opportunities expanded exponentially. A handsome guy, well spoken, and oozing with sincerity, Ara Parseghian became an overnight celebrity. Ara was forced to become the manager of his outside business affairs in addition to his coaching responsibilities and his growing family commitments. Juggling these priorities continued for the remainder of his coaching career. Eventually he had assistance, but he never had an official agent.

The list of engagements included many speaking events (with honoraria), participation in coaching clinics (for fees), part-time television commentary positions (local and national), honorary coaching fees for college all-star games, and product endorsements. The most lucrative of the multiyear commercial associations was with the Ford Motor Company. Ara appeared in national television spots (one time with Katie), in print advertisements, and as the spokesperson in the early years for Ford's "Punt, Pass and Kick" youth initiative. As part of that contract, the Parseghian family received new cars every year (Ara drove a Thunderbird and Katie a station wagon), and eventually Ara negotiated sweetheart deals for his assistant coaches.

Along with his outside work for compensation, Ara maintained a schedule of charitable commitments for the University of Notre Dame, the Multiple Sclerosis Foundation, and other worthy causes that requested his appearance to speak or play at charity golf tournaments.

One only has to look at the detailed calendar cards Ara kept every year to conclude that he was extraordinarily busy for most of the year — not just during football season. The amount of travel required was significant. This only was possible with the understanding of his immediate family and the able management of Katie Parseghian on the home front.

Katie essentially orchestrated the family's eventual move from Wilmette, Illinois, to South Bend, Indiana. The family's new home was designed and hastily built in South Bend to be ready before the 1964 football season. Ara's new job was all-consuming from his first day in January 1964. Katie and the children continued to live in Wilmette to finish the school year; Ara started his assignment in South Bend and returned home on weekends. Near the end of the school year, Katie wanted the children to become part of a smooth transition and took them on a weeklong visit to their new city to explore and learn about their new public schools. Karan would be a freshman at Adams High School. Kriss and Mike would attend Jefferson Elementary School. The family stayed at the Pick-Oliver Hotel downtown (since demolished). Upon returning to Wilmette, Karan was informed that she could not march with her class in her upcoming eighth grade graduation due to this absence. This was an unfortunate slight that her protective mother never forgot or forgave.

When the Parseghians owned homes in Oxford and Wilmette, the home football weekends meant housing and entertaining family. Ara's parents, his brother, Jerry, and Jerry's family were regulars. The increased job responsibilities at Notre Dame complicated matters, but that particular family tradition of gathering continued. In addition, Ara and Katie were also encouraged to entertain local friends, assistant coaches, and key university invitees at their home after a game. The reason for this was quite practical. South Bend only had a handful of decent restaurants, and they were packed to overflowing on game weekends. Entertaining at the head coach's home was far more efficient. Celebrations after a home win contrasted with the atmosphere after a loss, when the invited guests were polite enough to keep the event subdued and lighthearted. As Katie joked, though, "That didn't happen very often." Celebrations were the statistical rule. In Ara's eleven-season career at Notre Dame, there were fifty home wins, one tie, and only six losses.

The rhythm of the Parseghian household in that period was captured in a feature story by Mary Lou McGue that appeared in *Our Sunday Visitor* on October 8, 1967, titled "Mrs. Ara Parseghian, First Lady of Football Graces Grid Madness."

Huddled in an old blanket in the stands at South Bend's School Field last Friday evening sat a lovely dark-haired woman with a battered umbrella to protect her from the rain. Only a few recognized her in her dark glasses, worn not for anonymity but because others were broken and she needed the prescribed lenses to watch the action on the field. The eldest of her three children, 17-year-old Karan, had been chosen by the student body at John Adams High School to represent them as one of the attendants to the Queen for their school's homecoming festivities that evening.

Breathes there the wife of a true football fan who has not tasted a frustrating sample of what life must be like in the Parseghian household? For the dedicated spectator it lasts from early August through the ultimate playoffs, which many women will claim coincides with the first appearance of flowers in the spring.

Throughout this pigskin-dotted land of ours, women watch helplessly as the males in their lives enter a trance that reaches an apex around the first of October and lasts through the New Year's Holidays. Something like withdrawal symptoms begin to appear during the first months of each year and recovery is nearly complete in time to put up the window screens for hot weather. Among these addicted is a special breed whose fans name is legion — Notre Dame Fans.

Just as the Parseghians have in such a brief time become an important part of the Notre Dame football legend, their house appears to have always been there. Blending perfectly with other older homes in the block, after enthusiastic greetings from a black poodle named Bridget and another puppy of uncertain ancestry known as JB, Mrs. Parseghian explained that the house was completed for them in a record nine weeks.

When her engagement was announced, the name Parseghian caused the same difficulties with pronunciation there that it did on large scale when achieving national prominence. With a twinkle, she recalls that a clerk in one of the local stores congratulated her and asked, in all seriousness, "Will you be living in this country?"

Mrs. Parseghian enjoys cooking and has become adept at preparing many Armenian specialties but says, "Life is so helter-skelter here so much of the year that there are few opportunities to really prepare a husband-type sit down dinner."

Mrs. Parseghian does not accompany her husband on most of the trips he makes because her duties as mother come first. Neither do she and the children attend games played away from Notre Dame, preferring to watch or, as last Saturday, listen to the play-by-play on radio, free to give vent to their emotions in their own family room. One reason is that she wants to be on hand to meet her husband and the team when they return to campus.

After each home game she is hostess to a varying circle of friends invited to an open house. She enjoys entertaining and the party provides sort of an unwinding buffer. Guests are encouraged to bring along their own out-of-town guests, so the number can range anywhere from five to forty, as it did after the first game against California. One of the guests who came along that day was TV's Merv Griffin.

Mrs. Parseghian speaks matter-of-factly about her solo duties as a parent for much of the year. There is acceptance that his work requires almost total submersion during the football season. They all know that he would have liked to have been at School Field for the important event in Karan's life last Friday night. But there was no question in any of their minds that he could be anywhere but at Purdue Memorial Union in West Lafayette with his squad.

Somehow Katie has achieved a remarkable self-sufficiency with no obvious self-pity, at the same time remaining completely feminine. Her own personality is part of the key to her equilibrium — knowing what must be done and doing it with love. Her creative instincts enable her to spend time alone to good advantage.

This year she is serving as treasurer for the Ladies of Notre Dame, an organization of faculty wives.[1]

The burdens of being the cheerful innkeeper, party planner, and hostess all fell on Katie's shoulders. She handled it beautifully. Returning from the stadium after home games, Ara mingled with the crowd, as was expected. On rare occasions, with a small group of very close friends, Ara would try his hand at playing the piano, 1940's and '50s standards — something he picked up on his own after watching his sister take lessons as a child. This was a cherished memory by those in attendance because it was so rare and completely unexpected.

Away games offered a welcomed respite for the family. The university rule at the time was that spouses were not invited as part of the traveling party using chartered aircraft. So, Katie and the children had their own rituals to cheer on the team at home. They would gather around the radio in the family room and listen to the game via the Mutual Broadcast Network. (Notre Dame's later TV appearances were almost always home games.) If the team won, Katie made bowls of popcorn and the four of them celebrated in private. There was lots of popcorn over the years.

The division of household tasks was very well-established — Katie was in charge of everything. Ara freely acknowledged this, and the division continued throughout his lifetime. Ara wasn't particularly handy around the house nor was he especially mechanically inclined. The only tools he was truly comfortable with were his golf clubs. Katie expressed no resentment when Ara needed to relax or blow off steam on the golf course. The small-town Ohio girl was resourceful and comfortable around household maintenance and mechanical issues, so she took over.

For the children, integrating into a new school routine wasn't difficult. In Wilmette, what their dad did for a living was no big deal. New classmates in South Bend were still clueless as to what it actually meant to have the head football coach as a dad, and they treated the newcomers with relative normalcy. That would change over the years as the Parseghian children matured and their classmates became aware of Ara as a national figure. In the spring of 1964, the larger South Bend community was in a crisis of malaise and worried about more serious issues than who would coach the Irish. Notre Dame football hadn't been an uplifting factor for a number of years. More importantly, the auto maker Studebaker had ceased manufacturing operations in South Bend in 1963, leaving massive unemployment and economic uncertainty in its wake.

Ara thoughtfully made some significant concessions to family life to strengthen family harmony. For example, he did not travel to recruit high school players as a matter of personal policy. He left that task to his assistant coaches. This meant he could spend more time at home in the offseason. Over eleven years there were hundreds of potential recruits. (Notre Dame followed Big Ten guidelines and limited scholarships to 120 total, or an average of 30 per year — more than today's NCAA limit of 85 total). Coordinator Brian Boulac could only recall two occasions when Ara made a home visit to a potential recruit, and neither was successful. Ara saw his role as the "closer" once an interested young man and his family visited campus. Notre Dame's picturesque campus and strong educational reputation could almost sell itself to the right recruit. This classic auto sales technique — to hold off on finalizing a deal until the manager (coach) was consulted — may have been carried over from Ara's summer experience as a car salesman. Among the players I interviewed who said yes to Ara's personal invitation to join the team, each can recall specific details of their one-on-one meeting with the coach — citing it as the turning point in their decision making. Ara was an effective closer.

Starting in his years at Northwestern, Ara became an attractive option on the coaching staffs for postseason all-star games. Reliably, Northwestern's season ended without a bowl invitation. For the Parseghian family, the all-star coaching invitation meant the expectation of a true holiday (Christmas through New Year's) vacation away from cold northern climates: locations such as Miami, San Francisco, and Hawaii provided welcomed relief from gray midwestern winters and quality family time with minimal stress. After 1969, Notre Dame entertained bowl bids regularly and the destination vacation pattern continued, but with added stresses for the coach and less family time.

Each summer there was a planned vacation to a resort on Lake Michigan at Portage Point Inn. There, Ara and brother Jerry's families joined forces. The laid-back resort boasted a nice beach, communal family dining, and plenty to do. This was a highly anticipated outing, especially for the cousins. It may have been the one time every year when Ara was the most relaxed, spending time with close family and removed from the demands of his otherwise grueling personal schedule.

When Ara was at home and out of football mode, he was an engaged father. Daughter Kriss tells the story of when she once babysat for Jim and Mary Hesburgh (Father Hesburgh's brother and sister-in-law), who lived directly across the street from the Parseghians. Alone with the children, she heard noises outside the Hesburghs' house. She called her dad, who was wearing his pajamas and bathrobe and eating ice cream, asking for help. Ice cream still in hand, he walked right over and found nothing out of the ordinary. He instructed Kriss to go home to bed. When the Hesburghs returned home, they found Ara in his robe waiting for them instead.

Looking back, Katie wondered how they made it all work — all the expectations and moving pieces. But they did.

CHAPTER 17

TUG OF WAR

Historians mark November 1, 1955, as the beginning of the conflict now referred to as the Vietnam War, which ended on April 30, 1975. Ara's final season coaching at Miami University was 1955. Therefore, this conflict encompassed the entirety of his combined nineteen-year coaching career at Northwestern and Notre Dame. The significance of the war spilled over into every aspect of American life, including college football. The repercussions have lasted a long, long time, and the subject deserves special attention.

It would be fair to state that the Vietnam War had little direct effect on life in America until 1963. That year, the Kennedy Administration sent a small group of military advisors to the independent Southeast Asian country struggling with democracy. As Ara was finishing his eighth season at Northwestern, the general populace, the student body in Evanston, and his football team had no clue what was about to confront them. The shocking assassination of John F. Kennedy on November 22, 1963, consumed the attention of the American people and effectively ended a period of wishful national optimism known as "Camelot."

The arrival of Ara Parseghian on the Notre Dame campus in January 1964 coincided with the new Lyndon Johnson Administration sending approximately 23,000 US military "advisors" into Vietnam. That number escalated to over 184,000 by the end of the year. The Fighting Irish were in the process of completing their most successful football season since Leahy's last in 1953. It was good enough to earn national championship accolades from the National Football Foundation and Hall of Fame. The campus spirit in South Bend couldn't have been higher. Head Coach Ara Parseghian was featured on the cover of *Time* magazine. But for many of the all-male graduates in May of 1965, the reality of the Vietnam War loomed large.

In the 1940–1965 timeframe, Notre Dame was often referred to as the "Catholic West Point." A measure of this designation was assigned because of the commitment which had been made to Reserve Officer Training Corps (ROTC). Notre Dame was one of a small number of national universities that hosted all three branches of military ROTC, the Army, Air Force, and Navy (Marines included). Entering freshmen had an option to select two semesters of required classes in physical education or to take a year of military science in the ROTC. In fact, Rockne Memorial (where the Football Office was located) and the ROTC Building were directly across the street from each other. Every year the entering class was roughly divided equally between the two options. The military option had the lure of scholarships, which enticed tuition-challenged students to participate. The upshot was that after freshman year many continued with the military programs and Notre Dame graduated hundreds of freshly minted officers with regularity. In 1965, and thereafter, the pattern continued for another few years — until the effects of the Vietnam War became manifest. Today, Notre Dame still maintains a strong and dedicated ROTC presence in all three service branches, but not nearly so pervasive in raw numbers as it once was.

What Ara thought of the Vietnam War in 1964, 1965, and 1966 — contemporaneously — can only be speculated about. Sixty years later, practically nobody remembers, or admits to, being in favor of the war. The military participants who endured the war have lived an isolated life without the same public recognition bestowed on them as on previous generations of veterans. But at the time, national sentiment initially favored sending American troops halfway around the world to fight a Communist enemy in jungles and rice paddies (a home field advantage for the enemy). Favorable views didn't cut across political party lines in the early days. Democrats were in power. As a staunch Democrat, Ara probably went with the party's position. And along with the consciousness of the entire country, his mind probably did an about-face as months stretched into years and years of conflict.

During the 1960s, national network news (CBS, NBC, ABC) aired as a once-a-day program that lasted exactly fifteen minutes, including commercial breaks. The faces of people fighting in the war didn't get much airtime. Newspapers and magazines were the dominant media and this undoubtedly protracted the gradual change of opinion in the country. The casualties mounted overseas, and these eventually touched all corners of the nation.

Historians identify the Tet 69 Offensive, which started on February 23, 1969, as the turning point against citizen support for the war in the US. The year1969 was marked by increased domestic unrest. More American troops were sent overseas, and more casualties returned home. At the peak, over five hundred thousand military personnel were engaged. Young men attending college were initially shielded from participation in the conflict through student deferments. In an attempt at fairness in selecting recruits for military service, a lottery system was instituted for all eligible males born before 1951. If you were a male in college on December 1, 1969, you likely still remember where you were for the national radio broadcast of draft lottery numbers tied to your birthday. Male college students were now in the crosshairs to be called and serve in the increasingly unpopular Vietnam War. Protests spilled over to a preponderance of college campuses where, for all practical purposes, classes were suspended in the final weeks of the 1970 spring semester.

Tucked into Ara's private files and recently uncovered is a poignant story from a letter sent to Professor Charles Rice by a Marine veteran who served in Vietnam in 1968.

Dear Professor Rice:

The greatest football team that ever played for Notre Dame never attended a class on campus and never played a game in South Bend.

The letter explains in detail that the author served during the Tet Offensive under severe and often dangerous conditions. To occupy themselves during the rainy season, the Marines would go out and play tackle football on the muddy road that ran down the middle of their unit. Someone came up with the idea of contacting college teams in search of equipment and uniforms they could use in their games. The letter continues:

> It seemed a brilliant idea at first, but pretty soon enthusiasm faded. We received a letter from USC, which included an order catalog to be filled out to get items from the USC Student Store. We were privates making $100 a month, and naturally could not afford the store prices. . . .
>
> The rain was really bad that day, as I looked outside what we called our "hooches" and saw an army truck outside with a tarpaulin on top, in front of our hooch. Inside the truck were boxes from a guy named "Ara," mailed from South Bend, Indiana. The effect on a combat marine of opening up a box from back home and finding a gold helmet is incomprehensible. We were given jerseys, helmets, as well as gifts and letters from the Notre Dame Student Body. . . .
>
> Our little team had 5 players, and I was the only one to come back from Vietnam alive, and even at that, I was wounded 5 times in combat.

The Vietnam War touched or altered the lives of the entire all-male student body at Notre Dame. The football team was no exception. These are Ara's handwritten notes found on a yellow legal pad about the changing times and how to address his football team (with minor edits for clarity):

> Interesting times
> Demonstration dissent, plus political / race / economic / religion reasons and opinion
> Update you on yesterday — 9 squad meetings Wednesday participated in March (10)
> expression we want to do something about — latest decision, camaraderie — we want to make sacrifices
> Some logic is needed, I've attempted to apply logic to the problem
> You are all intelligent educated

Am I OK?

our governmental marching is based on checks and balances

lately the paper is just full of articles criticizing or supporting the decision officials in Washington are trying to change the policy

your objections should be aimed there

success in any venture is built on several factors — loyalty, teamwork, cooperation, pride, determination, hard work

We are in a position to show that the strength in our program in loyalty, set up example for another to follow

this country is torn with disunity — athletes and specifically football knows that success can only come with loyalty, unity, families and respect

let's apply the logic. First of all, you have accepted a responsibility (class) through late May

you have accepted April 6 to May 9th spring practice and game to follow

under fundamental logic these commitments must be fulfilled before other activities

the student body is as I understand it considering a boycott against the blue and gold game. To hurt and assault your own students, St. Joe Valley Club to improve who?

The strike (sacrifice) To destroy property (illogical) To ram your head into a wall and get another bump is logical?

To assault your own family when an unpopular community decision is made logical.

My appeal is to your common sense which at times is uncommon

Fulfill your commitments!

The profound difference between athletic "heroes" and heroic actions during a war would be made clear to the Notre Dame team and student body through the experience of one of their own.

Robert Patrick "Rocky" Bleier arrived on the Notre Dame campus in the fall of 1964 as a recruited football player from Xavier High School in Appleton, Wisconsin. While he practiced with the 1964 team, Rocky saw the actual games from the grandstand since freshmen were not eligible to play. He got his chance in 1965 and performed well in spot appearances as a sophomore in a predominantly running offense. This earned him a starting role as halfback in the 1966 backfield that included Nick Eddy (halfback), Larry Conjar (fullback), and sophomore quarterback Terry Hanratty. Rocky incurred a lacerated kidney injury at Michigan State in the 10–10 tie game. As a result, he listened to the final team victory, 51–0 at the University of Southern California, on the radio from a hospital bed in South Bend. In his 1967 senior season, he was named team captain.

The 1966 National Championship Team only allowed thirty-eight points in a ten-game season. In point of fact, the defensive units (first and second string) only allowed twenty-four points, including six shut-outs. The remaining fourteen points were the result of busted plays where Rocky Bleier played a key role. One came on a muffed pitch-out against Purdue which was recovered and run for a touchdown. The other was against Navy, when a blocked Bleier punt was recovered for a touchdown. Bleier has gone on to become an accomplished motivational speaker. On occasion he will, with humble humor, retell these botched plays, wondering why he never got credit for two additional touchdowns — the ones he helped score for the opposition. When his teammates are in the room, this is done, tongue in cheek, to highlight the incredible record that the 1966 defensive unit racked up.

The Pittsburgh Steelers drafted Rocky in the final round and he made the team in 1968. He played in only ten games before he was called up by the US Army. This was considered an administrative snafu by the Steelers' head office since professional athletes were usually accommodated in some fashion, say in the National Guard, that allowed them to serve and continue playing. Thus, Rocky became one of only a very small handful of professional athletes who actually served in Vietnam.

After boot camp, Bleier was shipped out to Vietnam in May 1969, about one year to the day from his graduation from Notre Dame. He served as squad grenadier (40 mm, M79 grenade launcher) in the 196th Light Infantry Brigade.

On August 20, 1969, while on patrol in Hiep Duc, Rocky's company was ambushed, and he took a rifle bullet in his left thigh. Laying on the ground, an enemy grenade landed nearby, and the shrapnel ripped into his lower right leg and injured his foot. He was evacuated and spent nearly two months facing multiple surgeries and slow recovery in Army hospitals. Released from a hospital in Kansas, he was finally on his way home. But Rocky wanted to take a detour to stop at Notre Dame and spend time with his coach, Ara Parseghian, along with some of the teammates that he had played with only two years earlier. Coincidently, the game against USC was at home on October 18, 1969.

In an email to the author, Bleier wrote the following:

> I was on recuperation leave from the military and wanted to stop by Notre Dame on my way home and say Hi to Ara and the coaching staff.... As busy as Fridays are the day before a home game, with former players and alumni all wanting to say Hi to Ara, it was a mad mess at the Convocation Center. I caught him between meetings and he ushered me quickly into his office where we had a catch-up chat ... but it was Col. Stevens who asked if I would first present the Flag to the Military Honor Guard before the game on Saturday, in which I replied of course I would. Then he hesitated and asked if I would speak at the pep rally that night ... I really didn't want to. I had nothing to say and you know how those rallies where at the Old Fieldhouse, it was about the team and the fans and besides the game was against Southern Cal ... so it was huge ... but he talked me into it ... of course I was right ... the fans where cheering and hollering "We're number one!," "Ara stop the rain," "Beat the Trojans." etc., as players, assistant coaches and then Ara himself spoke. He finally introduced me ... I limped up on one cane and said, "It has been two years since I last stood before you as a former captain and a lot has happened to me in the two years, some good, some bad.... The good is that I met a couple of people just like you that had dreams and aspirations ... the bad is that I had to leave some of them on the battlefields in Vietnam," and I broke down and cried in front of 4,000 fans, the night before the highly ranked USC game. There was a silence, then some polite clapping and the pep rally was over ... I felt badly.... that was no way to leave the fans and the team the night before such a big game.

At halftime the following day, hobbling to the microphone with two canes, Bleier was introduced to the stadium crowd by Father Hesburgh. The sold-out crowd went silent, and there were very few dry eyes in the House that Rockne Built. It was pretty obvious that Rocky might never walk again normally, and playing football again was out of the question. If you were one of the 59,075 in attendance that day, there was now a familiar name and a face attached to the Vietnam War. And he was one of their own — Rocky Bleier.

Rocky's story of personal rehabilitation, recovery, and professional football success is extraordinary. He played ten more seasons with the Steelers on a team that amassed four Super Bowl Championships. He was featured on the cover of *Sports Illustrated* three times. Among Notre Dame football players, only Joe Montana has more covers to his name (ten). (It is an unfortunate irony that neither player is eligible for the College Football Hall of Fame because neither was designated an All-American in college.)

Rocky was awarded a Purple Heart and a Bronze Star. Today, Bleier is recognized prominently at the Pentagon with a plaque in the Corridor of Wounded Warriors.

In 2020, the NCAA recognized Rocky Bleier with the Inspiration Award, "for people who used perseverance, dedication and determination to overcome a life-altering situation and most importantly are role models giving hope and inspiration to others."

The American government removed military personnel from Vietnam in 1973. The Vietnam War officially ended in 1975. The US human toll reads 58,220 dead and over 1,600 missing in action. The South Vietnamese military lost over 200,000 lives. Civilian casualties are estimated at two million. Between one and three million lives were lost by the other side. But the wounds are unending.

A total of 2,709,918 American men and women served in the entire Vietnam Theater of Operations, 9.7 percent of their generation. Unfortunately, an exact count of Notre Dame students who participated in the Vietnam War is undeterminable, as is the ultimate number of fatalities from all causes, direct and indirect.

The United States established diplomatic relations with Vietnam on July 11, 1995. The country has emerged as a viable trading partner and a popular vacation destination. Many American tourists, including Rocky Bleier, have returned for their first visit in over fifty years.

CHAPTER 18

NO JOKE

If Ara Parseghian had a favorite joke he enjoyed telling, it has escaped the memories of those who knew him well. He wasn't a joke-telling kind of guy. But in contrast to the often serious photos of Ara in coaching attire, there is a rich legacy of good humor that he shared with his closest friends and associates. This seeps out in stories told about pranks he pulled and in the self-deprecating humor he shared in his prolific letter writing.

THE SHOT PUT

This practical joke was reported by Tom Pagna with Bob Best in *Era of Ara*:

> We had a shot-putter on our track team (at Miami, OH) named Tom Jones. He could put the shot around 56 feet, and in 1952 the world record was only 60. During our spring practice sessions Ara wanted to have some fun with him. So, he had Paul Shoults, his defensive backfield coach at Miami,

Northwestern and Notre Dame, make a wooden ball the size of a shot and paint it black. On the way to practice Ara and Shoults, who had the counterfeit ball concealed, approached Jones, hard at work on his specialty. "Gosh that looks easy," Ara began. "I bet any guy with some muscle and half a brain could throw that farther than you." Naturally that boiled Jones' competitive blood and he challenged Ara to a match. Jones went first and he threw well over fifty feet. Shoults ran out to measured and in the process switched the shots. He brought the wooden one back. "I've never tried this before so at least you can do is give me a couple of warm up throws," said Ara. Jones agreed, and Ara began fumbling with the shot shifting it around several different ways in his hands. "Is this the right way to hold it?" he asked slyly. His bait was dropped, and he figured it was time for a toss. The first one was totally effortless and went about forty-five feet. Jones was amazed but not yet worried. Shoults came back and the next throw was nearly fifty-five feet. Jones was completely silent. "I think I've got it," Ara added, "this one will count." By now a crowd gathered. And with absolutely no form at all Ara launched forward and threw it well over sixty-five feet. Jones finally caught on to the looks and broke up with the rest of us.[1]

A KICK IN THE BUTT

Ron Dushney was a good football player, part of the talented Notre Dame sophomore class in 1966. He became a backfield regular in 1967 and 1968. Ron's biggest challenges arose in practices. It seemed that every time Ara was watching he got self-conscious and made mistakes. Finally, Ara lost patience. "Dushney, if you screw up again, I'm going to kick your ass." That made a miscue inevitable. True to his word, in front of the entire starting team, Ara asked Ron to bend over. Then he gave him an affectionate and light kick in the butt. Everybody laughed at the friendly gesture and this broke the tension. Thereafter, every day before practice began, Coach Ara asked Ron to bend over and repeated the playful kick in the butt. The team got into this ritual — symbolic that Ara cared about all his players and wanted them to perform at their best physically and mentally. The ritual was reprised one last time at the fiftieth anniversary dinner for the 1966

National Championship Team in 2016. The assembled crowd laughed enthusiastically and stood in ovation.

STOP THE SNOW

Ara inserted a self-deprecating story many times in the speeches he gave, obviously struck with the irony involved and the positive reaction it always got from an audience. This particular moment was recounted by Tom Pagna and Bob Best as follows:

> I remember the adversity Notre Dame fans experienced before Ara came here in 1964. But after we won our first five or six games the students became drunk with their newfound power. One game late in the season it began to snow and the students started chanting, "Ara stop the snow! Ara stop the snow!" Ara walked over to me with a puzzled expression and said, "That's ridiculous." He paused for a moment and then gazed back quizzically, "Do you think I could?"
>
> Just to show you how the years change a person, during one of our games last year it was snowing off and on, and at one point the students renewed the cry of their predecessors. "Ara stop the snow! Ara stop the snow!" This time there was no hesitancy in his voice as he asked me, "Do you think I should?"[2]

LOCKER ROOM SURPRISE

No one was immune from Ara's pranking impulses, especially not his assistant coaches. They became somewhat used to the coach putting them on.

Joe Lee was a very loyal and diminutive maintenance man at the Athletic and Convocation Center. Joe was especially attentive to Ara's every wish. It occurred to Ara that this helpful allegiance presented an opportunity to really surprise his staff. He instructed his friend Joe to slip into the locker of the assistant coach Wally Moore just before practice was over. When the staff assembled in the locker room after practice,

Ara waited for that coach to open up his locker. Upon doing so, Joe jumped out toward a shocked Wally. Prank delivered.

DIGGER'S OFFICE FURNITURE RELOCATION

When the move putting the Notre Dame Football Office into the new Athletic and Convocation Center transpired in 1968, the furnishings for the largest staff and revenue generator in the Athletic Department were all new, sturdy, and quite comfortable. Other sports didn't fare so well and received bare-bones furniture and hand-me-downs. When Digger Phelps came in as head basketball coach in 1971, he raised a complaint about the disparity in office furnishing. Athletic Director Moose Krause was sympathetic. New furniture was delivered in the summer of 1972. But this furniture, selected personally by Digger, was more residential and had a distinctive French Provincial look. Very pleased with himself and his selections, Digger busted into a football staff meeting one morning and invited everyone to come and see his new office furniture — which they did.

Afterward a plan was hatched. The next morning the entire football staff arrived early, and with the help of janitors, moved every stick of furniture out of Digger's office area and distributed it, piece by piece, to nooks and crannies around the voluminous building. Digger arrived shortly thereafter to an empty office suite. Fuming mad, he immediately realized that he had been pranked, then busted into the football staff meeting down the hall for the second day in a row — giving Ara and his staff precisely the reaction they were waiting for.

A PRESENT FROM "DUKE"

An unlikely friendship blossomed between Katie, Ara, and actor John Wayne (who was born Marion Robert Morrison in 1907 and died in 1979). Wayne was a University of Southern California partisan, having reportedly lost his football scholarship due to a body surfing accident. Letters and notes in Ara's personal files reveal a spirited friendship. All of Wayne's correspondence was simply signed "Duke." Dinners together were the rule when the Parseghians were in Los Angeles, especially after Ara was retired. Good-natured ribbing formed a common thread in the relationship. At one point a large box from Duke was delivered to the Parseghians's home. Upon opening it, Katie and Ara found an unlikely object. It was a flimsy, molded-plastic helmet spray painted red and gold and originating from the uniform of the Trojan Marching Band — obviously gifted to the actor at some point.

Ara thought long and hard about an appropriate thank you note. Finally, he and Katie formulated the following response: "Dear Duke, We received your very unusual gift. At first, we were perplexed as to exactly what it was. Finally, after inspecting if from every angle and trying to imagine a use, the answer came to us. Obviously, this is the replica of a very ancient urinal. Thank you very much."

This object was displayed prominently in Ara's former office.

CIGARS FROM JOHN MCKAY

During Ara's coaching tenure at Notre Dame, the most bitter rivalry was with USC, led by Head Coach John McKay. The two coaching legends were respectful and polite away from the scheduled games every year, many of which eventually determined the national champion. But it would be fair to say they weren't buddies. So, it was surprising to discover the following exchange in the files from 1975, when McKay accepted the head coaching job with the NFL's Tampa Bay Buccaneers.

Dear John,

A number of my friends sent me the article by Tom McEwen after your press conference on December 4 or 5.

I know you indicated that you will miss the Notre Dame games most and that you enjoyed beating the Roman Catholic school coached by a Presbyterian.

In view of my enormous contribution to your success, I think it is only fair that you share with me the financial awards that have been bestowed upon you by the Tampa owners.

You can well imagine the time-consuming problems of standing in a welfare line. Of course, each week I scout the window openings and have been able to get my welfare check by getting up earlier.

In the event you do not see fit to reward me for my 11 years of help, I would be more than happy to settle for some of those ample Tampa cigars you alluded to in one of your earlier press conferences.

In the meantime, I will watch with great interest the draft and the progress of your new challenge. I realize it will not be easy but I am sure you will do an excellent job in this new challenge.

Best wishes for a Merry Christmas and Happy New Year with continued good health and happiness,

Ara

The return note from John McKay, dated January 7, reads as follows:

Dear Ara,

Just a short note to thank you for your letter and your support.

Under separate cover I'm sending you some fine Tampa cigars . . . as long as I am in Tampa you will need not worry as I will send them monthly.

In a more serious vein, I will certainly miss our great rivalry. Sincerely, without a doubt, you are one of the finest coaches I have known. I hope that our paths will cross again — you have a standing invitation to Tampa and a golf game.

My best to you and Katie.

Regards,

John

Boxes of Tampa cigars were often gifted to Ara thereafter. Ara enjoyed a good cigar on occasion, but handing these out to friends with the above backstory made them much more flavorful.

CELEBRITY CAB RIDE

During his career Ara was a frequent visitor to New York City. An experience there became one of his favorite stories to tell at banquets.

Standing outside his hotel with his bags in tow, Ara needed to hail a cab to the airport. The fellow in line in front of him seemed to recognized him and offered to share a cab since he was also going to LaGuardia. The ride went well and the conversation turned to football, as might be expected. Disembarking from the cab the gracious passenger paid the full fare. In so doing, he told the cabbie he could go home that evening and tell his family that he had driven a very famous person — Notre Dame Head Football Coach Joe Kuharich!

AN INTRODUCTION BY ART BUCHWALD

This is the text (saved in Ara's personal files) of an introduction of Ara by famous *Washington Post* syndicated columnist and humorist Art Buchwald given on May 17, 1972, probably at a Multiple Sclerosis Foundation dinner.

> Despite his fame on the gridiron, we do not know too much about Ara Parseghian. He is a mystery to all of us. Except for the fact that he feeds his Notre Dame players bananas and palm leaves three times a day, there is little printed information on him.
>
> Well, I heard I was to speak here tonight. I asked for a biography of him and here's what I received. The bio provided by the Public Information Office . . . of the University of Texas.
>
> Ara Parseghian concluded his season as Notre Dame football coach with sixty-six wins against twelve defeats. This makes him the second greatest Notre Dame coach ranking only thirty-nine games behind the greatest Fighting Irish coach of all time . . . Pat O'Brien .
>
> Ara is responsible for producing some of the greatest All-Americans of modern-day football and has been named Coach of the Year, the Athlete of the Month, and Armenian of the Century.
>
> But this is nothing compared to his greatest accomplishment. Ara Parseghian is the only coach in the United States who has never received a suggestion to send in a football play from President Richard Nixon.
>
> When I asked Coach Parseghian before the dinner how he explained it, he said modestly, "I guess I'm just lucky."
>
> Born in Akron, Ohio on May 21, 1923, Ara grew up like any kid, throwing rocks at lampposts, pouring ink on girls' pigtails, and smoking Marvels behind the railroad tracks. But when he was about twelve

something happened to change his whole life. He found an old, abandoned Ford station wagon in an empty lot, and as a lark he started opening and closing the doors.

A talent scout from the major advertising agency who handled the Ford account was driving by and he couldn't believe it. He stopped and said, "Son where did you learn to open a shut doors on a station wagon like that?" "I don't know," Ara said, "I guess it just comes naturally to me."

The advertising account executive said, "Son, someday they're going to have a thing called television and they're going to need people like you to do commercials. If you study hard and practice not only on the doors but also opening and shutting the windows, you may one day become a rich man."

So, Ara Parseghian, who up until that moment, had been a drifter, decided he would devote his life to making TV commercials for station wagons.

But when he finished college, Ara discovered that no one wanted a station wagon door opener who was unknown.

A kindly man at Ford said, "If you can get to be the coach of Notre Dame and have a winning season, we will sign you up for our commercials."

With this as an incentive, Ara went to Notre Dame and applied for the coaching job. He told them the truth when they asked him why he wanted the job. "If I can coach at Notre Dame and produce a winning team, I'll be able to earn a living on TV selling Ford station wagons."

The alumni board was struck with his frankness. Since in their last season Notre Dame had two wins and seven losses they figured they had nothing to lose. And so, they signed him to a three-year contract.

The rest is history. Ara Parseghian has sold more Ford station wagons on television than any other coach in football.[3]

CHAPTER 19

GAMES THAT
MATTERED,
1967-1974

This is a logical point to divide Ara's career at Notre Dame into two distinct halves. But there is still an interesting season to mention before an administrative change at Notre Dame regarding bowl game participation defined the second part of the Parseghian coaching legacy.

The 1967 season began with high hopes and expectations. The problem that eager pollsters faced was that personnel changes after 1966 were unaccounted for. Of the thirty-three players who saw regular action in 1966, twelve graduated (Rhoads, Sieler, Duranko, Regner, Goeddeke, Page, Swatland, Lynch, Gmitter, Horney, Azzaro, and Eddy) and a majority of them were disbursed among various NFL training camps. (Some eventually had distinguished professional football careers.)

Another pattern was emerging, one that even the students noticed. It was always assumed that to win the national championship title the Irish would have to be undefeated. A single loss knocked the team out of contention. Thus the pollsters interest in Notre Dame waned after an initial defeat. Many of them had no love for the reborn Catholic team in the first place. The alarming pattern of predictable hurdles that Notre Dame had to overcome had names — Purdue University, Michigan State University, and the University of Southern California. Win against all of these teams and the percentages were favorable for No. 1 contention. In Ara's first six seasons (1964–1969), his record against these teams in aggregate was eight wins, seven losses, and three ties. Ara's teams were undefeated against every other team on the regular schedule over these six years!

In many ways, 1967 was the inverse of 1965. There was an overabundance of offensive firepower. But the defense lacked depth and experience, especially against the teams with explosive offences. The 1967 season opened with a convincing 41–8 win at home over California.

The tables turned the following week in West Lafayette when Notre Dame played against Purdue and suffered a 21–28 loss. While the Boilermakers had lost Bob Griese to the Miami Dolphins, they replaced him with a talented sophomore named Mike Phipps. Offensively the Irish were not sharp. Quarterback Terry Hanratty threw the ball for a then unheard of sixty-three times, completing twenty-nine passes, but also four interceptions. Having learned a lesson playing against the Irish the previous year, Boilermakers Head Coach Jack Mollenkopf double-teamed Jim Seymour the entire afternoon. That was the story of the game and the beginning of a repeat championship season unraveling. One loss to a ranked team and a national championship became only a remote possibility.

The knockout punch came two weeks later against Southern Cal in Notre Dame Stadium, a 7–24 loss. Here again the restructured defensive unit had no answer for the added dimension that Coach John McKay had discovered at a junior college, O. J. Simpson. The Irish held a 7–0 lead at the half. But the second half was all Simpson, all the time, and an exhausted defense couldn't make stops. The Notre Dame offense wasn't helpful either, turning the ball over four times on interceptions. After just four games the defending national champions had a record of 2–2. Loss number two knocked Notre Dame out of contention for a repeat national championship for good. The Irish were able to dig deep and win their remaining six games for a final record of 8–2 and finishing ranked No. 5. The University of Southern California, now with a future Heisman Trophy winner, finished as national champions.

Ara's 1968 team also finished ranked No. 5. The challenging pattern continued. An early season loss to Purdue at home (22–37) deflated expectations for the remainder of the season. The super sophomores of 1966 were playing in their senior year. A close loss to Michigan State in East Lansing (17–21) probably hurt the most. Officials neglected to make an obvious holding call against Jim Seymour late in the game, and this oversight changed the result. Ara was livid. Danger lurked around the corner right after the next game, a win against Navy. In a practice scrimmage, quarterback Terry Hanratty injured his knee and required surgery. Sophomore Joe Theismann had been waiting in the wings with just three games to play. He held the offense together and thus began his notable career as a Notre Dame quarterback. There was redemption of sorts at the Los Angeles Coliseum, where the Irish were able to knock Southern Cal out of a repeat national championship by earning a 21–21 tie. The final blow came on a handoff to Coley O'Brien, playing halfback, with a throwback pass to Theismann to make the winning score. The Irish defense held O. J. Simpson to fifty-five yards on twenty-one carries — the least productive day in his otherwise extraordinary Heisman Trophy year.

Ara's teams were so respected that at 7–2–1 they were ranked No. 5, behind Ohio State University, the University of Texas, Penn State University, and Southern California. In his first five seasons, all of Ara's teams finished ranked in the top 10. There was one consensus national championship in 1966, and one contested national championship in 1964.

While nobody knew it at the time, the 1969 season would provide something more to play for if the Irish were to ever again stumble in the regular season.

The year 1969 represented a significant changing of the guard in the playing personnel. There were no holdovers from the 1966 national championship team. The players recruited in 1967, first eligible to play in 1968 as sophomores, were coming of age. But the team chemistry was changing. The hunger for national recognition in 1964, accelerating to a championship season in 1966, had lasting elements of common purpose and experience through the 1968 team. But the 1969 team couldn't lean on recent history to establish their identity. Thus began a cycle of constant rebuilding that characterized the second half of Ara's coaching tenure at Notre Dame. 1969 was also the threshold year for a new incentive to attract and motivate the next generation of athletes — the prospect of a postseason bowl game.

The emergence of Joe Theismann at quarterback characterized the next two seasons, 1969 and 1970. To the surprise of Ara and the other coaches, Joe was not only a crafty runner but an able passer, especially when he was on the run. In addition, he possessed two characteristics that are difficult to teach, leadership (albeit bordering on cockiness) and good football instincts. He understood the geometry of the game in multiple situations.

An away loss to Purdue in the second game of the 1969 season (14–28) put the Irish behind the eight ball for early national championship consideration. A 14–14 tie against Southern Cal at home extinguished all hope (a possible winning field goal literally bounced off the cross bar). But the team was blessed with future All-American talent: defensive tackle Mike McCoy, Bob Olson at linebacker, and offensive linemen Larry DiNardo, Jim Reilly, and Mike Oriard. The team finished the season with five consecutive wins and an overall record of 8–1–1.

Then an unexpected event changed Notre Dame Football forever. The administration agreed to allow the team to play in a postseason bowl game for the first time since the 1924 Rose Bowl. The stated rationale for a change in course was driven by a revised academic calendar which scheduled final exams before Christmas Break, something that actually happened in 1968.

Behind the scenes other factors weighed heavily. First, since Notre Dame was an independent school the revenue from bowl participation didn't have to be shared with a conference and could be significant. Second, the Irish were in danger of brand dilution once they lost a game or two in the regular season. This also had revenue implications. How much lobbying by Ara to the administration impacted the decision would be speculative. Clearly, he was pleased with this development. Importantly, all his future teams would have something to play for should their national championship aspirations be snuffed by a regular season loss or two.

On November 17, 1969, it was announced that Notre Dame would play No. 1 ranked Texas in the Cotton Bowl (Dallas, Texas). It was a media matchup of two highly regarded college football programs on New Year's Day (1970).

On the evening of the announcement, this author grabbed a Coke in the near-empty LaFortune Student Center and was approached by a fellow with cameras draped around his neck, obviously a professional photographer. "Where's the pep rally?" he asked. It was near the end of the semester on a weeknight and there was no celebration to be had anywhere over the bowl game news. "I'm from UPI and I was sent down here from Chicago to get a photo of the campus reaction. What do I do?" The student said, "Follow me" and walked the UPI man across campus to the Architecture Building (since renamed Bond Hall) where busy sophomores were working late into the night on their final projects. A "reaction photo" was staged. Two students held the *South Bend Tribune* headline aloft with about fifteen students inside the building jabbing "No. 1" fingers into the air. The photographer stood outside an open window to capture the faux "mayhem." The scene was all over in five minutes and the students went back to work. By the next morning a UPI photo of the event was featured in virtually every newspaper in America. At the turn of the millennia the *Chicago Tribune* designated this photo as one of the twenty most important images of Notre Dame Football in the twentieth century.

GAME SEVEN, JANUARY 1, 1970
Notre Dame vs. Texas, Cotton Bowl
(Dallas, TX), Lost 17-21

This football game is significant for many reasons. It was the first bowl appearance by a Notre Dame team in the modern era. It was also the first bowl game for the head coach as a coach (he appeared in one as a Miami player). Thus the learning curve was quite high for all concerned.

A December 8, 1969, memo from Ara to Father Joyce, highlighted the obvious administrative challenges. The preliminary budget was assembled by Ara and Business Manager Bob Cahill. They attempted to be detailed and accurate. The football side of things was estimated to cost about $80,000. This did not include costs for the marching band or any other administrative people. It included expenses for travel, lodging, food, team allotments and incidentals, gifts, and entertainment. Ara was able to procure courtesy cars from Ford at no cost, which were made available to the team members and traveling party. One of the unwritten goals was for the team and the administration to have a sufficiently positive experience such that future bowl invitations would be welcomed.

What follows is an excerpt from Ara's annual report to Moose Krause and Father Joyce:

> A comment certainly is an order regarding our Cotton Bowl venture. It was a great experience for all involved and in spite of the many problems, the team performance and effort were exceptional. I was pleased with the determination of our team and, obviously, disappointed with the final score. The first bowl game in forty-four years required many organizational details. Now that we have the experience of a bowl contest, I'm sure that future preparation, in the event that we are invited and accept, should be less difficult. I would strongly endorse a letter to the NCAA suggesting a booklet of rules and recommendations for bowl bound teams. This would answer many questions and eliminate the anguish that we encountered.

The game on the field held intrigue of its own. Texas had an exceptional team. The main concern was stopping the vaunted and unusual (at that time) Texas Wishbone Offense (today generically known as the triple option). They had the talented players to run it to perfection and that season no team had stopped them.

The Longhorns had added emotional motivation because one of their defensive backs, Freddie Steinmark, had been diagnosed with cancer and had his leg amputated during the season. He was on the sidelines on crutches for all practices and the game. After his passing only months later, Steinmark became one of the historic stories of personal courage for Texas Football and still is part of the permanent lore of the storied program.

Tom Pagna noted, "This team had made up a 14-point deficit to previously undefeated Arkansas in a nationally televised game at the end of the season and clinched the Southwest Conference title. This prompted President Richard M. Nixon to walk into their locker room immediately after the game and pronounce them National Champions."[1]

Overall, the Irish (previously 8–1–1) had a lot to overcome. Practically nobody gave Notre Dame any chance of winning. It was a defensive struggle throughout. Irish linebacker Bob Olson was named Defensive Player of the Game. Led by Joe Theismann, Notre Dame went ahead 17–14 with seven minutes left to play. The Longhorns answered with a final drive that took over five minutes. Final score: Texas 21, Notre Dame 17. The game was statistically as close as the score. Notre Dame had 410 yards of total offense in 70 plays while Texas had 448 yards in 78 plays. Former President Lyndon Johnson visited both locker rooms after the game. The final AP ranking placed Notre Dame at No. 5.

Pagna weighs in again: "Overall, the bowl experience had been a good one. The players to a man agreed it would be a fun memory. Our hotel rooms, the food, the social gatherings all contributed to making it an enjoyable paid vacation for our families. And of major importance, the University gained over $200,000 for its minority student scholarship fund. Except for the loss, everything about this venture had been positive."[2]

The 1970 season had all the earmarks of potentially being one of the best ever for Notre Dame. Theismann became a dominant college quarterback and he found a crafty receiver in Thom Gatewood. Eventually both were inducted into the College Football Hall of Fame, and Gatewood was only the second Black player from Notre Dame after Alan Page to be so honored.

The Irish had rolled through their first nine opponents undefeated. No team scored more than fourteen points and there were three shutouts (although the last was a tight 3–0 win over LSU). The final hurdle separating the team from a possible national championship was the finale against Southern California.

GAME EIGHT, NOVEMBER 28, 1970
Notre Dame at Southern California
(Los Angeles Coliseum), Lost 28-38

Gameday was uncharacteristically rainy and sloppy at the Los Angeles Coliseum. A nervous Ara Parseghian never relished playing Southern Cal away from home. The advantage of scheduling the Trojans in Los Angeles late in the season was that favorable weather was virtually guaranteed. Not on this day, unfortunately, with four inches of rainfall. Managing the game around the weather became the challenge.

Two early offensive miscues led to two short-yardage Trojan scores. They proved to be the difference in the game. The offense wasn't able to hold the ball and keep the Notre Dame defense off the field with enough gas to hold the Trojans late in the game. Theismann would throw for 526 yards in this game — a school record. But it wouldn't be enough to prevail. Ara Parseghian walked into the Los Angeles Coliseum four times in his first seven seasons — three visits with a national championship on the line (the fourth resulted in a 21–21 tie in 1968). He was denied twice in the cavernous vestige of the 1932 Olympic Games.

GAME NINE, JANUARY 1, 1971
Notre Dame vs. Texas, Cotton Bowl
(Dallas, TX), Won 24-11

Fortunately, Texas wasn't a team that depended on speed and passing as much as it depended on deception and physical execution in the backfield. Ara had a plan after having a year to analyze the first meeting of the teams. Here are the comments he shared (as found in Ara's personal files).

> This New Year's Day we have an opportunity to avenge our last year's defeat to the Longhorns of Texas. In order for Notre Dame to win, it is imperative that we stop their wishbone offense. We must know and carry out all our own team defensive assignments. Our tackling must be sharp, along with great team pursuit! Gang tackle their ball carriers. Basically they are running the same offense as last year, which is the blast series (hike, 4, 6, and eight) plus a few other plays. They will use the pass very sparingly, but we have to read our keys, and react accordingly. We can win this game, but it will take a 100% team effort for the full 60 minutes. Get yourself ready mentally and physically for a tough, hardnosed game. Beat Texas!

The so-called mirror defense, or, as Ara privately described it, the "Okie Doke Defense," was effective.

Pagna explains further:

Ever since the narrow loss to Texas the year before, Ara had been analyzing the wishbone offense and toying with ways to harness it. He came up with a plan that was masterful, but risky. He called it the mirror defense. The basic principle was to focus certain defensive backs on the Texas halfbacks and quarterback and certain linebackers on the fullback. These defensive people mirrored the running backs. This could be a defensive look the Longhorns hadn't seen before. Ara figured that this unfamiliarity would ruffle them enough to stall their offense. But as a man for man defense, one mistake by any player could cost us more than any other defense. This one demanded perfection. . . .

They (Texas) fumbled nine times, losing five, and soon abandoned their running attack for a passing attack. That's what Ara had been hoping for. Texas was a great running team but not passing, something it didn't have much experience with. Not only that, but our offense was moving so well that Texas was thrust into a score-or-else situation, a problem for a Wishbone team.[3]

The game was 24–11 favoring the Irish with twenty-four seconds left to play in the first half. The score held. At the end of the game, the Texas thirty-game winning streak, the longest in the nation, had been ended. Pagna shares more reflections:

Nebraska looked like our main competition at that point for the National Championship. They were able to play LSU in the Orange Bowl that night, and if the Tigers could only win, the national title would be ours. They gave it a great try, but Nebraska pulled it out. Most of us watched the game from our rooms and were disappointed to see Nebraska squeak by. Just to make sure the pollsters wouldn't regard our win over Texas too seriously, Nebraska Coach Bob Devaney told the press, "Not even the Pope would vote Notre Dame No. 1." He didn't and we finished second.[4]

The 1971 and 1972 seasons were disappointing by the standards that Ara had set at Notre Dame. The AP/UPI rankings for these years were 13/15 and 14/12. These were the lowest rankings Ara received in his eleven years at Notre Dame. A 16–4 combined record over two years would be considered a success at most schools. Once again, two losses to USC were the crucial tripping points.

The 1971 season was especially taxing on the team. At 8–2, they were invited to the Gator Bowl. The team was asked by Ara to vote on participation. In a close vote, they elected to defer and effectively end the frustration and their season. This was a bitter disappointment to Ara and the coaching staff. It was the last time that Notre Dame players would be granted veto power over a bowl decision. Forever after, important decisions of this nature were made at the upper administrative level.

The 1972 season was equally challenging, especially after an early season 26–30 loss at home to the University of Missouri, coached by Dan Devine (a future Notre Dame head coach). Again, the 8–2 Irish were invited to a bowl, this time against the No. 1 University of Nebraska in the Orange Bowl. Reflecting back, Assistant Coach Brian Boulac observed that *this* was the bowl game that the Irish probably should have passed on. The Nebraska team was loaded with talent, including Heisman Award winner Johnnie Rodgers. The outcome was embarrassing: a New Year's Day, primetime loss of 6–40. It was the most lopsided loss in Parseghian's career at Notre Dame. The Irish never were in contention against the Cornhuskers.

On January 2, 1973, very few college football observers would have predicted the surprising reversal of fortunes for the Notre Dame team a year later. What accounted for the change? Tom Pagna's speculative perspective on the societal change on campus is illuminating.

> The students, too, seemed to be moving in a new direction. The years of counterculture had run their course. Maybe it was the Vietnam War ending or perhaps being different was a fad they had passed, but students now were only bothered by the age-old concerns of getting good grades, finding a job and who to date on Friday night.
>
> Female students had been admitted to the University, and they brought with them a fresh spirit. Their male counterparts were a little better groomed and appeared more eager to join the world again. The Notre Dame tradition of racing to the window every time a girl walked in front of a dorm had ended. Co-eds were becoming commonplace, and they were giving the school a different personality.

And for some reason, football fit in perfectly with this new look. The students were once again enchanted by the fall football pageantry. For the long-time Fighting Irish fans it was like the good old days.[5]

The Irish literally steamrolled their opponents over the course of their ten-game season. Statistics don't lie. This team outscored their opponents 358–66.

In his annual report to the administration on June 27, 1974, this is how Ara summarized the 1973 season.

Without question, the 1973 season was one of the greatest in Notre Dame Football history. It seems as if all the pieces finally fell in place and the result was an undefeated season, the Sugar Bowl victory, and the National Championship recognition. This was without question the highlight of the decade that I have spent at the University. In previous years, in 1964 and 1966, we had won the MacArthur Bowl and in 1966 we had won the National Championship, but, unfortunately, there was some question by the sportswriters relative to the Michigan State game. The conquest of 1973 was one of the greatest comebacks in Notre Dame history.

In reviewing the annual report of 1972, I note that I commented that we would have a fairly solid offensive football team, but our concern was with the defensive phase of the game. However, I also mentioned in my report that we had concentrated very heavily in our recruiting to bring in defensive players, those that had distinguished themselves at the high school level in that phase of the game. At that time, I felt there would be a significant percentage of freshmen that might be able to make a contribution to our defensive team. Well, this came to fruition with the outstanding performances of Luther Bradley and Ross Browner. The defensive unit was bolstered immensely and as it turned out, the defensive team of 1973 was probably one of the better ones that we have had in my ten years at the University.

I would have to single out the field leadership that we had on the '73 football team. Obviously, a coaching staff can prepare a ballclub, but once the game starts the coaches are on the sideline and in the press box and the leadership must take place on the field. I honestly believe that the three-captain system that we were greatly concerned about when the appointments were made worked exceptionally well. Frank Pomerico leading the offense, Mike Townsend leading the defense, and Dave Casper being the

Team Captain worked far beyond our expectations, as well as that of others. When one considers that important field decisions have to be made, attitudes created and maintained on the field, I honestly feel the captains contributed to our success in 1973 immeasurably.

In view of the 1973 season, I would have to say that balance probably played a very important part in our success. We had an outstanding offensive unit directed by Tom Clements; the defensive team was bolstered by the good fortune of having the freshmen make an immense contribution; and our kicking game with seasoned, experienced veterans played an important role. When we took the field for a ballgame, we knew that we could win any one of three ways . . . with our offense our defensive units or our kicking team.

The season set up a marquee matchup with the University of Alabama in the Sugar Bowl on the evening of January 1, 1974. It was the first time since 1966 for a No. 1 versus No. 2 matchup, and the first time in memory of that happening in a postseason bowl game. It was the first ever meeting of two storied football programs, matching two highly successful coaches, Paul "Bear" Bryant and Ara Parseghian. Both squads knew they were playing for the national championship. No further motivation was necessary.

GAME TEN, DECEMBER 31, 1973
Notre Dame vs. Alabama, Sugar Bowl
(New Orleans, LA), Won 24-23

Before the game, Father Hesburgh took Ara aside for a moment outside the locker room. "Coach, I've never asked you for anything before. But I'd really be pleased if we could win this game." This uncharacteristic request by the nationally respected university president was prompted by the manner in which Father Ted had been treated at events and festivities before the game. It seems that when he was introduced, his name was consistently botched: Father Hesburger, Father Hessman, Father Hamburg, and so on. The errors were so frequent that he believed the slipups weren't accidental. He'd had enough of it.

Tom Pagna and Bob Best's 1975 narrative has the benefit of being read and then approved by Ara and Katie before publication. Therefore, it is presumed to be as contemporaneous and as accurate as any record now available.

> Since renewing our bowl involvement this was the first time the National Championship was at stake for the winner. Refreshingly, that gave our players a completely different attitude toward preparation for the game. Their vote to compete this time was unanimous and they didn't carry with it any contingencies. They just wanted to play and win. On their own, they decided to stay on campus to practice instead of going home for Christmas. So, we worked as hard as possible in our snowy climate and left for New Orleans four days before the game. . . .
>
> It had rained much of the day and early evening and overhead the lightning was freely visible. Ara put the team through a few timing drills but fearing the lightning, soon whistled them into the locker room. By the time the bands and guest performers had cleared the field for a return, the storm had ended.[6]

The game was very tightly played for four quarters. The teams were well matched and both teams were in a position to win at the end. With a third down deep in their own territory and ahead by a single point, the Irish were faced with a do-or-die decision. The challenge: to get a first down and hopefully run out the clock for a win. Both possession and position were at risk. An offsides call against the Irish put them back another five yards at this crucial point in the game. Then came the play of the game. It is probably the only play most people still remember from this important game or season.

Pagna continues:

> Casper was our intended receiver, but Ara had inserted a second tight end, Robin Weber, to disguise our pass plans. With the snap the Alabama secondary converged on Casper, leaving Weber virtually free. He was running a deep pattern toward the Alabama sideline. Meanwhile in the end zone, Clements was forced to get the pass off. Two of our players had missed blocks, and an Alabama tackle who should have been on

the ground by now lurched toward Tom and barely missed his pass. Weber did some stretching of his own, and after juggling the ball momentarily he cradled it for his first Notre Dame reception — a 35-yard gain. Now we had breathing room, and with an additional first down we ran out the clock.

With one clutch call that would make national headlines, Ara went a long way toward removing the label his enemies insisted on sticking him with ever since the 1966 MSU tie. This wasn't any better than scores of other plays he had come up with in pressure situations, but it would become the most publicized.[7]

Coming back to the locker room Ara said, "They gave us two things out there," he screeched in a hoarse voice. "One is the Sugar Bowl Trophy!" We cheered that for several minutes and then he continued, "Two is the MacArthur Bowl, symbolic of the National Championship!" With that we were given a visual description of the word bedlam. It continued for nearly an hour. . . .

"The pass from Clements to Weber with seconds to go was the key to the win," Ara explained to the media. "It was a win or punt situation. If we hadn't made the first down Alabama would surely have been in field goal position with us punting from our end zone."

"I definitely feel we're the National Champions. We beat the leading scoring team in the nation. They are an excellently disciplined team. We beat a great football team and they lost to a great football team."

A tall man in a black and white houndstooth hat came through the doorway. The players made a path for the Bear as he headed for Ara. He congratulated Ara and then asked, "Where is "Mark Clements [sic], I wanna shake his hand." . . .

Naturally the joy of our present accomplishment enveloped us. But with the loss of only five seniors to graduation we were dreaming about doing all this again next year.[8]

The legendary Alabama coach had it right. The most consequential play of the game was in actuality an improvisation by Notre Dame quarterback Tom Clements. The Clements-to-Webber pass is without question the most memorable single play in Ara Parseghian's career at Notre Dame. It was the only photograph of game action (a color photograph from the end zone) framed and hung in the coach's personal office. Of all the thousands of plays run by his teams over Ara's career, this was essentially a broken play, one not found in the playbook. But the play, with the weak-side tight end slipping off a block and becoming open for a possible pass (dotted line), was added to the 1974 Playbook, and named "Alabama 73."

One of the overused words for an author is "remarkable." Sometimes the word is used to describe something that doesn't merit this designation. In this case, however, the word applies. Ara wrote a letter to Bear Bryant weeks after the game. It is a remarkable gesture and puts the depth of Ara's sensitivity and character on display.

February 7, 1974

Dear Bear,

I am fully aware, from having experienced it myself, how disappointed you must have been after the Sugar Bowl game. I have felt for a long time that a close loss is far more difficult to take than one that is decided by a larger margin. However, I feel it is important that I pass on the sentiments that we here at Notre Dame feel.

The game was a historic first. The first meeting of traditional rivals, the North versus the South, the religious implications, the press having entered into it by blowing statements out of proportion in previous years. . . . I really don't think that I have to list all of the pre-game involvement because you are well aware of the circumstances. In view of all this, I personally approached the contest with some apprehension. However, after reflecting back on the events of the Sugar Bowl, I feel compelled to write this letter.

First of all, I speak on behalf of myself as well as our coaching staff. We have a great deal of respect for you and your staff and squad. It only takes one game for competing schools to evaluate the total preparation and dedication of an opponent. Our people were impressed!

Much has been said about Alabama fans and Notre Dame fans, and yet I found them to be some of the most courteous that I have encountered for a number of years. I have played in stadiums in both the North and the South at Notre Dame and have been viciously abused and harassed on more than one occasion. I have also been physically accosted by thrown bottles, cans, ice, etc. For one to put the game in its proper perspective, discarding the one-point differential, I honestly believe that Notre Dame fans, coaching staff, administration, and this certainly includes this Head Coach, have come away with a renewed respect for one another.

The tradition of the two schools is well known and I think it is good for college football that we will meet in 1976. Hopefully, it will lead to other scheduled games with the Crimson Tide in the future.

I know they call you "the Bear" and you like to present yourself as a folksy, little old Arkansas boy, but I am renaming you "the Fox." You are right on top of what is going on. In standing across the field from you for a full game, I totally understand why you have won 231 games. The respect that the football world has for you has been earned and you justly deserve it.

Paul, I am not prone to normally writing this kind of letter, but under the circumstances I feel a compulsion to do so and I want you to understand that everything that is in this letter are the true sentiments of everyone at the University of Notre Dame.

Best personal regards,

Ara

The appreciation for Ara, and for a continued bright future for Notre Dame Football, was never more apparent than at a banquet honoring his ten years of success held after the 1974 Spring Game. Over 1,100 were in attendance. The highlight was Ara being named the first ever Honorary Notre Dame Alumnus, a designation that has been reserved and used only sparingly since. In his remarks accepting the honor, Ara said the following: "There is an old cliche that is very true that says 'it is far easier to win a championship than it is to retain it.' The success of 1973 will make the job and the ambitions and hopes of 1974 more difficult."

The lifetime bonds of friendship among students at Notre Dame were strengthened by the success of Ara Parseghian and the Irish football team. That became obvious on the first day of 2024, which marked the fiftieth anniversary of the Sugar Bowl win over Alabama and the national championship. Tony Jeselnik, class of 1971, sent an email challenge asking his pals if they remembered where they were when Tom Clements passed to Robin Weber in that fateful game. The responses were illuminating. Everyone seemed to remember exactly where they had been watching the game on television that night and what they were doing — military service, graduate schools, law schools (including one at the University of Alabama).

Tony Earley is the retired CEO of a large electric utility. In 1973 he was a junior naval officer having passed through the Navy's ROTC program at Notre Dame. His vivid and poignant submission to the email chain was: "I think we all remember where we were for this one. I watched it in the Officer's Club on the Subic Bay Naval Base where it was the next morning. My submarine was scheduled to get underway at noon. As soon as Robin Weber caught the pass, I sprinted to our pier and crossed the gangplank with only minutes to spare. It was worth risking a Court Martial." When asked for permission to include his story in this book, he provided the following details: "You are certainly welcome to use it. One amusing detail I didn't include was that my Commanding Officer was watching the game across the room. He was a USNA grad but a big ND fan. I positioned myself near the door so I could get out first when he started to leave. What I failed to remember was that he had a jeep and driver. When I got outside and saw that, I had to sprint to the pier and crossed the gangway just ahead of the Skipper."

Just when everyone was celebrating the national championship and the prospect of contending for a second in 1974, fate stepped in. The culmination of unanticipated events eventually led to the surprise resignation of Ara Parseghian at the conclusion of the 1974 regular season. It began with a scandal implicating six rising sophomore football players that exploded over the summer.

Pagna and Best chronicle the situation as follows:

The players, all sophomores to be enrolled in the Notre Dame summer session, had a girl in a dormitory room after hours. She was there of her own volition, but later decided to call the police and charge our players with rape. Though the authorities were contacted, she never did file a formal complaint. That made no difference, however, because the story was out. A violation of Notre Dame Rules had taken place, and the school officials were forced to act. . . .

The school officials eventually settled on suspending them for one year with the possibility, not a guarantee, of re-admission. . . .

As had been University policy, the names of the players and their offense would not be made public. But by the time the school made a simplistic announcement that "Six students had been suspended for a violation of University policy," the whole world knew who the six players were, and they had been involved in some sort of sexual activity. The *South Bend Tribune* carried a story pointing out that no formal charges had been made by the girl, and the wire services used information from that account to augment the University statement. But the sensationalists around the country had their day. A Los Angeles newspaper used the headline "Rape at ND" even though the story it carried pointed out that rape charges weren't filed. The *New York Daily News* headed it's writeup with "Sex Scandal Ousts Six Notre Dame Gridders." It made little difference that both stories clarified the facts. Many readers didn't go beyond the headlines and even if they did it was just prejudgment. Ara's greatest fear was materializing — insensitive editors were going to magnify the offense and mark these young men for life. . . .

If ever a team with spirit, talent and momentum was going to carry over from the year before, this had figured to be the one. Now that was extremely questionable.

Ara was morose, less dynamic and energetic than I ever remembered. His hair flecked grey, almost suddenly. The wrinkles in his face were more prominent. He didn't seem as tall and lost the bounce in his step. He no longer laughed or clowned, and our staff meetings were all business. He was tired and stooped, almost totally preoccupied. Where his radiant eyes formally pierced your mind, they now drifted in a distant gaze. . . .

We speculated that his daughter Karan had taken a turn for the worse or that he was concerned with the preparations for her upcoming wedding date. Rescheduling our late season game with Georgia Tech to September 9, would mean advancing the fall practice period. It would also mean opening the season two days after Karan's wedding.[9]

After two away wins with large margins at Georgia Tech and Northwestern University, the Irish returned for their first home game on September 28. They were ambushed by an old nemesis, Purdue, 20–31. Purdue was coached by Alex Agase, Ara's former assistant at Northwestern and arguably his best friend in coaching. The Irish played uphill in the rankings after that with seven consecutive wins. Quietly, one of these games became momentous.

GAME ELEVEN, NOVEMBER 2, 1974
Notre Dame vs. Navy, Veteran's Stadium,
(Philadelphia), Won 14-6

On an unseasonably warm day in Philadelphia, on the hard baseball turf of Veteran's Stadium, the Irish were almost ambushed again by a motivated Navy team. The last time Notre Dame had lost to Navy was in 1963 (prior to Ara's arrival), with Heisman Award winner Roger Staubach at quarterback. In 1964, Staubach's senior season, the Irish dominated in a 40–0 romp. The Middies had never made a respectable showing in the succeeding nine meetings, with embarrassing lopsided scores. Thus, the expectation in Ara's eleventh season was that beating Navy could almost be assumed, especially by the reigning national champions. But as the sports adage goes, "on any given Saturday," and so it was.

Tom Pagna captures the moment well:

> That brought us to the game that produced the most critical decision of Ara's career. Offensively we moved the ball all over the field against Navy, but fumbled or threw an interception to stall each drive. Navy's defense, an excellent unit under Head Coach George Welsh, played its best game of the year, while Midshipman punter John Stufflebean kept us pinned in our own territory with a 48-yard average on the day. Navy connected on two field goals and took a 6–0 lead into the fourth quarter. With ten minutes to play Clements threw a six-yard touchdown pass to Pete Demmerle, and freshman kicker Dave Reeve gave us the lead with his point after. Freshman safety Randy Harrison picked off a desperation pass attempted by the Middies and returned it for a 40-yard touchdown to insure a 14 to 6 win.
>
> "It's a win, that's all that counts," Ara commented after the game, but it was one that he and Notre Dame paid a high price for. The pressures of

the game encouraged him to hop off his merry-go-round and see where it was taking him.[10]

Katie clearly recalled the scene when Ara arrived home after the flight from Philadelphia. "He threw his bag across the threshold and exclaimed, 'I've had enough of this.'" He talked it over with Katie and his brother, Jerry, and Ara resolved to resign at the end of the 1974 season.

Ironically, something erupted twenty-eight days later that almost changed his mind. After wins at home against the University of Pittsburgh and Air Force, the 9–1 team had one final game against Southern California at the Los Angeles Coliseum. Most Irish fans who remember this nationally televised game wish they could forget it. The Irish took a 24–6 lead against the top-ranked Trojans into the locker room at halftime. But USC's Anthony Davis took the second half kickoff for a 102-yard touchdown. This was the beginning of the most disastrous momentum lapse in Ara's career. Davis was to score four touchdowns on the day and twenty-six of the first twenty-seven Trojan points. Before it was over the Trojans scored forty-nine unanswered points in seventeen minutes. Final score, University of Southern California 55, Notre Dame 24. Southern Cal would emerge as national champions at season's end. Davis might have won the Heisman Trophy except that his stunning performance came after voting was concluded. He finished a close second to Ohio State's Archie Griffin.

An embarrassed head coach almost changed his mind about retiring in order to avenge the loss. If he had changed his mind, this game, despite the score, would have qualified as one of the games that mattered. When Ara did finally announce his retirement a week later, the press speculated that he may have been asked to step down after the USC loss. Rumors swirled about racial dissension on the team. There was no factual basis to support any of the rumors. Ultimately, Ara knew he had made the right personal decision for the right reasons.

The Orange Bowl invited Notre Dame to a rematch with Alabama on January 1, 1975. The Crimson Tide were undefeated going into the game and virtually nobody gave the now-humbled Irish a chance in this rematch — especially with an assumed dispirited Irish team and the obvious revenge motive from the Sugar Bowl in 1974 being hyped by the entire Alabama fan base.

GAME TWELVE, JANUARY 1, 1975
Notre Dame vs. Alabama, Orange Bowl
(Miami, FL), Won 13-11

Tom Pagna paints this picture, starting with the pregame team meal:

Gentlemen, I said, there aren't more than a half dozen people outside this room who think we can pull this game off. The writers pick us as 11-point underdogs. Your mothers and fathers, your friends and neighbors are all saying prayers that we won't be humiliated. They reflect what Southern Cal did to us a month ago. They are positive we've got black-and-white problems, that we are torn apart with internal problems, that we quit in the second half versus USC. Why should we bother to show up tonight?

There's one very good reason. Ara Parseghian is too great and too humble a man to ask this team to win one for him. He won't do it. I sure as hell will. I'm not too humble to ask you to dedicate yourself to win this one for Ara. We've got to execute and play our hearts out. But we can win![11]

Ara addressed the team at the half:

"Win this game. Let's show them why we're Notre Dame and the tradition we have," Ara shouted, interrupting the previously subdued tones in the lock room and alerting the players it was time to get ready for action. "The last time we went out in the second half we got ourselves in trouble," he continued (reminding them of the Southern Cal game a month earlier when they led 24 to 6 at the half, only to suffer one of the most embarrassing losses of his career, 55 to 24.) "This is our chance to redeem ourselves to go out there and beat — this football team."

"This will be the last time I walk out of this locker room at halftime and I want this win. I want it for Notre Dame. Let's get out there."[12]

Pagna continues the story:

All of our doubtful players saw action at least for whatever few plays they could muster. The game was emotional, electric and a labor of love by all the players and assistant coaches. Wayne Bullock scored a four-yard touchdown in the first quarter after Al Samuel recovered a punt at the

Alabama 16. Mark McLane ran nine yards for a second touchdown to put us up 13–0. Alabama kicked a field goal before the first half and added eight points with 3:13 to play.

There were those who thought Alabama could overcome a 13–3 halftime deficit and capture the National Championship. But many of the spectators were pulling for the underdog Notre Dame — more particularly, for its coach Ara Parseghian. He had become the latest Notre Dame football legend, and this was his last game with the Fighting Irish.

The Tide was rising again in the closing minute, but defensive back Reggie Barnett intercepted a Richard Todd pass and clinched the victory. That cost Alabama the National Championship and gave us a 10–2 record. Even with the rash of misfortunes we experienced, we came within two quarters of an undefeated season — one against Purdue and one against USC.

It was a festive group of men in the locker room. Ara entered with tears of joy glistening in his eyes. What he had to say to all of us wasn't important, it was just being there to hear him say anything. That high-pitched voice of his was whining like never before. He spoke in staccato phrases, trying unsuccessfully to get them out without cracking.

"I've never had a victory in my coaching career with a group of guys so dedicated," he bellowed. "I'll remember this forever. This was my last game at Notre Dame. I'm never going to forget any one of you. What a great football game! You beat an undefeated team that was ranked No. 1. You were the underdogs. You showed all those who were down in the mouth about us! Father Toohey, come on over here and say the prayer. We've got a lot to be thankful for."

That ended the demands of his 243rd game, and 24th season as a head coach. It was his 170th victory against fifty-eight defeats and six ties, which put him among the top thirty winningest coaches of all time and second only to Knute Rockne at Notre Dame. At fifty-one he was young to be leaving football with such impressive credentials.[13]

This is from Ara's 1974 football season report to Moose Krause under the category of resignation (copy found in Ara's personal files):

There have been many rumors and speculation on my decision to resign. The release that accompanied the announcement was totally correct. I was physically, mentally, and emotionally exhausted. Not only had I been the

Head Coach at Notre Dame for eleven years, I had held the same responsibility at Northwestern for eight years and Miami of Ohio for six years. One quarter of a century on the field had somewhat drained me. I felt the need to step aside for at least one year. The decision was not hasty or impulsive. I had mulled it over for quite some time. In retrospect I think it was a wise decision. Leaving Notre Dame was not easy. My eleven years were filled with excitement and many of the moments will be long remembered. The coaching responsibility at Notre Dame is unique, and the pressure I felt was self-inflicted. In all of the eleven years, I have been most appreciative of the Administration's position relative to time demands. It was apparent to me that there was a genuine concern for the football coaches' problems.

With this last report, I send my best wishes to everyone in the Athletic Department who will have the responsibility for continuing a proud tradition. I also include my grateful thanks for the cooperation our football program received from the Administration. Success is based on teamwork . . . my good fortune was to have that for over a decade.

Very sincerely,

Ara Parseghian

FOURTH QUARTER

(1975-2017)

CHAPTER 20

DECISION TIME

The circumstances surrounding Ara Parseghian's decision to retire as head coach at Notre Dame have often been the subject of speculation and misinformation over the years since 1974. What follows is a straightforward narrative developed from eyewitnesses to the events. Fortunately, there have been a number of these reliable sources, and their memories of this important event are quite detailed.

In summary, self-imposed stress was the culprit. Correspondence written after the fact by Dr. Nicholas Johns, Ara's personal physician, fully support the medical aspects of his decision.

The build-up to Ara's decision included many factors that individually didn't tip the scales, but collectively added to his decision process. One consideration often cited was the health of the Parseghian's oldest daughter, Karan, who was dealing with recently diagnosed multiple sclerosis. This news, of course, would weigh heavily on any parent's heart. But in the fall of 1974, Ara and Katie were celebrating the September marriage of Karan to James "Jim" Burke. It was a good match; instinctively, the Parseghians were comforted that Karan was now in loving hands for her future. To this day, Katie has nothing but unqualified admiration for the manner in which Jim, and thereafter the couple's two sons, made accommodations for Karan's well-being and comfort. Katie simply says, "Jim is a living saint." The couple welcomed two boys, James and Michael. James has become a world-renowned and respected doctor in the area of autoimmune diseases, including multiple sclerosis.

The changing dynamics of recruiting and preparing a different generation of young football players may have contributed to Ara's decision to retire as well. When one looks back, though, this factor has probably been overemphasized. Parseghian was instinctive about reading human nature and then finding the incentives to motivate young men toward a common goal. His philosophy was best suited toward hardscrabble kids from immigrant families, especially those in the now-declining Midwest. He had been one of those kids himself. And there were still lots of such young men and parents from backgrounds who would appreciate what Notre Dame had to offer.

The increased need for speed in the skilled positions put a burden on the coaching staff to identify and recruit the right guys to fit the changing personnel needs. All of the major college programs in America were suddenly enlightened to the difference players' speed was making. The pool of speedy players was finally and permanently expanded to include Black players in every corner of America. Although churchgoing was quite often an integral part of their family values, not many of these young men came from Catholic backgrounds. Notre Dame was making inroads in the area of attracting diverse players that could succeed and keep the team nationally ranked.

The profound disappointment Ara internalized after six Black players were suspended in the summer of 1974 added to the difficulty of his job on the field. But that wasn't his first concern. Ara viewed the event as a shortcoming of his own leadership — that he let these young men down somehow. He could be hard on himself. In this case he was.

As much as anything, the demands of a schedule that provided no downtime had a cumulative drip-drip-drip effect on his psyche and likely cemented his decision. In his final season, Parseghian's Notre Dame salary was $35,000 (this would translate into about $250,000 when adjusted for inflation today), well below then-competitive standards at the time. Ara still needed supplementary income as the family provider. That required a number of days on the road away from home. There were constant requests for additional personal appearances, many from people who were championing worthwhile causes. Saying no to these created a pressure of a different kind since selfish instincts weren't part of his personality or character.

And then, there was the "big one," the relentless pressure to win games on the field and compete for a national championship. This steady pressure over his coaching career compounded season upon season. With Ara's years of accumulated experience along with a stable and capable coaching staff, the factors for continued success were in place. Ara believed that his job was secure, especially in the eyes of Fathers Hesburgh and Joyce — the only people that mattered. But the personal expectations he internalized became demons that tormented him without relief.

Katie remained sensitive to the rumors being floated at the time that Ara was fired because of the poor showing at Southern California, a 24–55 loss after leading at halftime. These were one hundred percent without foundation.

In the final analysis, mental and physical exhaustion from the combined factors tipped the scale for Ara. A circumspect person, Ara took stock of his own health and didn't like the trajectory he discovered. He needed a fundamental change in his life. The idea of retiring had been fermenting for months. Katie knew that the time had come to make a permanent change when Ara threw his bags across the threshold as he returned home from the late-season Navy game in Philadelphia on November 2, 1974, a game the Irish narrowly won in the fourth quarter (14–6). Ara understood he was reaching a breaking point, and the decision was made. He had inspired his teams with the mantra "We have no breaking point." There was a line he was determined not to cross, though, the line protecting his family and his personal health, not his ego or accomplishments. This was a decision born of Ara's personal strength, and without question, it was one of the most significant decisions of his life. Once made, it was irreversible. How it would be implemented had yet to be determined.

The timeline on how Ara's decision actually unfolded has been reconstructed with approximate calendar dates as follows:

Ara hopes to broach the subject of retirement with Father Joyce on the plane ride home from the Southern Cal game on Sunday, December 1. However, Father Joyce is not on the charter. He is on his way to New York for the National Football Foundation's Hall of Fame Induction Dinner on Tuesday, December 3.

Upon Father Joyce's return to South Bend, Ara meets with him in person and announces his decision to retire from coaching at Notre Dame at the end of the 1974 season. This is probably on December 4 or 5.

A surprised Father Joyce questions Ara about the finality of his decision. He suggests a week for thoughtful reconsideration.

Midweek, around December 10 or 11, Father Joyce calls Katie Parseghian at home to make sure Ara is committed to his decision. He floats the idea of having Ara take a year of sabbatical after which he could resume his position as head coach. Ara and Katie discuss this possibility at home.

At the end of the week, likely on Friday, December 13, Ara meets with Father Joyce and informs him that after careful reconsideration, his decision to retire is final. Ara brings a list of names of candidates for Father Joyce to consider as his replacement. Father Joyce, while obviously disappointed, responds that the list isn't necessary because there are contingency plans already under consideration.

At this point on the calendar, December 13, the only people who know what has transpired are Father Joyce, Ara, Katie, Jerry (Ara's brother), and presumably Father Hesburgh. Even Athletic Director Moose Krause is not in the loop.

On Saturday evening, December 14, the Parseghians are guests at the home of their close friends Patricia (Patty) and Art Decio in Elkhart. Breaking away from the party, Ara and Art meet in a private home office. There he tells his good friend about his decision and that Father Joyce is spearheading the flow of information. Now the group in the know has expanded by one.

Returning home from that party, Katie and Ara are met in their driveway by their son, Mike. He informs them that a television report has been broadcast locally announcing that Ara would be leaving Notre Dame "according to informed sources." No additional family members had been aware of Ara's plans up to this point in time. Now the speculative information has been expanded to a wider audience — before even immediate family members had been informed.

Early on Sunday morning, December 15, Moose Krause visits the Parseghian home after being informed about Ara's departure by Father Joyce. Meeting with Ara outside in his car, Moose indicates his surprise; he had been unaware of his friend's thoughts of retiring. Immediately he offers to resign his position so that Ara could succeed him as athletic director. Ara declines his friend's kind offer.

Later on Sunday morning, official news still hasn't been disseminated. Ara personally calls the homes of the assistant coaches and informs them that a coaches' meeting is being convened before noon. Micki Boulac receives the call without any inkling of what was going on; her husband, Brian, was attending Mass at Holy Cross Church with their daughters. A curious Micki immediately calls Martha Shoults, wife of Paul Shoults (the assistant coach with the longest association with Ara), wondering what might be going on. Martha doesn't know details either, but says her husband, Paul, is already on his way to the meeting.

At the late morning meeting of his assistant coaches on December 15, Ara informs them of his decision in person.

On Monday, December 16, the university formally announces Ara's retirement and that the new head football coach will be Dan Devine, at the time the embattled head coach of the Green Bay Packers in the NFL.

Father Joyce likely made the selection of Dan Devine with minimal consultation with Father Hesburgh. Devine was rumored to have been on the short list back in 1963 before Ara's hire. There was a personal family connection with Devine that appealed to Father Joyce, and in all likelihood, no other candidate was ever seriously considered.

One of the questions always raised among people intimate with Notre Dame football history is why Assistant Coach Tom Pagna wasn't the logical candidate to succeed Ara. Embedded in the narrative above is the answer: Ara was in fact offered the option of a year off. The presumption is that during that sabbatical year, either Pagna or Shoults would have been elevated to the position of interim head coach. Had Pagna gained interim head coaching credentials, he could have become the heir apparent at the end of Ara's career at a future date. Without those credentials, however, he would not have been a strong enough candidate. The mistake of naming a head football coach at Notre Dame without previous head coaching experience was a lesson that Fathers Joyce and Hesburgh didn't need to learn a second time after their experience with Terry Brennan. History reports that on only one occasion at Notre Dame has such a promotion worked out well. That fellow's name was Knute Rockne, in 1919.

A lingering question, like an unpleasant smell, hung over the surprise unveiling of Ara's decision. How did the press (in this case television networks) know that Ara was thinking of leaving Notre Dame before his immediate family members, the athletic director, and his assistant coaches were informed? The circle of people in the know was small and altogether trustworthy.

By process of elimination, Ara concluded that Father Joyce had probably informed Green Bay Packers Coach Dan Devine about what was likely to happen. Indeed, the source of the news leak was eventually traced back to Green Bay. Ara viewed this as a breach of trust by Devine, or his confidants, and a lack of courtesy that placed Ara in an uncomfortable and awkward position with people he cared about.

One of the courtesies granted by Moose Krause to Ara after his retirement was office space in a remote corner of the Athletic and Convocation Center, administrative support, and access to all the athletic and fitness facilities. It came as an annoying surprise to Ara in January 1975 when he couldn't access the coaches' locker room because the lock had been changed by order of Devine. The slight was soon corrected by Krause, but never completely forgotten.

Thus, the relationship between Ara and his successor began with distrust. It never improved. Ara quietly avoided future association with Devine in order to protect the careers of some of his assistant coaches who were retained under the new coach. Michael Parseghian was a rising junior at Notre Dame and still interested in participating on the team; Ara did not want to jeopardize his son's opportunities. Much to his credit, Ara never publicly criticized Devine while he was head coach at Notre Dame. He had too much respect for the difficulty of the job.

The sudden resignation of Ara Parseghian prompted a deluge of letters from admirers. These were all saved in Ara's personal files and ranged from being written by former players, parents of former players, alumni, friends, and a number of Armenian Americans who had never met the coach but felt a kinship. Some prominent football coaches added their best wishes to the mix.

The most insightful reaction came from one of Ara's closest friends, Head Coach George Allen of the Washington Redskins (now Commanders). On a simple card he handwrote the following, "Ara, you did the right thing. George."

CHAPTER 21

SECOND HALF

When a victorious Ara returned to South Bend early in January 1975, he may not have fully appreciated the abrupt and profound change coming to his life as he emptied the spacious office of the head football coach on the ground floor of the Athletic and Convocation Center.

Starting as a junior halfback at Akron South High School in 1940, Ara had been fully engaged in the game of football for thirty-four consecutive years, first as a player and then as a coach. The practices, the locker rooms, the games, the sounds, the smells, the camaraderie—all were suddenly gone. It had been Ara's decision to walk away, so any second thoughts had to be suppressed and the future had to be embraced despite the uncertainty. Yet, it must have felt like he was diving off the high board into a pool of uncertain depth.

Ara Parseghian retired from being active in the football realm as a young man at the age of fifty-one. He would live until the age of ninety-four. This required doing something new and challenging for the next forty-three years of his life.

MAKING ENDS MEET

The disappearance of regular direct deposits to the family bank account was the most obvious sign of a new normal for Katie and Ara. Thanks to Moose Krause, Ara received the following courtesies: a new reserved parking spot, an office on the second floor of the Athletic and Convocation Center near the athletic director, secretarial assistance as necessary, and access to university facilities. After his retirement, the only contact Ara had with the football program was through informal communications with those of his assistant coaches who had been retained.

Ara felt more than a little annoyed when a reliable source informed him that his replacement, Dan Devine, received a contract paying him $75,000 annually. That was over twice what Ara was paid by the university in his final season. (There are no secrets in small office environments.) By the time he left coaching, more than half of Ara's annual gross income came from outside sources. These commitments continued, especially the contract with Ford, and they cushioned the financial shortfall. Katie and Ara, children of the Great Depression, were prolific savers; this habit further alleviated their short-term financial stress.

REFLECTIONS AFTER THE PERIOD OF ADJUSTMENT

One might expect some regrets or second thoughts after a radical change in careers. But this doesn't appear to be true, as Ara's letters to Fathers Hesburgh and Joyce make very clear.

September 17, 1975

Dear Father Ted,

First of all, let me say that I am embarrassed with this tardy response. It was fully my intention to write and thank you for the eleven great years you made possible for my family and me. In retrospect, it will probably be the most enjoyable decade that all of us in the Parseghian family will ever enjoy.

Notre Dame means a great deal to my children because their formative stages of life occurred in the past eleven years in the Notre Dame environment. As you know, Mike is now a junior in pre-med and to my delight he is doing very well academically. Obviously, I'm not going to broadcast the fact that he inherited his mother's intellect!

I certainly share your sentiments regarding the warm and close association that existed between the Administration and Athletic Department during my tenure. Coaching at Notre Dame was a great experience for me personally. One that I enjoyed until the last year where I felt a tremendous physical, mental, and emotional strain. It has been a little over nine months since I made my difficult decision, but that time has allowed me to reflect and evaluate my resignation. I am totally convinced that I made a very wise choice. I miss working with the staff and young athletes very much. I miss, too, the strategic game preparation, but the self-inflicted pressure I imposed upon myself became an enormous drain. These past nine months have convinced me of that.

In any event, I want you to know that everyone in the Parseghian household has great admiration for you and what you have done for Notre Dame. If there is any way I can be of assistance, I would consider it an honor to be called upon.

Warmest personal regards,

Ara

Dear Father Ned,

I have enclosed a copy of the recent letter I wrote to Father Hesburgh. It was my full intention to write to both of you and acknowledge my appreciation for your cooperation and help in making possible a successful football program during my tenure. All of the things I have expressed to Father Ted are the same sentiments I feel for you in our eleven-year association. I enjoyed our visits in your office on matters that I would bring to you for counsel. Sharing the team's success and occasional failures as we made our annual football road trips will be long remembered.

Father, more important, it's a great feeling to be able to make a decision such as I did and be able to continue our friendship. Too often the reverse is true.

If I can be of any assistance to you, please call on me.

Warmest personal regards,

Respectfully yours,

Ara

Hardly the mention of an opening in the college or professional football coaching ranks for a number of years after Ara's resignation didn't include speculation that Parseghian was on the short list under consideration. Ara was adamant that he wouldn't even entertain a football-related job until after a calendar year away from coaching as a personal cleansing period. He stayed true to this.

Responding to this speculation many years later, Ara commented:

> There were a number of opportunities for almost a decade both at the professional level as well as a return to college football. I think I established as time moved forward that I was serious when I stepped down after the 1974 football season. There were a number of years when people continued to speculate about my return to the game, but now most everyone is convinced that I won't return to coaching.
>
> I've never counted the number [of offers], but offers go back as far as my coaching days at Northwestern. I did consider, or should I say reviewed, the possibility of a couple of exceptional financial offers. But my heart has always been with the college game. Additionally, I liked the university environment to raise my children and that had a big influence on my decision to stay in the college game.[1]

Discovered in his personal files was a very detailed, typed, single-spaced, formal contract proffered to Ara in 1970 by the Miami Dolphins of the NFL. It is multiple pages and includes all the boilerplate language that an NFL contract would have been required to include. All the contract needed from Ara was his signature and a postage stamp. The essential terms were an initial salary of $50,000, generous bonus provisions for performance, and a pathway to earn out a 3 percent ownership interest in the team. Obviously, Ara decided not to pursue this option.

Many years later Ara was asked by Don Shula, who did become the Dolphins coach, if he had been contacted by the team. Shula was speculating that he might have been the Dolphins' second choice. The ever-gracious Parseghian responded that it never happened. Shula went on to become the winningest coach in NFL history with 347 career victories.

Along the way, he also became a very wealthy man. The two coaches remained friends. Both are enshrined in their respective Halls of Fame.

THE LAST GAME

It may surprise readers to learn that Ara coached one last game after leaving Notre Dame. The date was July 23, 1976. The game pitted a team of college all-stars against the Super Bowl Champion Pittsburgh Steelers at Chicago's Soldier Field. The game was called at halftime due to severe thunderstorms — with the collegians trailing. Games like this between college all-stars and professional teams have not been scheduled again.

It is interesting to note that Coach Knute Rockne coached a final game in a similar venue prior to the tragic plane crash that took his life in March 1931. It was the height of the Depression and New York Mayor Jimmy Walker arranged for a team of former Irish players to suit up against the New York Giants in the emerging professional league as a fundraiser benefit for people in need. The out-of-shape collegians were overwhelmed by the fit professionals. The sold-out game in December 1930 was officially Rockne's last.

INSURANCE BUSINESS

Serendipity struck mid-1975 when a group of local South Bend entrepreneurs solicited Ara to become the public face, rainmaker, and partner in their specialty insurance business. Thus, Ara Parseghian Enterprises was established with South Bend offices downtown in the new, high-rise St. Joseph Bank Building on 202 South Michigan Street. The focus of the agency was to broker credit insurance between automobile dealers financing their own cars with national reinsurance companies. Ara's early experience as a part-time car salesman added a sympathetic presence at dealer locations and at dealer group sales meetings. His now long-standing association with the Ford Motor Company corporate offices helped open doors throughout the Midwest. A successful business was born and a financially lucrative second career was launched. The loss of his coaching salary was soon not missed.

This is how Ara described this venture:

> We have an insurance agency with fifteen employees. Some of my former coaches at Notre Dame joined us, namely John Ray, who was defensive coordinator; Wally Moore, offensive line coach; Doc Urich, wide receiver coach; and all of them are doing an outstanding job. We also have Gene Knutson, a Michigan grad who also played at Green Bay, and Dan Martin, a marine in World War II, is our president. We definitely have a football flavor in our agency. Basically, we apply the same principles that we used when we were coaching. We are highly respected and successful.

ON AIR

Ara further enhanced his income by becoming a television color commentator during the college football season. The money was very good. But the real attraction was that he could stay involved with the sport he loved, and especially the people in college coaching.

The document from Ara's files offers further insight:

> Broadcasting allowed me to continue an association with college football without the pressures of winning on Saturday. I got to see old friends and make new ones. I had the opportunity to watch teams practice, look at films, observe the changing strategy offensively and defensively, and comment during the course of the game. I can leave after the contest, feel compassion for the loser and elation for the winner and wake up Sunday morning without having to face the trials of reviewing game films with my team.
>
> I was with ABC for six years. Chuck Howard called me in 1975, my first year out, and asked if I would like to do color commentary. I appreciated the opportunity but felt my first year out of the game would be difficult and wanted to wait a full year to see if I could live with my decision. In 1976, Chuck contacted me again and it was to be my first of six years with that network.

When I joined ABC in 1976, I was asked to do Notre Dame games. Frankly, I was a bit apprehensive because I knew it would be a difficult assignment, but after some discussion, I agreed. I did ND versus USC, ND versus Alabama and two Pitt–ND games over a period of two years. I remember in the first ND game that I did, I referred to ND in my commentary as "we." The first commercial break that we had after that comment, Keith Jackson reminded me it was no longer "we" and my job was to be neutral. I tried very hard to be impartial. To my complete astonishment, it was not the opposing teams that complained about my work, it was my successor. Chuck Howard and I discussed the matter, and it was mutually agreed that I wouldn't work ND games. I had no objection because at best, it was a no-win situation.

Ironically, for many years the Notre Dame fan base thought Keith Jackson had anti–Fighting Irish bias because of the manner he covered the games. As Keith assured me, this was not the case. Jackson's personal agent, Jim Harper, was the son of former Notre Dame Head Coach and later Athletic Director Jesse Harper (the person who recommended Knute Rockne for the head coaching position). Keith was just strict about maintaining neutrality, including the constant review of his own game tapes. The friendliness and mutual respect in the Jackson–Parseghian broadcast booth felt by the viewers was genuine. The two enjoyed rounds of golf together on the road as time permitted.

The most controversial broadcast event in Ara's career came at the 1978 Gator Bowl in Jacksonville, where he worked with Keith as the number one ABC college football broadcasting team. The night game between Ohio State and Clemson was close into the fourth quarter, the Buckeyes ahead 17–15. What happened next is an unforgettable moment in college football broadcasting history. A Buckeye pass during a sustained drive (likely to result in a score) was intercepted by Clemson's Charlie Bauman. He ran out of bounds on the Buckeye sideline where he was then punched in the neck by Head Coach Woody Hayes. It was all captured live on TV to a national audience. A bench-clearing brawl ensued. Unfortunately for Keith and Ara, the overhang of the upper level of the stadium partially blocked their view of the incident in real time. They were reluctant to initially report what everyone at home had just witnessed for themselves — focusing instead on the brawl, which they did observe. Thus, the controversy.

The backstory, which was never reported, harkened back to the early days of Keith Jackson's broadcasting career. He was instructed by the producer of a game from the control booth to read a statement that the last touchdown was being dedicated to a particular young man, identifying the man by name, who was dying in a local hospital. Keith initially declined the request, but the producer insisted. Reluctantly, and without sufficient knowledge of the background, Keith read the statement as he had been instructed. Unfortunately, the young man in the hospital was watching the game — but didn't know he was dying until he heard it in Keith's statement. From that day forward Keith vowed to only report on what he actually witnessed and in a manner he was comfortable with. Since he did not initially see Hayes's punch himself, he followed his strict personal rule.

Woody Hayes was fired by Ohio State Athletic Director Hugh Hindman the following day after he refused to resign. This was not the first outburst by Hayes of punching or shoving players or referees in public. But now it was national news, embarrassing to the university and to the entire state of Ohio.

Katie, who was in Jacksonville when the event occurred, recalled the incident clearly forty-one years later, for two reasons. First, that evening was the couple's thirtieth wedding anniversary. And second, Ohio State Athletic Director Hugh Hindman, one of Ara's teammates at Miami, had been with them in Greenfield, Ohio, on the day they were married.

Once again, Ara's personal files offer perspective:

In 1982, CBS bid and won the opportunity to co-share the college telecast. That summer, CBS was assembling a new team and they called me to see if I was interested in joining them. The assignment would be in the New York studio with Brent Musburger on the pre-game, half-time and post-game shows. I called Chuck Howard to discuss my CBS opportunity. Don Bernstein [ABC public relations for college broadcasts] said Chuck was doing the British Open and wouldn't return for about a week. CBS was pressing me for a response. So, I decided that the

CBS offer was interesting and challenging and elected to sign. When Chuck returned from Europe, he called me and expressed his disappointment. He felt I should have given him the opportunity to compete. We parted on amicable terms, and even though we are competitive today, we remain friends.

It's a pleasure to work with Brent Musburger. He is truly a team player and very versatile. He is the consummate sports nut; and it doesn't make any difference whether it's football, baseball, basketball, golf, or hosting in the studio, Brent is exciting, interesting, and knowledgeable. He's one of the hardest workers I've ever been around. He's always prepared. He draws people into the telecast and his announcing technique allows his color man to express game thoughts. The CBS booth format is not restrictive, and the result has been more dialogue in a smooth flow. Rick LaCivita, a great producer, was instrumental in the change.

We are expected to be at the game site by Thursday to watch the home team practice. Before that we've been on the phone with both head coaches or their offensive and defensive coordinator. We've talked to the sports information director about names, numbers, and any personal things about individual players that might be interesting to the fans. Thursday night we have a production meeting, coordinating all the information and itinerary for Friday and Saturday. We also will review videotapes of the two teams if they are available. Friday morning we visit coaches' offices, look at films, talk with the head coach or his top assistant to get more information. In the afternoon, we watch the home team practice and sometimes the visiting team will have a light workout. If they arrived too late to practice, then we meet with them that evening before another production meeting. Brent Musburger and Rick LaCivita on a number of occasions travel to the visiting teams' campus on Wednesday to the practice and get additional information. Saturday morning we meet again to update everyone on new developments and then to the stadium for the game. There are rehearsals for our openings and a double check on electronic communication. Generally, we hit the kickoff pretty much on the anticipated schedule and after the telecast, we scatter to our homes to start to prepare for the next show. You have to throw out all names and numbers you memorized and worked on and start on the two new teams. College football is fun, but doing the telecast requires a lot of preparation.

Ara Parseghian announced in May of 1989, that he wasn't going to continue with the rigors of broadcasting college games. The folks at CBS Sports were both surprised and disappointed.

MIAMI UNIVERSITY TRUSTEE

Quite unexpectedly, Ara was asked to join the Miami University Board of Trustees. He served his alma mater in this capacity for nine years (1978–1987). It was a labor of love.

Also serving on the board at the same time was Charles "Charlie" Mechem Jr., a successful attorney who then became a successful business executive as chairman of the board of Taft Broadcasting in Cincinnati. Charlie was a student at Miami during the time Ara was completing his degree. "My first glimpse of Ara was when he had been playing for the Browns and came back as a student, walking around with a Browns' warm-up jacket. I thought it was the coolest thing I'd ever seen."[2]

Charlie is generous in his praise of Ara as a trustee. "You think that when a guy like Ara is asked on the Board it is because of his notoriety or because it is to fill an honorary position. At the time the Miami Board was quite small — only nine persons. The surprise was the intense level of engagement Ara had. He was always well prepared. On ticklish issues he'd become thoughtfully quiet until called upon."

"I asked Ara once what made a good coach. He answered, 'Most coaches think a couple plays ahead. I like to think five plays ahead, and I expect the next play won't go well and then think about what I would do.'"

Both Ara and Charlie were asked to become the chairman of the board of trustees. Both declined for the same reason. It required significant time and both had other responsibilities.

The two stayed quite close thereafter. When Ara's grandchildren needed financial help, it was Charlie, along with former ND football manager Jim McGraw, who chaired two separate fundraising dinners in Cincinnati that raised hundreds of thousands of dollars.

Eventually, Mechem became Commissioner of the LPGA (Ladies Professional Golf Association) and continued to serve on multiple corporate and charitable boards. He met and knew many of the most prominent people not only in sports, but in business, entertainment, and politics. Asked who he would name as people he really looked up to in life, Charlie answered, "On that very short list I'd include my dad, my first boss as a young lawyer, Neil Armstrong (a Taft Broadcasting board member and friend) . . . and Ara Parseghian would certainly be on my list."

RUDY, THE MOVIE

The movie *Rudy* created a sensation and renewed enthusiasm for Notre Dame Football when it was released in 1993. It purports to be the true story of Daniel "Rudy" Ruettiger, who dreamed of attending Notre Dame and playing football for the Irish and did so against all odds. Rudy was not the first walk-on player to make the team, and he certainly was not the last, but he became the most famous, much to the consternation of those who came before or after. The arc of the story is true. But many of the details were crafted in Hollywood to enhance the story. The real Rudy was on the Notre Dame practice team for two years, only one of which was coached by Ara Parseghian. The claim that Ara promised Rudy in 1974 that he would dress for one game in 1975 is dubious. By the middle of the 1974 season Ara had decided to resign and wouldn't have been inclined to make a promise he couldn't fulfill. The travel list for Ara's last game at Notre Dame, the 1974 Orange Bowl, does include prep-team players, including Daniel Duettiger (an obvious typo).

However, Ara did maintain an interest in Rudy's success after both had departed Notre Dame. Ara and his business partner Dan Martin invested in a start-up home improvement business with Rudy in South Bend. Unfortunately, the venture wasn't a success. When the movie *Rudy* was scripted, Katie recalls that Ara was asked to play himself in the production. He declined. For the premier of the film in South Bend the Parseghians were seated with Rudy's parents at the formal dinner and then attended the screening at South Bend's State Theatre as honored guests.

Assistant Coach Brian Boulac was adamant that "Rudy played his ass off." In the end, this is the central message of the film and why it has endured as one of the most successful sports movies in history. The chances of good things happening tend to increase when you work your ass off.

CHAPTER 22

ABOUT AN EIGHT

Katie Parseghian remembers fondly, "Ara loved his golf."

The day that Ara Parseghian first picked up a golf club is not recorded, but it predates his first foray into organized football. It was probably one summer day in his early teens when he hitchhiked to Loyal Oakes Golf Course, Norton, Ohio, to earn caddy money during the Depression. Ara's passion for the game continued until he could no longer swing a club safely, well into his early nineties.

People close to Ara, especially his fellow golfers, would not be surprised to learn that Ara kept meticulous records for many of the rounds of golf he ever played, probably starting as a student at Miami University. Intensity was an unsuppressed character trait in Ara when competitive athletics were concerned. Unfortunately, these notebooks have been lost in rounds of another kind—housecleaning purges. They would have been as close to handwritten personal diaries as the coach ever came, including dates, names, places, scores, money owed, and comments.

Without attaching much psychoanalysis to the subject, initially the game of golf probably was a symbolic avenue of acceptance and social advancement for a first-generation immigrant child with an ethnic last name. The equation was simple. Well-dressed men with good jobs (during economic hard times) played this game for fun and relaxation while paying kids to carry heavy bags across manicured acres of grass. A smart young fellow like Ara would have noticed that good golfers were admired by their contemporaries. Therefore, he would have concluded that becoming a golfer might be something to strive for.

Ara was blessed with unusual athletic ability, especially muscle memory. He was naturally left-handed in how he wrote and how he pitched in baseball. The golf clubs available to him as a caddy, most likely temporary clubs intended for visitors, were exclusively designed for right-handed players. Thus, Ara learned to play the game of golf right-handed (not an easy transition). Owning a personal set of clubs would have been beyond the Parseghian household budget during the Depression. Time on the golf course was probably limited to off-hours or days when the course was closed, so much of the improvement in Ara's game came naturally. Becoming a good golfer developed into a lifetime passion which was fueled by his sense of competitiveness (and explains the notebooks).

Unlike team games, the object in competitive golf isn't (usually) to inflict a beating to your fellow opponents. The object is to strategically beat the golf course and beat your last best effort. This makes beating opponents a "more polite" but not irrelevant factor in play. Success is totally within the golfer's personal control. The game suited Ara to a tee! And he became increasingly good at it. At his best he was consistently a four or five handicap player and he maintained this for a number of years as an adult.

Improvement at golf rarely happens quickly or in a straight line. Being the caddy master at Firestone Country Club, coaching the golf team at Miami, and giving informal lessons at the country club across the street from the first Parseghian home in Oxford — these were the stepping stones for his upward trajectory. As students, Katie recalls that she and Ara would go out for walks in the evening on the Miami golf course with the specific purpose of searching for golf balls lost in the weeds. (One of their shared personality traits was thriftiness.)

On October 11, 2019, Jack Nicklaus (age 80) was the invited guest of Charlie Mechem Jr., former Chairman at Taft Broadcasting Company, to a reunion held at the Camargo Club in Cincinnati, Ohio. The question arose: "Did you ever play golf with Ara?" Jack answered, "I know I played with Ara at least one time. But I don't remember where it was. Ara was a good golfer. I think he was about an eight (handicap)."

To put this comment in perspective, former Notre Dame Football Manager and Ara's frequent golfing partner, Jim McGrath, recalls that when Ara was seventy-nine, he was proud of saying that he still shot better than his age most of the time. That would make him "about an eight" handicap approximately when he played with Nicklaus, who is arguably one of the greatest golfers of all time. One wonders what Jack's own handicap was at age seventy-nine?

A photo of a younger Ara was saved in his files. It is of a group gathered at the first tee, at what Katie today guesses would be a Bob Hope Desert Classic. The others in the picture are Otto Graham, Arnold Palmer, and former president Dwight D. Eisenhower.

When a person is accomplished at playing golf, the game should become more enjoyable. Certainly, the opportunities to play with other good golfers multiply. Ara's celebrity status was confirmed in 1964. After that, he was on the A-list for celebrity golf tournaments (almost all of them with a charitable slant). The list of other celebrities he played with and got to know personally through the game of golf quickly expanded.

A special friendship tops the long list of golfing greats and celebrities with whom Ara shared a golf course. As early owners and annual winter residents at Marco Island, Florida, Katie and Ara became close friends with fellow residents Mary and Gene Sarazen. Both couples had condos on the top floors of the two original buildings. Known as "the Squire," Sarazen (1902–1999) was born Eugenio Saraceni in New York from Italian immigrant parents. In 1932, he was named the Associated Press Male Athlete of the Year. Like Ara, Gene was self-taught in the game of golf. Still rated as the eleventh greatest golfer of all time, Sarazen was the first PGA honoree of the well-earned Lifetime Achievement Award in 1999. Sarazen is one of only five professional golfers to win the Career Grand Slam with victories in each of the four major tournaments (along with Ben Hogan, Gary Player, Jack Nicklaus, and Tiger Woods). The winner of thirty-eight professional tournaments, Sarazen is also credited with inventing the modern sand wedge. Little wonder that two guys with similar backgrounds became fast friends.

Katie Parseghian provided even more details about their shared friendship. Gene and Katie shared the same birthday, February 27. This meant that they were always invited to a joint birthday celebration and shared the spotlight together at the Marco Island Country Club. Ara and Gene would spend free time on the sea wall at Marco watching the beachgoers pass by.

Ara's most frequent companion on courses close to home in Indiana, and sometimes in Florida, was George Thomas. They became lifelong friends. He was originally the golf pro at Elcona Country Club near Elkhart, Indiana, when Ara first came to South Bend. George eventually served as the coach of the Notre Dame golf team. One of his significant claims to fame was that he was one stroke over the cut at the PGA Championship in 1965 at Laurel Valley Golf Club in Pennsylvania — shooting the same score as Arnold Palmer. This was the kind of guy Ara wanted to play with, a teacher and someone (slightly) better than he was in order to measure his own progress. After 1965, their friendship flourished.

One of the interesting aspects of their enduring friendship was that George Thomas was of Lebanese extraction while Ara was an Armenian of similar background. Both were steeped in Middle Eastern cultures and trying to excel as first-generation American guys in sports. They played together a lot, sometimes with the likes of Lou Holtz and "Hawk" Harrelson (former major league baseball player and Chicago Cubs broadcaster), along with many other competitive area golfers. Ara was a member at South Bend Country Club, and he frequently played at Notre Dame's Burke Course, Brookwood, Signal Point, and other courses nearby — wherever he was invited to a competitive game. One highlight of every summer was the Big Three Tournament, held at Brookwood Golf Course (owned by the Thomas family), which brought the coaching staffs of the three major college football programs in Indiana (Indiana University, Purdue University, and Notre Dame) together for an afternoon of fun.

Ara was always courteous and known as a generous tipper to the caddies he employed, likely harkening back to his own days as a caddy. He could be very thrifty in many things, but rewarding caddies was an exception. One of the Thomas sons remembers getting a $50 tip, which was the equivalent of many rounds of normal tips in the 1960s.

On the golf course, Ara wasn't nearly as generous with his opponents. He was a stickler for following every rule and railed against someone who wanted to illegally "improve" their lie. On the greens Ara believed that every putt had to be made, including those only inches from the cup. This habit sometimes turned into theater to infuriate George Thomas. He would then get into a shouting match with Ara, with each calling the other names disparaging the other's Middle Eastern heritage. It was funny to watch. Except for these friendly exchanges, they both were very focused golfers and not prone to emotional outbursts during play. This made playing with Lou Holtz, himself a credible golfer but with an altogether opposite emotional makeup, very entertaining.

The Thomas family graciously shared Ara's handwritten letter from when George passed to be reproduced here.

12–10–12

Dear Barbara and Family,

Life does move in strange ways. The past two years when Katie and I would leave for Florida, I felt George might pass on and I worried the entire winter. Our intentions were for Katie and I to return for the funeral. He survived two winters, and this year before we left George came to our house had a beer and some grape leaf "dolma" and claimed he had gained 10 to 12 pounds. He looked it too! He appeared to be much improved. And I expected him to be around when we would come back in April. Little did I know that he would be gone in three weeks.

George and I were good friends as you know. We had a natural appeal by ethnic background. He had a magnetism about him and our love of sports, particularly golf kept us close. He was a great competitor and his golf accomplishments all well documented.

Our fun was on the golf course. The competition was fierce, and we used words our mothers never taught us. He drove us all crazy being on his own time schedule — but we would all wait. Then he would show up with that silly half smile and after two holes all would be well.

George is with God now, but it won't be long before he will try to get permission to redesign the golf courses — and knowing him he just might get it done!

Katie and Ara

In Notre Dame's Cedar Grove Cemetery, which is reserved for faculty, staff, and benefactors, the unassuming, gray granite headstones for Ara and George are just shy of twenty-two feet apart. Both are likely to be adorned by golf balls left behind by admirers. On a manicured green, the distance between the stones would be a challenging putt, but makeable. Ara would insist there still are no gimmies!

CHAPTER 23

AT THE PODIUM

Public speaking is a challenge for almost everyone. Behavioral research suggests that it ranks with death and snakes at the top of the list of human fears. If a job description were to be written for a college head football coach, public speaking would likely not be part of the obvious criteria. Yet, as visibility increases in all sports endeavors, college coaches, as celebrities, are called upon to speak in front of large groups with regularity.

Ara Parseghian grew to excel at public speaking. Yet, there is no evidence that he had so much as a speaking part in a school play until he reached the ranks of head football coach. His character demanded dedication and excellence in all things that mattered. So with his typical enthusiasm, he became one of the most sought-after banquet speakers of his generation. However, unlike with golf, he didn't keep detailed records of exactly where he was (though some of this can be gleaned from his calendars) or exactly what he said. Katie's recollection is that he wrote notes on file cards before speeches to keep moving on a well-ordered track of what he wanted to say to a specific group. Poignant stories were included and often ad-libbed in the coach's own distinctive style. After a while, Ara became comfortable with a stable of reliable themes and stories and depended less and less on the card system.

In the course of his public life the speeches ranged in subject matter, from football (naturally), to life lessons from sports, leadership, medical research, and general thoughts about character. The total number of Ara's speaking events would easily number many hundreds (not including broadcasting), and the fundraising consequences of these events could be measured in millions of dollars.

With this as background information, it might be logical to expect that some of Ara's speeches would have been recorded or filed away and accessible today. That is not the case. There are only two notable exceptions.

Ara was asked to provide the Commencement Address at Miami University of Ohio in 1987. The invitation letter from University President Paul Pearson was quite specific: the speech must be submitted in advance. Working from a stack of notes and utilizing the word processing skills of his granddaughter Taran, he met the requirement (although he left a couple of voids to tell personal stories in his own way). Thus, one of the two known surviving texts of an Ara Parseghian public speech is presented below, directly from the submitted text (lightly edited for grammatical clarity). If you want to understand the man's character, there it is as a tour de force in expansive clarity.

The Fundamentals Don't Change

Acknowledgements: President, Chaplain, Distinguished Colleagues, Members on Stage, Summer School Graduates, Parents, and Friends

First of all, I must say, I'm honored that Dr. Pearson has asked me to make this commencement address. Little did I realize when I sat almost forty years ago at my own commencement in Withrow Court, that I would be invited to address the Summer School Class of 1987. Looking out at this audience, I see some of my classmates and friends, and I'm sure they are surprised and possibly a bit shocked at my presence at this podium. After all, they knew me as a student, a coach and most memorably, a practical joker. And to this day they continue to implicate and tie me to practical jokes of which I was totally innocent.

Secondly, I want you to know, I envy you graduates because I would love to be in your shoes. Challenges, opportunities, adventures, excitement, and yes, success and failure wait for you. I experienced them all. My first losing season, one of two in twenty-five years of coaching,

I did up right. In 1957, at Northwestern, we lost all nine games. What a traumatic experience that was; but I must say, I learned more from that one season than any of the winning seasons including undefeated ones. Everyone should experience the equivalent of a losing season because, believe it or not, you will profit from it. Now, I don't recommend any more than one — you can learn all you need to know in one failure. The key is to learn from past mistakes and the trick is to not repeat them.

When I sat down to decide what I might say to this graduating class, my memory was able to span several decades, specifically four since my graduation, and the thought crossed my mind that time has provided me the benefit of many experiences and possibly I might share a couple of them with you. Education is very important as we all know, but you now go forward to the next chapter in your life to expand on your training and hopefully achieve your ambitions. In the process, you will learn from your personal experiences.

Miami has meant a great deal to me. It gave me my education, it introduced me to my wife, my three children were born here, it gave me my first coaching job, and after one year as Freshman Coach at age twenty-seven, I was named to succeed Woody Hayes when he departed to Ohio State. I remember well Paul Brown's comment when he learned of my appointment: (Paul referring to me) said, "He doesn't know what he doesn't know!" He was right — experience was my short-coming. But youth, enthusiasm and energy were on my side, as it is yours — Miami had educated me and additionally was giving me a great opportunity: now it was my responsibility to meet the challenge. Yes, I made mistakes, but I learned from them — and the old football adage applies to all professions. It's not the mistakes you make, it's the ones you repeat that become costly.

The basic fundamentals of football and life haven't changed. In football, it's blocking and tackling, conditioning, motivation and execution of the basics. Yes, the strategy and tactics of offense and defense are continually toyed with, and yes, the players are bigger and better skilled, but it's the execution of the basics that count. The basic fundamentals of life — a sound mind and body and a thirst for knowledge remain today's cherished goals. Additionally, developing professional skills, staying abreast of technical advancements are an important part of your continuing education. All of these objectives become more difficult with the temptations that have flooded the world and will tempt you. Keep the basics of sound mind and body as your fundamentals and your life will be fulfilling, exciting, and successful.

In putting together my thoughts, two key words from past experience popped into my mind, and interestingly, they both start with the letter "C". (As you know, that's average in the grading scale), but the words and the meaning would rate "A" for your future. They are communication and confidence. I would like to discuss each briefly and stress their importance to your future.

Communication — Dictionary gives several meanings:
The transfer of information to impart knowledge from one to others.
Understanding one another
Expression of thoughts
Sending information from one place to another.

My time has seen a dramatic advancement in communication technology. When I was born, our communication facilities were relatively primitive. The world has shrunk — the advent of computers, satellites, and many other technological advancements has allowed the world to know immediately current events. It also has provided us with the ability to solve complex problems in microseconds. Yet, it's the basic, one-on-one communication that remains as most important. Coaching taught me that saying it once didn't guarantee the transfer of information, but not saying it at all, guaranteed no communication. To solve problems, people must communicate and understand one another. Now, I must confess that all of my communication efforts weren't always successful.

(ad libs) Interception Story, blessed with great quarterbacks, Jim Root — Dick Hunter — Thornton Meyers — Huarte, Hanratty, O'Brien, Theismann, Clements, Montana

Dictionary's description of Confidence — Self Reliance, Assurance without question.

Confidence is one of the most important qualities you can have as you move through the challenges of life — and it's a very fragile and sensitive thing. To inspire confidence, I preached to the team: "There is no circumstance that we can't overcome," regardless of what bad luck we encountered, we believed that we could come back. Years of experience had taught me that every game wouldn't bring us the luck that people talk about. Therefore, it's important to handle adversity just as you do success.

Unfortunately, adversity is a confidence robber, sooner for some than others. Another saying that we had was: "We have no breaking point." Our opponents might let the flood gates open when they were ten points behind, or fourteen, but the attitude we attempted to instill was: "We have no breaking point." Your confidence level will have a great influence on your life. We all get down occasionally, but the important thing is to bounce back as soon as possible — regain lost confidence. It can work miracles for you, and inversely, it can destroy you. Some years ago, I read a book called *Psychocybernetics* by Maxwell Maltz. He was a plastic surgeon who came to know about the attitudes and confidence level of people. He discussed extensively what he termed the "adequate self-image:" the belief in oneself. Your opinion of your abilities sets your individual limitations. If you think you're a poor sales person, poor business person, poor conversationalist, etc., then it's very likely you will conform to your opinion. However, if you have an adequate self-image, you can be what you want to be. You set your own boundaries and limitations. Confidence in yourself — belief in yourself — is paramount to living a successful and fruitful life. If you don't believe in yourself, who will???

Let me tell you of a dramatic story that supports my sentiments of the importance of confidence.

John Huarte Story

Now let me tell you what ND did for my confidence in the eleven years that I coached at the "Golden Dome."

Stop Snow Story

Another important point I would like to make deals with the climate of what is happening in this country today. I realize that it would be very easy for you to adopt a cynical attitude — what with:

Irangate, following on the heels of Watergate

Contragate

Prayergate or Pearlygate (Jim & Tammy Baker)

Boskeygate (business)

Sportsgate (agents, players, & death penalty to SMU)

It would be easy for you to adopt a negative view of our country. However, my experience and the daily newspapers tell me that all professions have people willing to compromise the rules — the medical profession, legal, politicians, religious, business, athletes — you name it, and you will find it in our newspapers, and the cop-out, particularly in the sports world is, "Everyone does it!" Nonsense — everybody doesn't do it. I believe that anywhere from ten to fifteen percent of the public is willing to compromise the rules. In other words, cheat. That's why we have courts, lawyers, judges, and penitentiaries. Unfortunately, when a doctor, lawyer, politician, business person, or sports celebrity is apprehended and punished, the entire profession is suspect and basically scorched in the press. The point I want to make to you is simple. There are many honest, decent people in society, and they far outnumber the violators. Your ability to distinguish lawbreakers from the honest citizen shouldn't be too difficult. The fact remains that everybody doesn't cheat, and a handful of law breakers shouldn't destroy your confidence in our society.

We've now concluded lengthy hearings on the Iranian problem, and it brought to mind the importance of "integrity" and "credibility." These words were used countless times and the challenges and temptations ahead may necessitate decisions on your part that might challenge your integrity.

What is integrity? Dictionary describes it as, "an unbroken condition, a virtue, a general moral excellence." I think it's one's ability to think, say and do the same thing. Then, you're never in conflict with your own principles. When you think one thing — say another and then deny responsibility — you're without integrity. Unfortunately, our Administration was caught in that dilemma.

Credibility — Dictionary states: "worthy words of belief, an honesty and sincerity." In my position of leadership as coach, I learned early that whatever rules I laid down had to be enforced uniformly. If they weren't, then my credibility was destroyed. My honesty and sincerity had to stand the test of time. One lie, one inconsistency would have destroyed my credibility. A coach corrupts a player — the player assumes it's the way things are done and it perpetuates itself. The same is true in all professions, government, etc.

It seems to me that Gandhi's [list of] seven sins say more in less words than anything I've come across that is truly fundamental. He uses just three words in each of his seven sayings, and they make a profound impression. Hopefully, you will digest and record them in your brain's computer. Let them soak in — because they say so much with such few words:

Wealth without work
Pleasure without conscience
Knowledge without character
Commerce without morality
Science without humanity
Worship without sacrifice
Politics without principle

The fundamentals don't change; if you execute them, you've solved many of life's problems. From now on whatever you do that is newsworthy — good or bad — will be followed by the words "graduate of Miami University." Make us proud.

May I wish each and every one of you good health and fortune — have some fun, and don't forget to smell the flowers. Life comes around just once.

CHAPTER 24

HALL OF FAME

In the spring of 1980, the National Football Foundation announced that Ara Parseghian would become a member of the new class of inductees to the College Football Hall of Fame. Remarkably, this was his first year of eligibility as a coach inductee. The other members of this class were: Tay Brown, University of Southern California; Glenn Dobbs, University of Tulsa; Sam Huff, West Virginia University; Eddie LeBaron, College of the Pacific; Bob Gain, University of Kentucky; Merlin Olsen, Utah State University; Bob Ward, University of Maryland; and J. C. Caroline, University of Illinois.

In 1980, the physical Hall of Fame shrine was located in Kings Island, Ohio, outside of Cincinnati. This was its first location. It subsequently moved to South Bend and then to Atlanta, the current location. But since the establishment of the National Football Foundation in 1947, the formal Hall of Fame Induction Dinner was traditionally held in New York at the Waldorf-Astoria Ballroom in early December. This is the same venue used to formally induct members of the Rock & Roll Hall of Fame, although that shrine is located in Cleveland. The dinner has been the primary fundraiser for the Foundation's administrative functions, which are also located in New York City. In 1980, the tickets were sold by tables of ten seats for about $2,500.

By tradition, this event has always been a black-tie, stag affair. It is one of the premier sports gatherings in America. Over two thousand men attend from all walks of life with a high concentration of notable former players, athletes from other sports, college coaches and athletic administrators, media personalities, captains of industry, and a few political figures added for good measure. Dinner was served on the main floor and on the two tiers of surrounding balconies. Those balconies were festooned with large banners representing the colleges, large and small, with a football tradition. A small orchestra on one of the balconies played background music and shortened versions of various college fight songs as each of the multiple speakers was introduced. The main stage featured three tiers of head table spaces for honorees and dignitaries. Appropriate acknowledgement was given to high-ranking clergy in the entourage.

The pre- and the post-dinner receptions, set in various suites dispersed throughout the two towers of the hotel, were part of the total experience. Visitors to New York from the hinterlands — the likes of Columbus, Ohio; Norman, Oklahoma; and College Station, Texas — indulged in the full Big Apple experience. Open bars with complimentary cigars were the motif, reminiscent of the Roaring Twenties. Finding a high stakes craps game wasn't out of the question in this annual celebration of testosterone.

The list of men at Ara's table, by his personal invitation, were: his son, Michael Parseghian (who needed to find a tuxedo at the last minute); his brother, Jerry Parseghian; Art Decio (businessman from Elkhart and personal friend); Eddie Niam (boyhood friend from Akron); Cy Laughter (Dayton businessman and organizer of Bogie Busters, a golf tournament benefiting multiple sclerosis); Dan Martin, Gene Knutson, and Ed Hayes (South Bend business partners in the insurance company); and John Ray and Wally Moore (both former assistant coaches at Notre Dame and also Ara's business partners). The University of Notre Dame traditionally reserved two additional tables each year for administrators and former players previously elected to the Hall of Fame.

The 1980 class of inductees selected Ara to give their acceptance speech. This is the text of what he said that night, the second of only two speeches saved by the coach and reproduced here from his personal files.

It's certainly my privilege and honor to respond on behalf of all the 1980 Hall of Fame inductees. I'm sure that I speak for all of us when I say how proud we all are to have been selected. It's one thing to learn that you have been chosen to become a member of the Hall of Fame, and then it's another thrill to realize, particularly as you look around the room tonight, the exclusive company you are joining.

I would be remiss if I didn't thank, for all of us, our universities, our coaches, teammates, and everyone who assisted in making this night possible. This distinguished honor allows all of the new members to reflect on our careers. The first time we put on football equipment, the first game, the first season, and all the thrills of a playing career, and in my case a coaching career.

I trust that I speak for the other inductees, when I say that never in our wildest dreams could we have envisioned from our first football involvement, a night such as this. And most importantly, the purpose of our football participation as players and coaches, never had in mind a distinction or honor of this magnitude. The rewards of our football activities are many because the very nature of the game provides so many carryover values. One might say it's a microcosm of what one is to face as he moves through his post-playing life. How well I remember Paul Brown's words, "You must earn the right to participate, to compete, to win." We all know the sacrifices that must be made. No one can buy their way into this game and that's why it's so well respected. Isn't it true in all of our lives, the things that we appreciate the most are the things we worked hardest for and truly earned?

Ara's final major sports award came in 1996, when he received the Amos Alonzo Stagg Award conferred by the American Football Coaches Association at their annual convention in January. Essentially, this is a lifetime achievement honor. The text that accompanied the award is as follows: "Ara Parseghian was looked at by our committee as not only an outstanding football coach and a leader in our profession, but an individual who has carried forth those principles that he 'taught and lived by.' He has become one of the great contributors to our society in the area of benevolence. He exemplifies what the Stagg Award stands for."

For readers who are not football historians, Amos Alonzo Stagg (1862–1965) was one of the earliest and most successful college football coaches through his seventy-one-year career beginning at the University of Chicago, and later at the College of the Pacific. He was the winningest college coach in history (314–199–36) until Bear Bryant broke his record in 1981. Stagg is the only member of the College Football Hall of Fame inducted as both a player and a coach.

The story goes that in retirement, Stagg lived in Oak Park, Illinois, near the University of Chicago where he once coached. A neighbor lady called one day to inform him that the neighborhood boys playing football on his side lot were ruining his lawn. He reportedly responded, "Madame, I'm not raising grass. I'm raising boys."

Ara was a fitting awardee for that kind of spirit.

CHAPTER 25

BITTERSWEET

Life is bittersweet. This may not be obvious to the young, but adults, with rare exceptions, usually come to grips with this stark reality.

The lives of celebrities, seemingly full of fame and fortune, capture the imagination of the public because it is believed that their lives are somehow charmed. It is easy to imagine an alternate reality, thinking "if only that would happen to me" in response to unfortunate circumstances affecting each of our daily lives. What if our momentary fantasies were tested against the benchmark of trading not only the shiny moments, but every life experience, the whole package? How many of us would elect to do this after some serious thought and contemplation? No right-minded individual would elect to trade places with Ara Parseghian, and by extension, with his immediate family, for reasons that will become evident in this chapter.

KARAN PARSEGHIAN BURKE

Many of the important events in Ara's life revolve around Miami University. Perhaps no moment was more consequential than meeting

Katie Davis as she was walking across campus. From a chance encounter began a family and a lifetime of commitments.

Ara and Katie's daughter Karan was born as he was assuming the position of freshman football coach. Daughter Kristan (Kriss) and son Michael (Mike) were also born during Ara's coaching tenure at Miami. Karan, a dark-haired beauty, distinguished herself as a studious first-born. Upon graduating from Adams High School in South Bend (1968), Karan matriculated at Miami — in the family tradition. One year later she was joined by her sister Kriss on the Oxford, Ohio, campus.

During Karan's sophomore year at Miami (1970), troubling physical signs emerged that became gravely concerning to both Ara and Katie. Karan showed some difficulty in walking. Knowing the family histories on both sides, the parents made immediate arrangements to seek medical expertise. This led them to a top doctor at the University of Michigan, Dr. Wallace Tourtellotte. Ara's letter thanking Dr. Tourtellotte follows.

October 22, 1970

Dear Dr. Tourtellotte,

Just a note to thank you sincerely for making so much time from your obviously busy schedule.

My wife and I were impressed with your handling of a neurological problem as well as a psychological one. We endorse everything you said and the enthusiasm and confidence you projected to Karan has to be encouraging to her. The key words of vanity and depression were important in your positive approach to solving the problem — the jogging and the steroids, was received by Karan with hope.

Your success in your field is easily understood as one listens. I may call on you to give a pep talk before one of my games.

On behalf of Karan, Katie and I are grateful. Thank you.

Sincerely,

Ara Parseghian

Ara and Katie were devastated by the initial diagnosis of multiple sclerosis, as any parents would have been. The full extent of Karan's illness was kept private from all outsiders as plans were made to adjust to a new family reality. Even Karan did not know her true diagnosis. But one of Ara's assistant coaches and closest confidants, Tom Pagna, had an inkling of what was transpiring.

> Ara and I were showering one day after the other coaches had gone. We were talking about Karan. I could see he was more concerned about her than usual. I shocked him when I asked, "How long have you known she has multiple sclerosis?" He looked at me and turned pale. He mumbled, "just recently" and did not say another thing the rest of the afternoon. The next morning, he called me into his office, he shut the door, walked behind his desk and gave me a look that told me I was in trouble. His ire must have been building all night. "How the hell did you know about Karan?" he hollered. "Karan doesn't even know. My secretary is the only one besides Katie and the doctor and if she told you I'll fire her right now. The doctor isn't even certain it is MS and I don't want Karan to hear it from someone else. We'll have to break it to her, but I've been troubled in my own mind how to do it."
>
> I chose my words carefully in response. "Ara," I began, "stop and think about it. Our lives have been intertwined for a long while now. I feel the same empathy for your family as I do for my own. I babysat for your sister who has MS. Katie's brother died from it. I have a friend who has it so I know the symptoms. I saw Karan dragging her leg and I just assumed she had it."
>
> He apologized for snapping at me. He slumped to his desk, put his head in his hands and fought back the tears as he told me all about it. After countless tests verified the suspicions over the next several months, Karan's doctor broke it to her. Helping her adjust to that reality was the most difficult thing Ara ever had to do.
>
> Like any other obstacle, as soon as he found out what it was, he made up his mind to go out and conquer it. He learned all he could about Multiple Sclerosis. He talked to doctors, he got medical journals — any way he could get information, he got it. Money was the bottom line to all the research. So, he threw himself into a money-raising campaign that continues today. He got upset when he found out how much some professional fundraisers lobbed off the top. He knew he could raise money, and he did. He even paid many of his expenses to make appearances for MS. God only knows how much he's raised or the time he has spent. But he felt if his efforts improved the lives of all those who suffer from the disease, it would be worth it, it would be time well spent.[1]

Both sisters, Karan and Kriss, transferred to Saint Mary's College in 1971, the all-female companion school to the all-male Notre Dame across the road (the old US 31). Kriss, along with many of the assistant coaches' children, was a frequent visitor to Notre Dame football practices and became familiar with many of the players. By her own admission, Kriss was more social than academic. Upon her arrival at Saint Mary's, she was assigned to room with Rooney Frailey, who went on to become one of the first female cheerleaders at Notre Dame. She has remained close to this sisterhood of cheerleaders ever since.

Jim Humbert was recruited as an offensive lineman from Cincinnati's Roger Bacon High School in 1968. He vividly recalls the first time he met Kriss Parseghian. He was on a recruiting visit and speaking with Coach Parseghian in the lobby of Rockne Memorial where the Football Office was located. Kriss busted through the front doors to approach her dad. Ara exclaimed, "Here comes trouble." Three years later, Jim and Kriss started dating. They were married in the Church of the Sacred Heart (not yet designated a basilica) on the Notre Dame campus. The Humberts welcomed three children (in birth order): Taran, Jamie, and Kaley. They eventually moved back to South Bend and lived only minutes from Katie and Ara.

At her sister's wedding, Karan was introduced to Jim Burke, a Notre Dame graduate (1971) and at the time a law student on campus. A relationship blossomed between them, which ironically Ara was the last to recognize. Katie finally had to clue him in, "Why do *you* think he keeps visiting Karan?" Beyond the assumed level of interest of the typical Notre Dame student, Jim didn't know much about the intricacies of football. But he did share Ara's interest in current events and their politics aligned. It was a good match. Soon after, a wedding was scheduled for Saturday, September 7, 1974 — in part because no football game was scheduled for that Labor Day weekend. However, an away game with Georgia Tech was added after the wedding date was set for September 9, just two days later.

Jim Murray was a highly-respected syndicated sportswriter for the *Los Angeles Times*. One of his most notable columns centered around Karan and Jim's wedding and appeared on March 9, 1975, after Ara's retirement.

"Ara's Longest 20 Yards"

When someone asks Coach Parseghian what his greatest victory at Notre Dame was, he will probably lie. . . . His greatest victory came three nights before the Georgia Tech game last year when he walked his daughter down a dark, deserted church aisle. . . . His worst defeat came the day the doctor confirmed the unthinkable: that his daughter had multiple sclerosis. . . . But the longest 20 yards he ever had to make in his life came with an audience of unseen statues looking on. It was a night game, lit only by sputtering candles and a sanctuary light. . . .

It was the eve of the Georgia Tech game. Ara's daughter was to be married the next day. Her wants were simple. . . . All she wanted was to be able to walk down the aisle. . . . So, Ara and daughter Karan arrived at a wedding rehearsal for two. . . . This was no breakaway run, this was a step by step, foot by foot effort of the will. No father of the bride was ever prouder. "I have never seen my daughter more radiant than she was coming back out of the church that night," Ara recalls. "She had made it." . . . The wedding the next day was one of the great victories the Notre Dame campus has ever seen.[2]

Karan and Jim Burke moved to the Akron area, his hometown. They had two boys, James and Michael. Ara and Katie visited frequently since Ara's mother and sister also lived there. Ara became more active in fundraising for MS and served as the honorary national chair of the Multiple Sclerosis Foundation.

Karan summarized her story sixteen years after her wedding as follows:

I was diagnosed with M.S. when I was 17 years old. My parents had the good sense not to tell me at first since they knew my "stop the world I want to get off" reaction would have kept me from going away to college. The symptoms then were easy fatigue and a slight limp when I was tired, so I accepted the doctor's explanation of "an infection in the spinal cord." Cortisone even cleared it up in those first years.

When I was a sophomore at Miami I found out the spinal infection was called Multiple Sclerosis, and I took the turtle-hiding-his-head approach and made my parents promise not to tell anyone. From the perspective of 16 years, and thinking like a Monday Morning Quarterback, that was a pretty dumb way to handle the news. And it was very lonely to keep the secret to myself. I must have hoped it would go away before anyone knew.

My sister was relieved when she found out it was "only M.S." She had imagined all these tests were for a rare African disease or something worse. My friends probably had similar wondering, worrying, and should have been confided in.

If anyone would have told me during those traumatic first "why me?" years that I'd marry a lawyer from Akron who didn't care about the M.S. and that we would have two little boys and that I'd be in a wheelchair and be happy I would have laughed at them. But those unexpected things did happen. It seems somehow that somehow over the 16 years I've learned to adapt. I take naps every afternoon. I know it will take longer to do almost anything. I know that overdoing will mean paying for it later. Life with M.S. is very livable—just more inconvenient.[3]

Karan Burke died of complications from multiple sclerosis in 2012, thirty-eight years after her wedding date.

What could be worse for parents than watching their child die, inch by inch, from a debilitating disease without a cure? The unfortunate answer to that question became evident only a few short years later.

CHILDREN OF CINDY AND MIKE PARSEGHIAN

Michael, the thirdborn of the Parseghian children, also graduated from South Bend's Adams High School in 1973 having a notable football career as a fullback. He entered Notre Dame and spent his freshman year cracking the books—not trying out for the football team. He did make the team his sophomore year, sharing the practice field with some Notre Dame notables, including Joe Montana and Daniel "Rudy" Ruettiger. Mike made some game appearances as well. But being the coach's son wasn't always comfortable. He deferred playing in his senior year in lieu of preparing applications to medical school. In the spring of 1977, he was accepted into the selective Northwestern School of Medicine in downtown Chicago.

Mike's greatest accomplishment at Notre Dame may have been meeting Cindy Buecher. Notre Dame had started accepting women in the fall of 1972. The two young Domers dated seriously. They married in Grand Junction, Colorado, the summer before Mike's med school started, then lived in a high-rise apartment conveniently located within walking distance of the Northwestern School of Medicine and hospital. Katie recalls these four years as happy times when she and Ara could visit Chicago for overnight stays, enjoying all the city had to offer.

After earning his MD, Mike decided to pursue a career in orthopedic surgery and was matched at the University of Arizona for five years of residency. Cindy and Mike were blessed with four children in succession, Ara, Michael, Marcia, and Krista. Theirs was a picture-perfect family story . . . until it wasn't. Everything changed in September 1994.

Here is a lengthy excerpt from "Former Irish Coach Parseghian Battling Odds in a Deadly Game," an article by Bill Koch in the Scripps Howard News Service:

Ara Parseghian understands that you get knocked down in sports occasionally, that things don't always go your way. When that happens, you pick yourself up and carry on. You find a way to overcome whatever it was that knocked you down. It's a lesson that has served him well in life.

Parseghian has never been knocked down the way he was last September when he learned that his three youngest grandchildren, eight-year-old Michael, six-year-old Marcia and three-year-old Krista—have a rare and fatal genetic disorder called Niemann-Pick Disease, Type C.

"There was a period of about a month of terrible grieving," Parseghian said. "There's no shame for a grown man to cry. You think about the hows and the whys of this. I don't expect every day to be a bright, sunny day. But I didn't expect this. Obviously, it was a shock. It stunned me."

Michael was the first of the three to be diagnosed with the disease after his parents noticed that his motor skills were poorly developed. The symptoms include poor coordination and an inability to put words together in speech.

Because it's a hereditary disease doctors suggested that Michael's younger sisters be tested. The three children don't know about the disease but the older brother Ara, eleven, does. The younger ones are likely to get the news next month when ABC's *2020 News Magazine* does a significant segment on the family. "We were wondering what impact that will have on the kids at school," Parseghian said. "We decided it was more important to try to raise funds and hopefully find a cure."

Parseghian said, "The girls are not showing symptoms yet. We've got a little time, maybe four to six years with them. Michael is the one we have a deep concern about. He's eight and he's showing significant symptoms. He's a terrific kid even though he has difficulty speaking. Every time you ask him how are you doing Michael it's always, 'good, good. Everything is fine.' At the public school he attends there's another kid who's partially blind. Michael is his eyes. The two of them are great buddies. Michael feels as if he's doing something productive. I'm sure he knows he's not up to par with the other kids, but he doesn't know the extent of it."

Parseghian says people have told him to pray for a cure. He does. But he says that's not enough. "I've always had a philosophy that praying and doing are two different things. If I just pray alone, I have a chance. If I pray and do something about it, that increases the chances."

"What happens when you're around them is that you're grateful they're there," he said. "The very fact that we've immersed ourselves in this project gives us hope. If you lingered with the consequences of the disease constantly, it would be a disaster. But we see progress. We see a chance. Maybe it's a small percentage, but we see that."[4]

For additional context, an excerpt follows from "For Dying Children, a Long Shot," a piece by Bruce Lowitt in the *Saint Petersburg Times*, Tuesday May 16, 1995.

Ara Parseghian and his family are fighting for the lives of three of his grandchildren.

"My grandchildren, they're here now," he says. "The rules say they can last into their early teens. Give me some time.". . .

"People tell me I'm heroic," [mother] Cindy Parseghian says. "You know, you would do this too, and it's not heroic. It's very selfish. If we do nothing, we know the outcome, and that's unacceptable. I know other children will benefit but I'm doing this in the hopes that I can save my children."

For her husband the frustration lay in the fact that he, a physician dedicating his life to healing, could do nothing medically for his children.

"I'm not so idealistic to believe that medicine can do everything," Michael Parseghian said. . . .

"I don't take anything for granted with these kids," Cindy Parseghian says. "We've always spent a lot of time together as a family; I don't know that that has changed. But every moment with them is pretty bittersweet. . . . They have dreams and aspirations just like any other child, they are not always long-term dreams. . . . I, as a parent—as any parent—want to make those dreams and aspirations come true." The steel in Cindy Parseghian's voice is returning, it's only for a moment. "That's what keeps us going."[5]

Niemann-Pick disease type C (NPC) is so rare that there are under one thousand cases currently diagnosed in the United States.[6] All three Parseghian children with NPC, Michael, Marcia, and Krista, eventually succumbed. There is a bench dedicated to their memory at the Grotto, a special place for reflection and prayer on the Notre Dame campus. Mike and Cindy's eldest child, young Ara, grew up to become a physician and lives with his family near his parents in Arizona.

The Parseghian Medical Research Foundation was established in 1994 with Ara as spokesman and Cindy in charge of the day-to-day operations. The foundation continues to achieve notable success. The Notre Dame community, especially former football team members, rallied around their beloved coach and his personal cause. Over $40 million (and counting) has been raised and numerous research projects have been funded. There has been some limited success in treatments, although a cure remains elusive.

Ara once mused, "There's a lot of things that I was exposed to as the football coach that I had carried over to my present tasks and responsibilities. Only now I'm recruiting, getting people to work on our behalf and motivating people to win a cause for us rather than a football game. It's a time-consuming thing. And, being seventy-two with a bad hip and knee I have to take a cane with me now when I travel. And, it isn't an easy thing now, but this is a challenge we have to win."

After his grandchildren were diagnosed, Ara Parseghian spent the remaining twenty-three years of his life working for a cure with no breaking point.

CHAPTER 26

DEAR COACH

Once Ara left Notre Dame, the mailbox at the Parseghian residence in Granger, Indiana, was often filled with letters addressed to the coach. There were those, young and old, who sought an autograph as a personal keepsake. More recently, some of these requests were incentivized by the value of collectibles on web marketplaces. This annoyance, while regrettable, was impossible for Ara to police effectively. So, he generously signed his name (one per request) and returned an autograph to all who submitted the requests, sometimes paying the postage himself to do so. The upshot is that if you are holding an Ara Parseghian autograph today, chances are close to one hundred percent that it is authentic although not rare at all, since thousands were freely given. This generosity of spirit emphasizes his character: Ara achieved fame but didn't take himself seriously. In his humility, he felt forever complimented that people remembered his contributions both on and off the field.

After leaving football coaching at the conclusion of the 1974 season, Ara Parseghian also received a steady stream of very personal correspondence until his death in August 2017. There are scores of these paper messages addressed to his home. These physical objects are meaningful in an age consumed with instantaneous communication that is often rushed and impersonal.

Ara saved and cherished all of them. In fact, there are so many letters and notes sent to Ara that a book of these highly personal messages could be assembled. Unfortunately, that is beyond the scope of this volume, although it would be a worthy undertaking. Most of the messages are so heartfelt that not including all of them in a published format might disappoint correspondents. It would be equally unfair to the reader to exclude any of these. Each is a marker of Ara's character in its own fashion. A sampling of these have been identified by the family as typical of what all correspondents had in their hearts. The letters and notes come from individuals in differing walks of life and arrived at different times in the coach's lifetime — perhaps a note regarding the work of the Ara Parseghian Medical Research Foundation, or a birthday greeting, or a get-well message. The representative selection below has been included so that any reader who lacks a personal association with Ara Parseghian can observe the profound effect that he had on the lives of so many he cared deeply about. The original format and wording of these letters has been preserved. Brief commentary accompanies many of the examples that follow.

August 11, 1974

Dear Coach,

I thought I would write you to tell you how things are going. I'm sorry to hear about what happened with the team. I was in South Bend around the 11th of July so I knew what might happen. I was hoping that the penalty would not be so severe. To me it doesn't seem to be corrective punishment, but then again, my own views and the views of administrative people have not always been eye-to-eye.

Some, most, all of the players that were brought in to fill camp couldn't play for you but they do try hard and unlike me practice every day.

Please pass my regards to the rest of your family. Also, please give my best to the coaches, team, and Big John the trainer.

Thank you,

David

Dave Casper was the team captain and an All-American who played four positions at Notre Dame. After college he played for the Oakland Raiders in the NFL and then enjoyed a successful career in business. He was inducted into both the Pro Football Hall of Fame (2002) and the College Football Hall of Fame (2012).

July 31, 2017

Dear Ara,

I want to thank you Ara for making such an impact on my life. I am sure you would never know that. Prior to becoming one of the first ND female cheerleaders in 1969, I really knew nothing about ND football and all the traditions. You were my introduction to not only Notre Dame football but to a role model of leadership, integrity and all that is good in this world.

Sometimes when I'm thinking about things and reflecting on life, I often reminisce about my days at Notre Dame and I recall the feeling in my stomach when we cheered and I want to cheer "Ara stop the rain." I never truly realized the importance of a mentor, a teacher, a coach, a father and the amazing impact one person can make through their actions. Thank you, Ara for being that special someone gift to all of us and for making the world a better place.

Terri

Terri Buck Lewallen graduated from Saint Mary's College in 1972. She was one of the first four female cheerleaders at Notre Dame in 1969, and arguably the most photographed coed on campus. She eventually married former Notre Dame football player Brian Lewallen. Funnily enough, they never met each other in college; they met at a Notre Dame alumni event years later.

July 2017

Dear Ara,

I just want you to know I am praying for one of the strongest and most inspirational men I know. You have motivated many directly and many more indirectly. You are the epitome of what a good man should be. So many are quietly joining in this prayer for your full recovery. Whether it was at Notre Dame in our first year in 1964, or during the years I was off getting a law degree and a business degree and then beginning my career elsewhere, or when I returned to the community after Michael's [Chris's father-in-law] death, you were there to encourage me. You and Katie have always been a gracious couple and you have always been open to Carmy and me. I enjoyed working with you in business, although I must say requiring me to spend hours with Johnny Ray in a car to visit other bankers may have been one of the greater rewards of your insurance business. I do admire what you accomplished in so many ways and in so many different venues. Knowing your strength, I know you will once again prevail. So, get well and we all hope to see you soon.

One more person you touched,

Chris

Chris Murphy was chairman, president and CEO of 1st Source Corporation and 1st Source Bank. As a student from 1967 to 1968, he was Notre Dame Student Body President. He met Carmy Carmichael through her father, Mike Carmichael, who was the chairman of the largest fundraising campaign for Notre Dame at the time. Carmy and Chris eventually married, raised a large family, and still reside in South Bend, where they remain active in a wide variety of community affairs.

September 9, 2014

Dear Coach,

As I reflect on these past six years, I wanted to tell you how much you have meant to me as a leader. Growing up, I watched you on television with my father, and I always wanted to play for you. Well, my height and genes thwarted that dream on the football field, but it came true in the fight against NPC. I have had the extraordinary privilege of being coached by you on the field of life. Personally, and professionally, you have been an incredible inspiration for me, as well as to our faculty who follow your lead in the fight and our students who research NPC and raise money for more research.

When people ask me to name my favorite place on campus, they generally expect me to say the Basilica, Touchdown Jesus, the Dome, or the House that Rockne Built. But I tell them my two favorite places are the Coach Parseghian statue and the bench at the Grotto for Krista, Michael, and Marcia. These are my treasures.

To me, the statue represents leadership, planning, and confidence. I was eight years old when you called that famous Clements-to-Weber pass that ended the game against Alabama and won the National Championship. You had so much confidence in your players and the courage to make such a bold call when everyone expected you to punt and rely on your strong defense. Now, when I have to make a tough call and take a risk, I often walk to your statue, and somehow the answer comes. The answer is often the same: Trust your team and it will all work out. That's why I've called some Tommy Clements' passes in the past six years as Dean. The statue reminds me of your confidence in our team that is fighting for those NPC kids and families — someday they will be carrying you from the field when our championship is won.

Coach, you have taught me so much about being a virtuous person — your grace, your humility, and your passion to fight have educated and inspired me, and I have seen your impact on many others. In this time of reflection in transition, I just wanted to say thank you for being my coach. You are the greatest coach ever, not only for what you did on the football field, but especially for what you have done on the field of life.

With extraordinary appreciation and admiration,

Yours truly in Notre Dame,

Greg P. Crawford

At the time of the letter's writing, Greg Crawford was the dean of science at Notre Dame. He enthusiastically embraced the goals of the Ara Parseghian Foundation, fighting for a cure for Niemann-Pick disease type C (referred to as NPC in the letter). He distinguished himself by taking multiple cross-country bicycle trips to raise substantial funding. He became the president of Miami University (Oxford, Ohio) in 2016, Coach Parseghian's alma mater and where he had his first head coaching job. In President Crawford's installation address to campus on October 10, 2016, he awarded Coach Parseghian the Miami University Presidents Medal.

June 11, 2017

Dear Coach,

I wanted to reach out and wish you a speedy recovery. I remember complaining to you about my four hip operations and you told me that you had five. I don't complain anymore.

You taught us many lessons during our time together 1967–1971, and after.

If you can play with pain you can play!

Don't fumble!

You did CALS with us and you were 44.

Go to class — get your grades.

Don't drink at Frankie's — everyone will know you there.

Tape your ankles.

Hit and recoil.

Hurry the count.

The new shoes you sent us in June better not look new on August 15.

Bonded for a lifetime.

I'm so sorry I reported for camp in 1967 with a broken thumb — I was a total dumb ass — broke it in a drunken fight. I tell everyone it's the thumb that made Joe Theismann famous. I tell all the young kids that one night can change your life!

You were the most understanding during our Vietnam conflict protest. I fondly remember that you didn't punish us who skipped a spring practice to attend an antiwar rally in April 1969. You taught us to tell the truth, much like my parents. When I was arrested at a party for underage drinking, I agonized for a few days before telling you. You responded by informing me that you had known for a few days, and you were waiting to see if I told you the truth. Did not dismiss me from the team because I told you the truth. Thank you, Coach!

When we broke the huddle and hustled to the line of scrimmage no one knew the play until the first sound 2, 4, 6, 8, go green. I remember this fact every time I see our whole team standing at the line of scrimmage looking at the sideline. It reminds me just how brilliant your scheme was. No wonder we had such success.

Much love,

Chuck Nightingale, #28

Happy Birthday Coach Ara,

I was a freshman in 1973 and had the occasion of my parents' first visit to me on campus. I was excited to show them our world-class sports facilities. While walking through the ACC, I saw you coming down the hallway. I nudged my father and said this is the Head Football Coach coming our way.

You stopped by my parents, introduced yourself, and said how proud "you" were that they entrusted their son to your care in the care of all the leaders at our University. Telling my father and mother how their choice to have me attend this great University will shape this young man now and affect the lives of all those he comes into contact in whatever walk in life he encounters. My parents were impressed, grateful, and still talk about your kindness and foresight. Thank you, Coach Ara, for our National Championship that year, your community leadership, and concern you showed to my parents. Thank you for my memories.

Happy birthday Coach,

Jerome B. Mayer, ND 77

Jerry "Irish" Mayer left Notre Dame as a commissioned Air Force officer. He served from 1977 to 1997, rising to the rank of Lieutenant Colonel as an F-4 and F-16 pilot, instructor, and flight examiner. From 1997 to 2020, he joined United Air Lines as pilot and a captain of Boeing 727, 737, 757, 767, and Airbus A-320/319 aircraft.

Dear Coach,

I was asked to write a fan a note about you. Here is how I responded (attached).

"You asked me to write a letter talking about my coach, Ara Parseghian. It is hard to put into words what Ara has meant to me, not just as a student athlete, but as a man going forward in my life. I can honestly say that I am who I am today based on the principles Ara taught me, when I was lucky enough to play for him.

His work ethic, his insistence on paying attention to details and his ability to be compassionate, but yet stern when the situation called for it."

A simple thank you just doesn't seem enough to a man who helped make me a man.

Sincerely,

Joe Theismann, #7

CHAPTER 27

THE LOOK AND
THE VOICE

Ara Parseghian possessed many distinguishing physical attributes that are unforgettable by those who came to know him, whether in a chance meeting or over a lifetime.

Ara wouldn't be considered physically tall — about five feet, nine inches, maybe five feet ten in cleats. But everything else about him added to his physical stature. The most accurate way to describe his body type would be to call it thick. In photos taken after he returned from Navy service, Ara stands muscular and fit.

His natural abilities in athletics kept him in shape throughout his lifetime. Time for physical exercise was an essential part of his workdays, an easy feat with an office in an athletic facility and assistant coaches who also pursued personal fitness. Exercising as a team of coaches helped to build teamwork, kept individual bodyweight down, and perhaps most importantly, relieved stress. Students and faculty alike remember Ara bounding on the handball court, swinging or putting on the Burke Golf Course, and even playing pickup hockey once Notre Dame football offices were moved to the new Joyce Athletic and Convocation Center in

1968. Even on ice skates he was a natural. There is no evidence that he ever played hockey as a youngster, but he skated with balance, flow, and self-aware determination, qualities that also made him graceful when he found himself on the dance floor. His physical abilities were an exceptional gift.

In later life he may have asked himself if he had overworked his skeleton. The hip injury suffered while he was with the Cleveland Browns in 1949 wasn't an apparent deterrent from vigorous physical activities until his late fifties. In the remaining forty years of his life, he endured eight different surgeries. Seven of those were for joint replacements (hips and knees). The eighth was for a kidney stone extraction, with kidney stones remaining a persistent concern thereafter.

The players and coaches who saw him working at his most serious moments have memories of The Look. This memorable pose of Ara's accompanied some displeasure. His head would be cocked and his nearly black eyes would bore a hole directly into the gaze of The Look's recipients, described by some as going: "through the back of our heads." Ara was usually not a screamer when it came to getting someone's attention. Generally, all it took for him to receive a response was The Look.

By people who pay attention to such things, Ara was a handsome man. His tanned skin and naturally wavy black hair enhanced a face that had character. As he aged, Ara's full head of hair became salt-and-pepper and then completely snow-white. His distinctive appearance made him immediately recognizable throughout his later life, especially after his success at Notre Dame. His overall presence and demeanor made him a very credible media spokesperson for the Ford Motor Company and as a college football commentator on television for ABC and CBS.

Everything about Ara became familiar to average Americans — his unusual ethnic last name (which was frequently mispronounced), his distinct visage, and his unmistakable voice. He didn't have a deep, resonant tone as might be expected of an authoritative coach or a smooth broadcaster. In fact, his husky voice was slightly high pitched and at times squeaky when he was excited. The texture has been described as "gravelly." Think of a rusty handsaw ripping through a chunk of hardwood. Ara sounded like he had a permanent case of laryngitis.

When Katie asked a granddaughter to describe her grandfather's voice, this was the poignant written submission.

"Grandpa's Voice"

To describe my grandfather's voice is not an easy task. You could give all the adjectives of pitch and vibrations within the ears — low, deep, loud, etc. . . . but his voice was more of a feeling. It was the feeling of a sound that makes you stop and truly listen.

It was a masculine, commanding sound full of layers. Layers of intelligent, carefully chosen words expertly strung together, that illustrated his true power to motivate and to give and receive respect.

It was layers of raspy chuckles that were filled with unending love, patience, and mischievous fun. His voice was filled with passion and drive mixed with kindness, fairness, and confident modesty.

It's a voice I have trouble listening to today in recordings as the pain of his absence still affects me, but the memory of the layers I hear every day.

Miss him.

Love,

Kaley (Humbert) Thornberg

CHAPTER 28

REPORT CARD

The tradition at all levels of education, prior to when computers took over, was that report cards were written by the teacher(s) by hand. A student's progress could be tracked in boxes designed to record grades or insert check marks. This provided a personal connection between the teacher, the student, and ultimately, the parents. Then there were the open boxes assigned to each grading period for the teacher to add handwritten personal comments. These notes were thoughtful markers of personal development and perhaps areas for improvement. The exercise required high touch, and one has to wonder if something of value has been lost by discarding the former practice in the name of progress.

Writing a biography sparks thoughts harkening back to the old-fashioned report card — at least in the mind of this biographer. Surveying a person's lifetime necessitates making judgments about what to include to help the reader fully understand the evolution of the subject's personality and character. In many ways, biographies are like expansive report cards.

Personal accomplishments and significant historical events, definitely assist as signposts in the process. Imagining how Ara Parseghian's life would have evolved without the exact series of inflection points is just one way to approach the challenge. A childhood in the Great Depression. His brother, Jerry, signing his high school football permission slip against their mother's wishes. Enlisting in the Navy during World War II and being part of the Greatest Generation, which led to his catching the attention of legendary coach Paul Brown. Then noticing Kathleen Davis because her slip was showing as she walked along the Slant Walk at Miami University. Sustaining the hip injury that ended his promising professional playing career. Having Woody Hayes extend an occupational lifeline when Ara needed it most. Then Hayes leaving suddenly to create an opening for a new head coach at Miami. Hearing confidence in his abilities communicated by Fathers Hesburgh and Joyce when he questioned his worthiness. All of these are pivotal moments in the life story of Ara Parseghian. Did he lead a charmed life? What could be characterized as good fortune instead of hard work? Certainly, nobody would dare to dismiss two of Ara's greatest challenges as good fortune: making sense of the cursed diseases that afflicted one of his daughters and later his three grandchildren.

Ultimately the writer and the reader are confronted with a simple decision. Has the subject been accurately and fairly portrayed in the important matters of personality and character, and is there consistency? If so, does the person merit significant attention in print? The significance is not only for what the person did but because of the essence of who the person was. Would you have liked to have known the person? Would they have been a good next-door neighbor, perhaps the ultimate test?

By now the reader likely has cobbled together some distinct impressions of Ara Parseghian. But before any final judgments are rendered, it may be worth underscoring what has been learned about the man, over and above the plentiful stories and the impressive coaching statistics.

Ara had a superior intellect, although it wasn't really apparent until he was assigned leadership positions, starting with his time in the Navy. His own report card grades (none survive) from Akron public schools probably wouldn't adequately reflect his abilities or his potential. Nobody from his youth references academic proficiency. To the contrary, references to his youth focus exclusively on his noteworthy athletic talents.

One of the evolutions, probably subconscious, was Ara's determination to succeed. That required Ara's discipline to make maximum use of his abilities — all of them. Thus, we see over time an intense personal focus that is one of the prominent distinguishing traits mentioned by anyone who ever played or worked for him. Managing that focus in constructive ways became a lifelong challenge.

Experiences can be great teachers. But this happens only if one pays attention and absorbs the lessons to modify behavior and improve. Ara was an intensely introspective person. Poise, organizational skills, and leadership qualities aren't dispensed at birth. They are learned behaviors. Ara had an agile mind and was a fast learner—when and where he thought it mattered. Success breeds confidence, a quality Parseghian embodied fully by the time he arrived as head football coach at Notre Dame. Yet arrogance never marred his makeup; a twinge of insecurity lurked in the background to keep him humble.

One might surmise from reading about Ara's coaching career that he might have been a micromanager. That wasn't the case. Instead, he valued the ideas and contributions of others and analyzed views from his trusted associates in a professional manner. He challenged others to be exacting and precise before proffering advice. Ara understood that leaders ultimately are required to make decisions, and he did so after sufficient reflection. On the field, these decisions usually needed to be made quickly, and he never hesitated there. Off the field, his slower decision-making process sometimes annoyed those around him because it felt like unnecessary procrastination. In all cases he took final responsibility; he detested blaming others and he never resorted to doing so in public. In private team practices, he referred to game mistakes as teachable moments, often pointedly. This is quite different, though, from diminishing the confidence of a player or a team for personal vindication.

It would be wrong to assume that Ara didn't demonstrate outrage at times. His private records reveal a person willing to attack corruption, lies, misstatements, and institutional unfairness when such matters were thrust his way. He was principled and outspoken, not one to go along just to get along.

Ara was not religious in the churchgoing sense. He held a skepticism of organized religion, perhaps a throwback to his stoic father's views having narrowly escaped the ethnic extermination that destroyed his Armenian family. Ara did integrate comfortably into the Catholic culture at Notre Dame. He held the university's customs and religious personalities, certainly Fathers Hesburgh and Joyce, in highest esteem. Having a relationship with a religious institution was so comfortable that Ara and Katie maintained their personal residence near Notre Dame after retirement when they could have lived anywhere. Respect from all corners of the Notre Dame community sprung from an understanding that Ara adhered to uncommonly high moral and ethical standards; those may be viewed as his personal religion.

There are no obvious strains of creativity in Ara's upbringing, at least not in the sense of music or the arts. He was a prolific communicator, though, and left behind a rich legacy in the written word. He applied a distinctive creative genius in approaching ways to prepare his football teams and to win on the field. Coaches at all levels admired his methods and they attended clinics where he spoke, hoping that some of Ara's creative genius would rub off. Most of the time it didn't. The root incentive for Ara's creativity was to surprise and be superior to an opponent — to win. Sharing the "special sauce" wasn't part of his instincts because then the advantages of an opponent's unpreparedness would be lost. In all matters other than proffering coaching insights, Ara had a very generous spirit.

Not surprisingly, Ara was at his best in competitive situations. He maintained a presence of mind and coolness during challenging situations. He preached a credo of having no breaking point, and he successfully imparted this drive to his players and staff through his own actions. He strove to build confidence in others throughout his life.

Those closest to him understood that Ara was an emotional person who thought and felt things deeply and expressed his feelings strongly. The outside world only saw glimpses of this. His family and closest friends were immersed in his intense loyalty, protectiveness, and support. Eventually, his football players came to understand this personality trait. As students they saw the intense and focused coach often brooding and prone to give them The Look when he was displeased. After graduation, the players crossed over a threshold to join the trusted cadre for whom he cared very deeply. Almost to a person, there are stories that demonstrate considerable time spent by Ara, gestures of generosity, and sensitive personal consideration for his "troops." This bond of service was returned in kind when in times of adversity Ara and his family leaned on his tight football fraternity for support.

Without intending to lionize Ara, it is apparent that his best traits and characteristics were sorely tested near the end of his football coaching career. One unmanageable factor added to the mix made all the difference in an otherwise unbreakable man. The pressures of prolonged stress eventually overwhelmed him. He could be hard on himself, and he ultimately realized that and knew that he couldn't change. He was introspective enough to assess what was happening and to walk back from the true breaking point. Ara's ability to honestly self-evaluate probably saved the people he cared about most in his life instead of pressing on and putting them in jeopardy by stress-induced restlessness, irritability, and insensitivity.

Changing careers at the early age of fifty-two and committing to heartfelt causes opened new avenues for Ara's very best qualities to be rejuvenated and shine. The less-stressed Ara was able to spend more quality time with Katie, his expanding family, and a slightly larger circle of trusted friends and associates, many of whom he knew from outside of football. Personal tragedies arrived swiftly and unexpectedly, and they were out of his control. Their arrival may have crushed a lesser person, but the quality that reemerged to serve Ara was his ability to creatively focus on actions that could address negative impulses, and then commit to working toward positive outcomes.

Jim Humbert, Ara's son-in-law and one of his former football players, believes that one word captures the essence of the man he knew so well: "integrity." Ara's daughter Kriss Parseghian Humbert provided the most succinct statement about Ara's overall character when she said, "My father always did the right thing." That final report card would be universally acknowledged by all whose lives Ara Parseghian ever touched. And, it would have been enough for Coach to proudly carry it to his final home.

CHAPTER 29

LAST RESPECTS

When Ara Parseghian celebrated his ninety-fourth birthday on May 21, 2017, he was in good spirits and in fine health for his age. He used a walker as support when getting around, but it didn't hinder his penchant for mobility, and his mind remained crystal clear. Stubbornly, he still drove — if only to make the weekly meetings of the ROMEOs (Retired Old Men Eating Out) at Papa Vino's, a favorite restaurant very close to his home.

In addition to Ara, the regulars at ROMEO lunches included Roger Valdiserri (retired Notre Dame sports information director), Jim Gibbons (former Notre Dame baseball coach and administrator), Mike DeCicco (former Notre Dame fencing coach and athletic academic advisor), and Art Decio (Notre Dame trustee emeritus and benefactor). Others would be invited to join from time to time with the stated warning that they pay for their own lunch. It was a weekly assembly of people with vast, historical institutional knowledge at Notre Dame.

Unexpectedly, and without provocation, Ara's hip began to ache early in June. It was the very same right hip that he injured while playing football for the Cleveland Browns. Over the years Ara had undergone eight surgeries, including hip replacements and knee replacements and one for a persistent problem with kidney stones. To a lay person, the official diagnosis was an infection in the joint. Because of Ara's age, another hip replacement was not possible; treating the infection with antibiotics was the only available course of action. Whether that would work or not was the question. Sadly, the answer soon became apparent that it would not. Son Michael Parseghian, an orthopedic surgeon specializing in joint replacements, would have been one of the first to understand the gravity of Ara's condition and the probabilities working against his recovery.

From that point on, the goal was to keep the patient, now hospitalized, in the most comfort possible. A move to Dujarie House on the Holy Cross College campus was arranged in the hope that partial rehabilitation would yield results that would enable Ara to return to the comfort of his home. The coach drove himself hard to hit the physical therapy goals that were set. Ara was living with constant pain, determinedly working against his own adage that "we have no breaking point." He was eventually cleared to leave rehab to the tearful applause of those managing his care.

With around-the-clock care, his return home was manageable at first. A hospital bed was placed in a spare bedroom and the soothing tones of Frank Sinatra's music, Ara's favorite, played in the background. Within days of being home the family observed a marked downturn and suspected that Ara had a stroke. The coach was officially under the care of multiple local physicians. But the doctor with the heaviest heart was his own son, Michael. He was medically aware that his father was actively dying. In addition to his personal grief, Michael had to deal with the grief of his mother and of his immediate family.

When it was obvious that the end was near, closest friends and family members were called for final visits. By that time Ara had lost consciousness. Micki and Brian Boulac were present when Father Paul Doyle, representing the Notre Dame community, was called to the house. Within a day of that final goodbye, Ara Parseghian passed into everlasting life on Wednesday, August 2, 2017.

Arrangements had already been set in motion at Notre Dame in anticipation of the worst. A video obituary, the text of which had been written by this author, had been prepared at Fighting Irish Media for release as needed. The narration begins as follows:

"Ara made all the difference," Notre Dame President Father Theodore Hesburgh reflected. "When I interviewed Ara for head coach I only asked one question, 'Will you adhere to the standards of integrity we expect at Notre Dame?' When he answered yes, the choice was obvious."

Introduced by Athletic Director Moose Krause in January of 1964, Ara went right to work. Everything changed . . . everything. Coach Parseghian's combination of enthusiasm, leadership skills, on-field innovations and attention to details catapulted Notre Dame into national championship contention in his very first season. This began a "return to glory" storyline for Notre Dame Football that lasted eleven years.

Led by Heisman Trophy winner John Huarte, the Irish came within one minute, thirty-three seconds of an undefeated season in 1964. That team earned the first of Coach Parseghian's three MacArthur Bowl recognitions. Two years later, in 1966, Notre Dame was named undisputed national champion with nine wins and a single tie — the legendary 10–10 game of the century at Michigan State. Another national championship followed in 1973, with a thrilling 24–23 victory over undefeated Alabama in the Sugar Bowl.

Coach Ara Parseghian's playbooks began, "Congratulations, you've joined the team," and ended with the words, "We have no breaking point." Thus, a new generation of coaches, players, students, alumni and fans became believers again in "Notre Dame Spirit."

The final arrangements for a memorial service on campus had already been prepared for the eventuality. Those arriving by air into the South Bend International Airport had to pass over Notre Dame Stadium and were sobered to see a black and white image of Ara in tribute on the massive video screen (at the time the largest in any college football stadium). It remained posted for a week.

On Saturday evening, August 5, an invitation-only wake was held in the Monogram Room of the Athletic and Convocation Center. In addition to close family and friends, the invitation was extended to members of Ara's teams (coaches, players, managers, and trainers). A contingent of Northwestern players also attended. Katie Parseghian personally greeted each person as they passed Ara's open casket. With characteristic stamina and poise, she shared a personal word with everyone. It had to have been exhausting, as hundreds of mourners waited patiently in line.

On Sunday afternoon, August 6, a Celebration of Life Mass was held in the Sacred Heart Basilica on the Notre Dame campus. It was not a funeral Mass in the tradition of the Catholic Church because it was held without a casket or incense. But this distinction lacked any practical difference. Because it was the Feast of the Transfiguration, the altar was vested entirely in white with a massive spray of white gladiolus. Two large, framed photos were placed prominently in front of the lectern, one of Ara and one of the entire Parseghian family (the same photo that adorned Ara's home office). The cavernous church was packed to overflowing. A special section was reserved for former players, taking up nearly one-third of the available seating.

The Mass was officiated by Father John Jenkins, then president of the University of Notre Dame, assisted by twenty Congregation of Holy Cross priests. Father Jenkins gave the homily. In it he said, "Ara was a great coach because he won football games. Ara was a great man because he changed lives. . . . Ara, pray for each one of us."

A well-prepared eulogy was courageously delivered by Tom Parseghian, Ara's nephew (son of Ara's brother, Jerry). In addition to the organ and choir music, a rendition of "Give Me Jesus" was provided with guitar accompaniment by country music performer Vince Gill (sitting in for his wife Amy Grant, a personal friend of Ara's daughter-in-law, Cindy Parseghian).

Once Mass ended and before processing out, the assembled crowd sang the Alma Mater, "Notre Dame, Our Mother," which originally had been composed for the funeral Mass of Coach Knute Rockne in 1931.

The last line rings true: "And our hearts forever love thee, Notre Dame."

Following Mass, a Memorial Celebration hosted by the Parseghian family and the university was held in the Purcell Pavilion at the Joyce Center. This event was open to the general public and an estimated crowd of five thousand attended.

The emcee for this celebration was Anne Thompson, NBC correspondent, Notre Dame alumna, and university trustee. With her sensitive guidance the event stayed upbeat and truly celebratory.

Four guest speakers with close personal ties to Ara rallied the crowd: Gregory Crawford, PhD, the president of Miami University of Ohio and a dedicated supporter of the Parseghian Foundation when he was the dean of science at Notre Dame; Lou Holtz, former Notre Dame head football coach; Digger Phelps, former Notre Dame men's basketball coach; and Peter Schivarelli, former Notre Dame football player and manager of the rock band Chicago.

The family chose the following quotation from Ara for the event program: "You know what it takes to win. Just look at my fist. When I make a fist, it's strong and you can't tear it apart. As long as there's unity, there's strength. We must become so close with the bonds of loyalty and sacrifice, so deep with the conviction of the sole purpose, that no one, no group, no thing can ever tear us apart."

Music was provided by the Notre Dame Children's Choir and the Notre Dame Concert Band. Vince Gill provided a special musical tribute concluding with "Go Rest High on That Mountain." The last official part of the program was the playing of the "Notre Dame Victory March," the only time it was played that day. It was difficult not to feel choked up singing the last line, "While her loyal sons and daughters march on to victory."

The 2017–2018 Notre Dame football team honored Ara Parseghian with a number of visual remembrances. The base of the goal posts at Notre Dame Stadium were wrapped in foam protective coverings with the name "ARA" boldly painted in vertical lettering. Team uniforms had an added small circular shoulder patch reading "ARA" in white embroidered lettering on a black background. The iconic gleaming gold helmets had their rubber face mask tabs converted from saying "IRISH" to "ARA" for the season.

At season's end Katie Parseghian reached out to request one of those helmets, even a used one, which she offered to pay for. A new one was soon delivered to her home as a gift from Head Football Coach Brian Kelly and his wife, Paqui. This helmet remains prominently located on a shelf next to the television in the den — Ara's old office. Katie placed electric votive candles under the helmet. They are lit every evening as she relaxes to watch the evening news. They are in remembrance of Ara, her daughter Karan, and her grandchildren Michael, Marcia, and Krista. At times she falls asleep for the evening in her lounge chair. The flickering lights are Katie's personal devotion of hope for when they will all be reunited again.

EPILOGUE

_____

Some of the most sacred ground at the University of Notre Dame is dedicated to the two cemeteries embedded on campus. One, located on the private road between the Grotto and Saint Mary's College, is reserved for Congregation of Holy Cross priests and brothers, with a very few exceptions made for resident bachelor professors, like Frank O'Malley and Paul Fenlon. Here, the white stone cross grave markers are simple and identical. This cemetery is the final resting place for Father Theodore Hesburgh and Father Edmund Joyce, both of whom provided extraordinary service to Notre Dame and were instrumental to the success of Notre Dame Football during Coach Ara Parseghian's eleven-year tenure.

Cedar Grove is the other Notre Dame cemetery, located at the southern edge of campus on Notre Dame Avenue, with an unobstructed view of the famous Golden Dome atop the Main Administration Building. The grounds at Cedar Grove are exclusively reserved for faculty, staff, members of the Sacred Heart Parish, and select others who have made a significant contribution to the university. All Notre Dame graduates are allowed to purchase space in the newer mausoleum structures. The cemetery was established in 1843, by Notre Dame founder Father Edward Sorin, C.S.C. It includes markers for some of the early founders of the South Bend Community. South Bend was historically incorporated after Notre Dame, Indiana, in 1865. This cemetery is the final resting place for many of the notable faculty members prior to, during, and after the Parseghian era. Names such as Robert Leader (art history professor, artist, and one of the World War II Iwo Jima flag raisers), Emil T. Hofman (legendary chemistry professor and freshman dean), Joseph Casasanta (long-time band director, composer of Notre Dame fan favorite songs and the Alma Mater, "Notre Dame, Our Mother"), Heisman Award winner Leon Hart, former Athletic Director Edward "Moose" Krause, and television personality and benefactor Regis Philbin (class of '53) — to name just a few.

It is here, at Cedar Grove on the Notre Dame campus where the remains of Ara Parseghian are laid to rest. His spot is on the northern edge, surrounded by narrow roads that create an island, in the shadow of newly constructed mausoleum structures. Until recently the grave was marked by a modest grey granite headstone that simply read: "PARSEGHIAN." Thanks to the efforts of Peter Schivarelli, former Irish football player and manager of the rock band Chicago, and working with the family, Ara's gravesite was enhanced in 2020. A three-foot bronze sculpture by artist Jerry McKenna was installed, depicting Ara being carried off the field after the 1971 victory in the Cotton Bowl. A life-size version of the same piece is located at the south entrance to Notre Dame Stadium at the Ara Parseghian Gate.

As a Catholic cemetery, Cedar Grove is considered sacred ground by the Church. As such, all remains, regardless of the person's religious affiliation, are interred using the same rite of committal. On a morning in late August 2017, Cemetery Manager Leon Glon performed this rite for Ara Parseghian, alone, in privacy. The concluding prayer from the *Order of Christian Funerals* is as follows:

> Loving God, from whom all life proceeds and by whose hand the dead are raised again, though we are sinners, you wish always to hear us. Accept the prayers we offer in sadness for your servant Ara Parseghian, deliver his soul from death, number him among your saints and clothe him with the robe of salvation to enjoy forever the delights of your kingdom. We ask this through Christ our Lord.
>
> May the love of God and the peace of the Lord Jesus Christ bless and console us and gently wipe every tear from our eyes: In the name of the Father, and of the Son, and of the Holy Spirit. Amen.

Cedar Grove Cemetery is an island of tranquility surrounded by the constant and varied activities that define the vibrant living entity of the University of Notre Dame. To busy passersby it honors in whispers the memories of so many generations of the Notre Dame family. It steadfastly withstands the changing Northern Indiana seasons. In the winter it is likely to be covered in pristine white snow with the dark grey profiles of mature trees standing as sentinels. Spring eventually arrives at Notre Dame with sprouts of green, but it never seems soon enough. Throughout the summer there is an expansive leafy canopy creating cooling shade with occasional spikes of sun breaking through.

If you were to plan a visit to Cedar Grove Cemetery, the optimal time would be in the fall — during football season. Cedar Grove is at its best just as the leaves are changing in late October or early November. After soaking autumn rains, the grounds are covered by a carpet of multicolored leaves. Even the slightest breeze will prompt the remaining golden flakes to drift down gently. A visitor to the cemetery on a football Saturday will be overwhelmed by the Notre Dame experience.

If you listen carefully, you might hear strains of the Band of the Fighting Irish performing from the steps at Bond Hall in their pregame ritual. The crisp air is alive with the aromas of nearby, elaborate tailgate gatherings. Overhead the cadence of helicopters sounds — their airborne presence necessary to safely manage the eighty thousand visitors descending onto the campus.

A steady stream of Notre Dame faithful pass the black, wrought iron fence separating the cemetery from the busy sidewalk on their way to the Hammes Bookstore, to a tailgate party, or to Notre Dame Stadium. The full range of generations is represented. Young families with babies in strollers and children in tow meander along the sidewalk, all wearing some version of Notre Dame or Irish gear in blue, gold, and green. Students hurry past, brimming with anticipation for an entire day of activities with friends. Elderly alumni slowly make their way as well, pausing with the comfort of fond memories, some dressed in Irish-knit sweaters, plaid woolens, and classic embroidered slacks with shamrocks or leprechauns, again in shades of blue, gold, and green.

To visit Cedar Grove on a football Saturday is an emotional experience. It is something to savor. It is an opportunity to be grateful for all that Notre Dame represents and for all the people since 1842 who have contributed to this very special place.

If you are privileged to make this visit, consider what the University of Notre Dame would have been without the echoes of the names that surround you. And understand one important fact. None of what you hear, see, or feel would be nearly the same — not even close — without the providential arrival of Ara Parseghian as head football coach in 1964.

Father Hesburgh said it best, "Ara made the entire difference. He changed everything."

NOTES

Chapter 1. Roots

1. Mike Miktarian (died December 7, 2007), personal letter sent to Ara Parseghian after his father's death, exact date unknown. Letter reproduced from Ara's personal files.

Chapter 3. Conwell Findley

1. It would be impossible to capture the state of college football relative to race in the early 1950s, Ara's first years as head coach, without mentioning the case of Johnny Bright. It became a landmark in college football history, a moment of illumination. On October 20, 1951, when Drake University was playing Oklahoma A & M University in Stillwater, Bright, an All-American and an African American, became the victim of an intentional, racially motivated, on-field assault. He was slugged three times away from play which broke his jaw and ended his college career. In the press box that day was a *Des Moines Register* photographer, Don Ultang. He captured a sequence of six black and white images of the play and the attack. They were published in *LIFE* magazine. Immediately, the NCAA required face guards on all helmets and tackling rules were changed to severely punish gratuitous attacks in games. For his alert camerawork, Don Ultang was awarded a Pulitzer Prize.

Chapter 4. The Player

1. On a personal note, the author's father, Donald Hubbard, also reported in on April 1, 1943.

Chapter 5. Oxford

1. This material is from a ten-page, typed document from Ara's personal files that is thought to have been written in 1995. The document appears to be notes from an interview, although no identifying details about the interviewer or potential publication are provided on the pages themselves.

Chapter 6. Football Is a Coaches' Game

1. John Underwood, *Football Is a Coaches' Game* (College Football Hall of Fame, Kings Island, OH, 1978), video script.
2. Tom Pagna and Bob Best, *Era of Ara* (Strode Publishers: Huntsville, AL, 1976) 33–34.

Chapter 7. Northwestern

1. "Wildcats — A History of Football at Northwestern," *The Daily Northwestern*, courtesy of Northwestern University Archives, 2023.
2. Article used with permission, © 1956 Tribune Sunday Magazine. All Rights Reserved. Distributed by Tribune Content Agency, LLC.

Chapter 8. Ted, Ned, and Moose

1. "Introduction," *Dome*, 1967.
2. "Introduction," *Dome*, 1967.

Chapter 10. Winning Mindset

1. Allen L. Sack, *Counterfeit Amateurs* (University Park: Pennsylvania University Press, 2008).
2. Bill McGrane, *All Rise: The Remarkable Journey of Alan Page* (Chicago: Triumph Books, 2010).

Chapter 14. Games That Mattered, 1964-1966

1. Originally published in Mark O. Hubbard, *Undisputed: Notre Dame, National Champions 1966 (A Football Family and the Game of the Century)* (New York: Vantage Press, 2011), 38–39. Used by permission.

2. Theodore M. Hesburgh, "Opinion Editorial," *Scholastic Magazine*, December 1964.

3. Theodore M. Hesburgh, "Open Letter to Notre Dame Community," November 1964.

4. Dan Jenkins, "That Legend Is Loose Again," *Sports Illustrated*, November 7, 1966, 78.

5. Tom Wright, "Ambush at OK Corral," *The Scholastic*, December 9, 1966, 19.

6. Dan Jenkins, "An Upside-Down Game," *Sports Illustrated*, November 28, 1966, 22.

Chapter 16. Home and Away

1. Mary Lou McGue, "Mrs. Ara Parseghian, First Lady of Football Graces Grid Madness," *Our Sunday Visitor*, October 8, 1967. © OSV. Article used by permission.

Chapter 18. No Joke

1. Pagna and Best, *Notre Dame's Era of Ara*, 34.

2. Pagna and Best, *Notre Dame's Era of Ara*, 156.

3. Art Buchwald, "Introduction of Ara Parseghian," May 17, 1972. Permission to print granted by Leon Buchwald, Art Buchwald's son.

Chapter 19. Games That Mattered, 1967-1974

1. Pagna and Best, *Notre Dame's Era of Ara*, 167.

2. Pagna and Best, *Notre Dame's Era of Ara*, 171.

3. Pagna and Best, *Notre Dame's Era of Ara*, 189–90.

4. Pagna and Best, *Notre Dame's Era of Ara*, 190.

5. Pagna and Best, *Notre Dame's Era of Ara*, 225–26.

6. Pagna and Best, *Notre Dame's Era of Ara*, 246.

7. Pagna and Best, *Notre Dame's Era of Ara*, 252.

8. Pagna and Best, *Notre Dame's Era of Ara*, 253–55.
9. Pagna and Best, *Notre Dame's Era of Ara*, 259–61.
10. Pagna and Best, *Notre Dame's Era of Ara*, 264.
11. Pagna and Best, *Notre Dame's Era of Ara*, 280–81.
12. Pagna and Best, *Notre Dame's Era of Ara*, 281–82.
13. Pagna and Best, *Notre Dame's Era of Ara*, 282–83.

Chapter 21. Second Half

1. The quoted material here and elsewhere in this chapter comes from a ten-page, typed document found in Ara's personal files that is thought to have been written in 1995. The document appears to be notes from an interview, although no identifying details about the interviewer or potential publication are provided on the pages themselves.
2. This and the subsequent quotes from Charlie Mechem Jr. in this chapter are from an interview with the author on October 11, 2019.

Chapter 25. Bittersweet

1. Pagna and Best, *Notre Dame's Era of Ara*, 23–25.
2. Jim Murray, "Ara's Longest 20 Yards," *Los Angeles Times*, March 9, 1975.
3. Karan (Parseghian) Burke, "A Personal Perspective," publication unknown. Document taken from Ara Parseghian's personal files and used by permission of James Burke (Karan's husband).
4. Bill Koch, "Former Irish Coach Parseghian Battling Odds in a Deadly Game," Scripps News Service, September 1994.
5. Bruce Lowitt, "For Dying Children, a Long Shot," *St. Petersburg Times*, May 16, 1995.
6. According to a recent study, there are approximately 42 new cases every year and about 943 cases total. See Barbara K. Burton, Alexandra G. Ellis, Blair Orr, Shilpa Chatlani, Kwangchae Yoon, Jessica R. Shoaff, and Dan Gallo, "Estimating the Prevalence of Niemann-Pick Disease Type C (NPC) in the United States," *Molecular Genetics and Metabolism*, 134, nos. 1–2 (2021): 182–87, https://www.sciencedirect.com/science/article/pii/S1096719221007411.

INDEX

Big Ten Conference, 25, 46, 60

Big Three Tournament, 260

Blache, Greg, 27

Blackburn, George, 37

Blaik, Earl "Red," 41, 44

Blanchard, Doc, 139

Bleier, Rocky, 75, 138, 142–44, 150, 166, 171, 173, 178, 183, 201–4

Bonneau, Aimee "Amelia" Louise (Mrs. Amelia Parseghian), 3, 9–10

Bonneau, Cecile, 4

Bonneau, Felicite, 4

Bonneau, Jean Baptist (father), 3

Bonneau, Jean Baptist (son), 4

Bonneau, Marte Marie, 4

Boulac, Brian, 74–75, 85, 88, 99, 160, 169, 183, 195, 222, 243, 256

Boulac, Mary Ann "Micki," 75, 243, 299

bowl games. *See* University of Notre Dame, football games; *specific games*

Bradley, Luther, 223

Brady, Scott, 183

Breen-Phillips Hall (Notre Dame), 84

Brennan, Terry, 48, 59–60, 84, 132, 139

Brickels, John, 37–38, 40–42, 44

Bride, Joe, 122–23

Bright, Johnny, 307n1 (chap. 3)

Brookwood Golf Course, 260

Brown, Cliff, 188

Brown, Paul, 12, 23, 30, 32, 37–39, 42, 44, 81, 102, 294

Brown, Tay, 270

Browner, Ross, 223

Bryant, Paul "Bear," 41, 224, 226

Buch, Harry, 128

Buch, Pat, 128

Buchwald, Art, 211–12

Buck, Terri. *See* Lewallen, Terri Buck

Buecher-Parseghian wedding (Sept. 1994), 280

Buecher, Cindy. *See* Parseghian, Cindy

Buffalo Bills, 33

Bullock, Wayne, 233

Burgener, Mike, 171

Burke, Dr. James, 240, 278

Burke, James F., Jr., 12–13, 239, 277

Burke, Michael, 240, 278

Burke, Karan (née Parseghian), xxi, 13, 40, 239, 274–79

Burton, Ron, 52

C

Cahill, Bob, 217

Callahan, Charlie, xxvi, 122

Caroline, J. C., 270

Cartier Field, 83

Casasanta, Joseph, 304

Case Western Reserve University, 48

Casper, Dave, 223, 225, 284–85

Catholic Church (faith), xxii, xxvii–xxviii, 11, 301, 304

Catholic University of America, 63

Cavanaugh, Rev. John, 58

Cavender, Regis, 161, 163

CBS Sports, 253–55

Cedar Grove Cemetery, 262, 303–5

Church of the Annunciation, Akron, OH, 10

Civil Rights Commission, United States, 26

Clements, Tom, 224–26, 231

Clergeau, Marie, 3

Cleveland Browns, 23, 32, 38

Cleveland Memorial Stadium, 33

Coach of the Year. *See under* Parseghian, Ara

First Central Trust Bank, Akron, OH, 10
First National Bank of Akron, 10
First Presbyterian Church, Greenfield, OH, 33
Football Office (Notre Dame), 73, 83–85
Ford Motor Company, 191, 247, 250, 291
Four Horsemen, 138
Frailey, Rooney, 277

G
Gagnon, Cappy, xxvi
Gain, Bob, 270
"game of the century" (Notre Dame vs. Michigan State, 1966), 300
    events leading to, 151–53
    media attention, 154
    official NCAA record, 75, 161–68, 171
    as played, 159–71
    post-game reaction, 172–73
    as reported by sports writers, 174–76
    statistics, 170–71
Ganjoyan, Avedis, 6
Ganjoyan, Gaspar, 6
Ganjoyan, Katchig, 6
Ganjoyan, Mechitar. See Parseghian, Michael
Ganjoyan, Melkon, 6
Ganjoyan, Parsegh, 3
Ganjoyan, Yeghsa, 6
Gatewood, Thom, 219
Gator Bowl (1971), 222
Gator Bowl (Ohio State vs. Clemson, 1978), 252–53
Gibbons, Jim, 298
Gill, Vince, 301–2

Gillman, Sid, 31
Gillom, Horace, 24
Gladieux, Bob, 143, 164, 166, 171, 174, 178
Glon, Leon, 304
Gmitter, Don, 143–44, 171, 183, 213
Goeddeke, George, 136, 144, 162, 171, 178–79, 213
Gossage, Gene, 52
Graham, Otto, 33, 53, 259
Grange, Red, 146
Granger, IN, 283
Grant, Amy, 301
Great Lakes Bluejackets (football team), 28–30
Great Lakes Naval Training Station, xxii, 13, 28–29
Green Bay Packers, 244
Greenfield, OH, 16–18, 32–33
Greise, Bob, 133, 141–44, 214
Griffin, Archie, 232
Griffin, Merv, 194
Grotto, bench (Notre Dame), 286, 303
Groza, Lou, 33
Gustafson, Andy, xxiv

H
Hackenberg, Dick, 59
Haley, Dave, 166, 171
Hall, John, 181
Hall of Fame. See Basketball Hall of Fame; College Football Hall of Fame; Parseghian, Ara
Hanratty, Terry, 97, 99, 141–42, 146–48, 150, 162, 170–71, 173, 178, 183, 214–15
Harbaugh, John, 44
Hardy, Kevin, 162, 165, 170–71
Harper, Jesse, xxvi, 252

Harper, Jim, 252
Harrelson, Hawk, 260
Harris, Bill, 23
Harrison, Randy, 231
Harshman, Dan, 75, 178–79
Hart, Leon, 139, 304
Hayes, Ed, 271
Hayes, Wayne Woodrow "Woody,"
    37–40, 44, 56, 102, 145–46,
    252–53, 294
Heisman Trophy, 126, 139, 144, 214,
    222, 231–32
Heneghan, Curt, 137
Hesburgh, Jim, 196
Hesburgh, Mary, 196
Hesburgh, Rev. Theodore "Ted" M.,
    xxvii, 25, 48, 58, 62–64, 77, 84,
    115, 126–27, 129, 135, 147, 189,
    294, 300, 306
Hindman, Hugh, 253
Hinkle, Tony, 29
historic games. *See under* University of
    Notre Dame, football games
Hofman, Emil T., 304
Holcomb, Stu, 50, 53, 57
Holtz, Lou, 260–61, 302
Horney, Dr. John, 161, 170–71, 213
Hornung, Paul, 48
Howard, Chuck, 251–53
Howe, Roger, 45
Huarte, John, 118–19, 126, 131, 300
Hubbard, Donald O., 308n1 (chap. 4)
Hubbard, Mark O., 309n1 (chap. 14)
Huff, Sam, 270
Humbert, Jim, 277, 297
Humbert, Kriss (née Parseghian),
    93, 297
Hunter, Dick, 286
Hutchins, Robert, 62

I
Indiana University, 46
Ingrassi, Loraine, 14
Iooss, Walter, Jr., 148
Iowa game, scheduled for 1963, 152
Irish Guard, 120
Ivan, Ken, 136

J
Jackson, Keith, 252–53
Jack Tar Hotel, Lansing, MI, 158
Jefferson Elementary School, 192
Jenkins, Dan, 133, 175
Jenkins, Rev. John, 301
Jeselnik, Tony, 228
Jeziorski, Ron, 183
Johns, Dr. Nicholas, 239
Johnson, Lyndon, 219
Jones, Clinton, 163, 184
Jones, Tom, 205–6
Joyce, Rev. Edmund "Ned," xxiii, xxviii,
    26, 48, 58, 61, 64–66, 77, 115, 129,
    147, 189, 217, 242–44, 294, 303

K
Kazmaier, Dick, 146
Kelly, Brian
Kelly, Paqui, 302
Kenney, Dick, 161, 163–65
Keyes, Leroy, 142, 144
Knutson, Gene, 251, 271
Koch, Bill, 280
Kraft, Dennis, 155
Krause, Edward "Moose," xxviii, 59,
    67–68, 147, 152, 155, 234, 242–44,
    247, 300
Kuechenberg, Bob, 146, 169, 171
Kuharich, Joe, 49, 60, 211
Kunz, George, 141, 144

MARK O. HUBBARD

is the author of *Undisputed: Notre Dame,*
National Champions 1966 and the co-author of
Forgotten Four: Notre Dame's Greatest Backfield
and the 1953 Undefeated Season.